A Great Political Classic

Over a hundred years ago, Alexis de Tocqueville, a young French nobleman and an astute political scientist, came to the United States to appraise the meaning and actual functioning of democracy in order to understand how it might serve to supplant the outworn aristocratic regime in Europe.

In *Democracy in America,* the classic treatise on the American way of life which he wrote as a result of his visit, Tocqueville discusses the advantages and dangers of the majority rule which he thought could be as tyrannical as the rule of the aristocracy. He analyzes the influence of political parties and the press on the government, the effect of democracy on the social, political and economic life of the American people, and offers some startling predictions about world politics which history has borne out. So brilliant and penetrating are his comments and criticisms that they have vital meaning today for all who are interested in democracy.

Richard D. Heffner, historian, radio and television commentator, and author of *A Documentary History of the United States,* has selected Tocqueville's most striking and pertinent passages to make this masterful political critique available in a compact, inexpensive edition for the modern reader.

Alexis de Tocqueville

Democracy in America

Specially Edited and Abridged
for the Modern Reader

by

RICHARD D. HEFFNER

A MENTOR BOOK

MENTOR
Published by the Penguin Group
Penguin Books USA Inc., 375 Hudson Street,
New York, New York 10014, U.S.A.
Penguin Books Ltd, 27 Wrights Lane,
London W8 5TZ, England
Penguin Books Australia Ltd, Ringwood,
Victoria, Australia
Penguin Books Canada Ltd, 10 Alcorn Avenue,
Toronto, Ontario, Canada M4V 3B2
Penguin Books (N.Z.) Ltd, 182–190 Wairau Road,
Auckland 10, New Zealand

Penguin Books Ltd, Registered Offices:
Harmondsworth, Middlesex, England

35 34 33 32 31 30 29 28

 REGISTERED TRADEMARK—MARCA REGISTRADA

Library of Congress Catalog Card No. 56-7402

Printed in the United States of America

CONTENTS

✫

* Roman numerals in parentheses refer to chapters of the original text.

BOOK II

INFLUENCE OF DEMOCRACY ON THE FEELINGS OF THE AMERICANS

BOOK III

INFLUENCE OF DEMOCRACY ON MANNERS PROPERLY SO CALLED

BOOK IV

INFLUENCE OF DEMOCRATIC IDEAS AND FEELINGS ON POLITICAL SOCIETY

INTRODUCTION
TO THE MENTOR EDITION

☆

ALEXIS DE TOCQUEVILLE arrived in the United States in May, 1831, and departed its shores for his native France once again in February, 1832, only nine months later. Yet for considerably more than a century now, Tocqueville's *Democracy in America* has provided its readers an unparalleled abundance of description, analysis, and prophecy concerning almost every aspect of the American scene.

The first part of the young Frenchman's classic critique begins with a brief description of the New World's physical dimensions, of the origins of Anglo-Americans and of America's most striking characteristic: democracy and the absolute sovereignty of the people. There follows a somewhat outdated summary of the workings of American government, then an analysis of the book's central theme: the tyranny of the majority in the United States.

In its second part, *Democracy in America* deals with the impact of democracy or majority rule upon the structure and dynamics of American society, upon the way Americans think and feel and act, upon the essential nature of our freedoms. It is here that Tocqueville actually makes his most unique and prophetic contributions to contemporary thought. For above all else Tocqueville's concern is for the development and survival of both freedom *and* democracy. And today at mid-twentieth century surely there is no other theme so meaningful or so imperative for Americans—and for free people everywhere.

First published in 1835 and 1840, *Democracy in America* remains pre-eminently a tract for our times.

I

Ever since the emergence of Jacksonian Democracy in the 1820's and 1830's, the most pervasive myth to dominate American political thinking has been our rather naïve—and mistaken—equation of equality with freedom, of democracy (or majority rule) with liberty. Long before the Age of Jackson, of course, Thomas Jefferson had set forth the proposition that "all men are created equal" as the philosophical basis of the Declaration of Independence. And as far back as the so-called "Revolution of 1800," majority rule had triumphed in America when the Federalist party—a minority party of "the rich and the well-born"—was permanently driven from national office by the numerically superior Jeffersonian Democrats. Yet our early leaders, even the Jeffersonians, were themselves essentially far from equalitarian in outlook. They believed in government *of* and *for* the people, but not *by* the people. And, more important, they were much too dedicated to the principles of individual liberty and freedom ever to equate them necessarily and irrevocably with equality and democracy.

Thus it was not until Jackson's time that equalitarianism became the over-riding theme of American life, with majority rule its most convenient rule of thumb. Then, American political thought and institutions underwent the most profound transformation as political control was rapidly shifted from an older aristocracy of education, position and wealth to the "common man," the average American. To provide for the untrammeled rule of the majority, restrictions on the suffrage were removed, property qualifications for office were abolished, terms of office were limited, and the number of appointive or non-elective positions was drastically cut down. In short, "King Numbers" came quickly to reign supreme, and popular feeling became almost totally involved with the notion of majority rule.

In public office, the new equalitarianism meant that all men were of essentially equal talents, that each American was capable of holding any position in government, and that democracy required a rotation in office to prevent the development of an untouchable bureaucratic elite or aristocracy. The notion that "to the victors belong the spoils" was the most forthright expression of this simple democratic instinct for replacing office holders whose party had been repudiated with those who were more clearly "the people's choice." And the roaring mobs that pushed and fought their way into Andrew Jackson's inaugural reception, that knocked over punch bowls, smashed glasses, and trod in muddy boots on White House tables and chairs, made it abundantly clear that at long last equality had become the hallmark of American life.

*   *   *   *   *   *   *   *   *   *

It was in the midst of this riotous early ferment of democracy and equality that Alexis de Tocqueville made his grand tour of the United States. And surely no other observer has ever as perceptively noted or so well described these now widely accepted twin themes of American life. Indeed, in the very Introduction to *Democracy in America*, Tocqueville wrote that—

> Amongst the novel objects that attracted my attention . . . in the United States, nothing struck me more forcibly than the general equality of condition among the people. . . . The more I advanced in the study of American society, the more I perceived that this equality of condition is the fundamental fact from which all others seem to be derived. . . .

While about democracy (or majority rule) the young Frenchman observed further on in his study that "The people reign in the American political world as the Deity does in the Universe."

Yet Tocqueville was merely reporting, not approving. *Democracy in America* is no paean to the virtues of equalitarianism and majority rule. Quite to the contrary—and this is precisely what makes it so provocative and valuable for us today —this classic study thoroughly *rejects* Americans' now more than century-old, magical equation of equality with freedom, of democracy with liberty. No one would deny that in the Jackson era Americans had ruthlessly swept away even the trappings of privilege and presumption, and had substituted the rule of the many for the rule of the few. But had equalitarianism and majority rule proved to be unmixed blessings? Tocqueville thought not. Indeed, what he had seen of the leveling doctrines that pervaded every area of national life led him to question whether Americans' liberties, whether Americans' older concern for individual differences and freedom, could actually long survive their new penchant for equality and democracy. For as conditions became more equal, Americans seemed more and more to take pride not in their individuality, in their personal liberties, in their freedom, but rather in their sameness. So that, as Tocqueville wrote: ". . . every citizen, being assimilated to all the rest, is *lost in the crowd*, and nothing stands conspicuous but the great and imposing image of the people at large."

Increasingly, then, Americans had subordinated their concern for the liberties and freedom of the individual to their new respect for—or fear of—the majority, the "great and imposing image of the people at large." It seemed clear that equality and democracy, far from going hand in hand with

liberty and freedom, had in the sacred name of the majority
raised up instead a tyranny over the minds of men as oppressive and as formidable as any in history: the tyranny of the
majority. And Tocqueville could write: "I know of no country
in which there is so little independence of mind and real freedom of discussion as in America."

* * * * * * * * * *

That Alexis Charles Henri Clerel de Tocqueville should have
been so critical of American democracy, that he should have
thrust quite so vigorously at its underlying assumptions, was
by all means appropriate. For the brilliant Frenchman was an
aristocrat through and through, the heir of a distinguished
tradition of good family, conservatism, and intellectual aloof-
ness and individuality that had no affinity at all to the rampant
equalitarianism which characterized Jacksonian America.

Born in Paris on July 29, 1805, Tocqueville was descended
from a proud old Norman family that for long generations had
been considered among the *petite noblesse*. Thus it required
no particular devotion to the villainies of the *ancien regime*
to make Tocqueville initially suspicious of majority rule. The
leveling doctrines of the French Revolution had already taken
a heavy toll within his own family and circle of friends. During
the Revolution his parents had been jailed, his maternal grand-
father, the Marquis of Rosambo, had been guillotined in the
name of "Liberty, Equality and Fraternity." And though his
father was ultimately returned to rank and position after the
fall of Napoleon, Tocqueville's own childhood had been overshadowed by memories of these earlier popular excesses. In
so many ways, then, he was both by birth and by circumstance
ideally suited to the role of hostile critic of democracy in
America.

Yet this is by no means all that must be said of Tocqueville's preparation for his famous journey to America. For if
it were, we would be obliged to discount the larger portion of
his commentary as purely the product of personal spleen and
vindictiveness. But our young Frenchman was actually no
reactionary nobleman, no mere displaced aristocrat bitterly
attached to an older order of things and vainly desirous of
discrediting the rapidly spreading new democratic impulse.
In fact we find that though Tocqueville never abandoned what
he considered the loftier ideals and values of his aristocratic
heritage, still his lively instinct for fairness and justice had
touched off in him an enormous sympathy for democratic
ideas. He had studied and been much impressed by scholarly
allusions to the seemingly inevitable progress of democracy.

And within France herself, the Revolution of 1830 had further convinced him that the whole spirit of his age tended increasingly towards more equal and democratic conditions and institutions. Tocqueville's concern, then, was not to damn democracy, but rather to discover the weaknesses and the strengths of this movement which promised to play such a dominant role in the future. Having discovered them, he might reconcile them with the best aspects of the old order. The great political problem of our times, Tocqueville wrote, was not the destruction, but rather the "organization and the establishment of democracy in Christendom. . . . The Americans, unquestionably, have not resolved this problem, but they furnish useful data to those who undertake to resolve it."

Ostensibly, Tocqueville and his friend Gustave de Beaumont had come to this country in May, 1831, for the sole purpose of studying our prison system. Both young aristocrats were magistrates, and, after all, a prison survey provided them an adequate excuse for visiting the New World. Actually, however, Tocqueville and Beaumont came primarily because of their intense eagerness to examine democracy at first hand, to see for themselves the actual workings of those equalitarian, democratic doctrines that must ultimately be France's destiny. Democracy would inevitably come to their beloved France and to the rest of the world. But if these two young men could detect its errors and shortcomings in America, then at home they might at least prepare adequate safeguards for the inevitable. As Tocqueville himself wrote:

> It is not, then merely to satisfy a legitimate curiosity that I have examined America; my wish has been to find there instruction by which we may ourselves profit. . . . I confess that, in America, I saw more than America; I sought there the image of democracy itself, with its inclinations, its character, its prejudices, and its passions, in order to learn what we have to fear or to hope from its progress.

And in his superlative study, *Tocqueville and Beaumont in America,* George W. Pierson writes of the young aristocrats' purpose in coming to America: "They would make *démocratie* safe for the world."

II

There is little question but that Tocqueville's single-minded concern for searching out the general principles of democracy in America—and for applying them to his native France— endowed his study with a timelessness and a philosophical scope that make it as important for our own period as it was for his. For here the reader is seldom caught up in a myriad of unrelated details concerning American life of a century and more ago. Instead, he is carried steadily along from one well-set-forth generalization to the next, always free to probe further those which are closest to his own interests. And the total picture that Tocqueville paints is coherent, well-integrated and meaningful.

Yet it was precisely because Tocqueville had such a definite purpose in mind when he came to America that he fell into a basic methodological trap. In his eagerness to generalize upon what he called "the image of democracy . . . in order to learn what we have to fear or to hope from its progress," Tocqueville frequently indulged in the most blatant kind of *a priori* reasoning. New to America, and basically unfamiliar with its mores and institutions, he would formulate an abstract principle upon the scantiest substantive evidence. And then he would use his further observations only as proof of these somewhat intuitive generalizations rather than as the basis of more objective conclusions. Lord Bryce, a British commentator on the American scene, who a half-century after Tocqueville would much more systematically examine *The American Commonwealth*, complained that though the Frenchman never consciously ignored a fact which might disprove his theories, nevertheless, "facts do not fall on his mind like seeds on virgin soil."

There were, of course, other limitations as well that detracted somewhat from the general excellence of Tocqueville's critique. Sometimes his subjectivity and his avid concern for the broad implications of democracy in America kept him from seeing its details with precision and clarity—kept him from distinguishing between those patterns of thought and deed which were genuinely democratic in their origin and those which were merely the product of a continuous frontier experience and an English heritage. Sometimes, too, Tocqueville's penchant for generalization kept him from seeing through to those many basic changes in American life that were starting to take place even as he wrote. Thus, to Tocqueville the American Presidency seemed to be almost an office without power. He described at length the forces that enfeebled the Chief Executive and seriously limited his influence. And he disparaged any likely Presidential potential for boldness and leadership. But all of this was at the very moment that crusty old Andrew Jackson was in the White House, challenging the Supreme Court, vigorously forcing his will upon the Congress, and establishing a pattern of strong Presidential leadership that would eventually be followed by Lincoln, Theodore Roosevelt, Woodrow Wilson and Franklin D. Roosevelt.

There was still another major area in which Tocqueville failed to discern important changes in American life. For he was very much impressed with the power of the various states and with what seemed to him to be the inherent weakness of the national government. In time, he felt, there might be as many as 100,000,000 Americans in 40 states, and the disintegrating, decentralizing effect of such growth and expansion would mean a further weakening of the bonds of union. As the national government would grow even more remote from the average citizen, so national allegiance would be totally supplanted by loyalty to the individual states, or at best to regional blocs of states. And, of course, Tocqueville's visit to the United States did actually coincide with the rise of sectionalism and the South's cry for "states' rights." He came at a time when antagonisms between East and West, North and South were particularly bitter and pronounced; so that it was only natural that he should assume still a further decline in the power and prestige of the national government and an ever increasing loyalty to state and to section.

What Tocqueville overlooked, however, in his quest for generalizations, were the many adhesive, nationalizing forces that eventually would bind together even more than 200,000,-000 Americans in 50 states, spread out over a whole continent and beyond. The industrial revolution, a widespread factory system, a vast transcontinental railroad network, endless highways, mass communications, the standardization of American food, clothing, shelter and even ideas—all of these have bound Americans more tightly together since Tocqueville's time. And our union has actually been strengthened, not dissolved or even weakened, with an enormous accretion of national powers and a marked decline of state and regional loyalties. Tocqueville felt that in civil strife the union must fall. But from 1861 to 1865 it survived the holocaust of the Civil War, and emerged stronger than ever before.

Besides, as Lord Bryce suggested, "It is a salutary warning to those who think it easy to get to the bottom of the political and social phenomena of a nation, to find that so keen and so industrious an observer as De Tocqueville, who has seized with unrivalled acuteness and described with consummate art many of the minor features of American politics, has omitted to notice several which had already begun to show their heads in his day, and have since become of the first importance." Among these Bryce included the growing influence of money in politics, the systematization and organization of party rivalry, and the rise of the reform movement (although Tocqueville and Beaumont had supposedly come here to study prison reforms).

At other points as well *Democracy in America* suffers grievously from omissions and misinterpretations that can be traced directly both to the author's too easy assumptions and to his desire not to report, but rather to summarize, interpret and generalize.

III

For all of Tocqueville's obvious inadequacies and the often rather distressing subjectivity of his approach, still many of his generalizations concerning politics, religion, government, art and even literature in democratic America are actually amazingly shrewd and perceptive in their way. This is what makes *Democracy in America* a great book. Even where his observations fail to stand up as credibly objective and accurate reporting on the contemporary scene, Tocqueville still ranks as something of a master prophet and political scientist. Many of his brilliantly intuitive insights into the dynamics of nineteenth century democratic life hold true for our own times as well, and one is over and over again astonished at the way history has borne out numbers of his most sweeping assumptions.

It is quite clear, for instance, that Tocqueville misjudged the immediate strength and importance of the American Presidency. Yet at the very same time, the Frenchman was incredibly shrewd in his estimate of just what factors in American life would eventually *increase* Presidential influence and authority far beyond even Jackson's fondest hopes. "It is chiefly in its foreign relations that the executive power of a nation finds occasion to exert its skill and its strength," Tocqueville wrote. But for all practical purposes, in his own time a nearly isolated America *had* no foreign relations. Separated by great oceans from the rest of the world, America was safe from foreign aggression, her interests abroad were still comparatively small and unimportant, her dealings with other nations still at practically irreducible minimum. And though the President might possess what potentially were "almost royal prerogatives," still, at the moment, physical isolation and a dearth of foreign relations thoroughly limited the Executive's opportunities for exercising these prerogatives.

Thus it was neither law nor the Constitution, but rather circumstance alone, that enfeebled Presidential authority. And it is to Tocqueville's credit as an analyst and prophet that he so clearly perceived what *new* circumstances would in the future necessarily revolutionize the influence of the Executive. If America were to become a great world power and her early isolation were to become a thing of the past, then the division of governmental power would be different by far. "If the existence of the Union were perpetually threatened, if its chief interests were in daily connection with those of other powerful nations," then "the executive government would assume an increased importance in proportion to the measures expected of it and to those which it would execute." And today few Americans would doubt that our own enormous concentration of power in the Presidency has resulted at least in large part from America's emergence as a great world power in the years since World War I. Now toward the end of the twentieth century, our foreign relations have increased tremendously in scope and importance, our Executive finds increasing occasion to exert his skill and strength. Consequently the President's "almost royal prerogatives" have now been largely realized, quite in keeping with Tocqueville's prophecy.

About Americans' economic pursuits, too, Tocqueville made many wise observations: about Americans' intense love of wealth, their growing preference for commerce and industry over agriculture, their potential for vast material success. Americans make progress in industry, he wrote, because of their enormous ambition and their almost single-minded devotion to profitable activity. Besides, great fortunes were still to be made; and Tocqueville foresaw the rise of a ruthless industrial aristocracy—the "Robber Barons" of the late 19th century. Yet here Tocqueville perceived a fundamental contradiction in the American economy that its later Marxist critics could never really grasp: that while the "manufacturing aristocracy which is growing up under our eyes is one of the harshest that ever existed in the world . . . at the same time it is one of the most confined and least dangerous." This, because its wealth was not exclusive, its success not accompanied by the extremes of widespread poverty, nor by the polarization of society into only the very rich and the very poor.

In a singularly brilliant chapter, "Why Great Revolutions Will Become More Rare," Tocqueville pointed out that revolutions are made to destroy blatant inequalities. And, admittedly, in democratic America enterprise and the love of wealth will produce a few massive fortunes. But the very poor will also be few in number, and the immense neither-rich-nor-poor majority of the nation will always hold the balance between them. Riches are well distributed in America, not concentrated; and the American class structure—as the Marxist can never see or accept—is characterized by fluidity rather than by stratification. "Without being exactly either rich or poor," then, most men possess "sufficient property to desire the maintenance of order, yet not enough to excite envy. Such men are the natural enemies of violent commotions; their stillness keeps all beneath them and above them still, and secures the balance of the fabric of society." In such a land, then, amidst the conservatism bred by well-being, revolution must indeed be rare!

* * * * * * * * * *

Few basic American character traits and social patterns escaped the discerning Frenchman: their addiction to practical rather than theoretical science, their pragmatic concern not for the lofty and the perfect, but for the quick and the useful ("They will habitually prefer the useful to the beautiful, and they will require that the beautiful should be useful."), their inherent restlessness and ambition, their mutability and constant feverish activity ("The whole life of an American is passed like a game of chance, a revolutionary crisis, or a battle."), and their unending quest for devices and short-cuts ("He who has set his heart exclusively upon the pursuit of worldly welfare is always in a hurry, for he has but a limited time at his disposal to reach, to grasp, and to enjoy it.").

In Part II in particular, Tocqueville's long catalogue of the influence of democracy—or equality—upon the intellect, manners, and feelings of Americans remains shrewdly pertinent today. The Transcendentalists of his own day seemed to escape Tocqueville altogether, but of the future of literature in the American democracy he was quite certain, and largely correct. Its practitioners would reach more and more millions, he prophesied, introducing democracy's trading, enterprising spirit into literature. And though some few writers of superior abilities would retain their individual brilliance and artistry, most writers would become tradesmen themselves.

> Style will frequently be fantastic, incorrect, overburdened, and loose,—almost always vehement and bold. Authors will aim at rapidity of execution more than at perfection of detail . . . there will be more wit than erudition, more imagination than profundity; and literary performances will bear marks of an untutored and rude vigor of thought. . . . The object of authors will be to astonish rather than to please, and to stir the passions more than to charm the taste.

In literature, as in the cultivation of all other arts, the so-called craftsman of democratic ages places a premium upon quantity rather than quality, upon profit rather than perfection.

Religion, too, must feel the effects of democracy. Its forms and strictures become less rigid, though it continues to provide a substructure of belief and self-estimation for men whose seeming political freedom would otherwise make life and thought intolerably nebulous and infirm. Even the writing of history must be effected by democratic tendencies, with its emphasis placed not upon chance or upon the singular deeds and accomplishments of individual heroes and leaders, but —appropriately enough—upon mass movements and general causes instead. How astute an observation this was, of course, has been amply demonstrated by an American historiography which, since Tocqueville's time, has long been dominated by determinists of one kind or another, all more concerned with the giant forces that mold society than with the individual men who compose it.

Tocqueville described and prophesied with equal perceptivity many other aspects of democratic America as well: the peculiarly important role of the legal profession, particularly of the judiciary, the power and vituperativeness of a free press, the extravagance of democratic manners generally, the range and intensity of the American's political interests ("He speaks to you as if he was addressing a meeting; and if he should chance to become warm in the discussion, he will say 'Gentlemen' to the person with whom he is conversing."), the long aversion to—and slow preparation for—war, and yet ultimately the capacity completely to mobilize the nation and to wage total, victorious war, the dangers of civil war inherent in the master-slave relationship between Negro and white.

The young Frenchman also ferreted out an exceptionally significant American phenomenon by drawing attention to the multiplicity of public associations ("Americans of all ages, all conditions, and all dispositions, constantly form associations . . . religious, moral, serious, futile, general or restricted, enormous or diminutive . . . to give entertainments, to found seminaries, to build inns, to construct churches, to diffuse books, to send missionaries to the antipodes . . ."). Such private groups give individual men strength and substance in minor matters, prepare them for larger responsibilities, and perform functions that government would otherwise assume.

Finally, of course, most prophetic of all, there is Tocqueville's shrewd estimate of America's future relationship with still another powerful nation:

> There are at the present time two great nations in the world, which started from different points, but seem to tend towards the same end. I allude to the Russians and the

Americans. Both of them have grown up unnoticed; and whilst the attention of mankind was directed elsewhere, they have suddenly placed themselves in the front rank among the nations, and the world learned their existence and their greatness at almost the same time.

All other nations seem to have nearly reached their natural limits, and they have only to maintain their power; but these are still in the act of growth. All the others have stopped, or continue to advance with extreme difficulty; these alone are proceeding with ease and celerity along a path to which no limit can be perceived. The American struggles against the obstacles which nature opposes to him; the adversaries of the Russian are men. The former combats the wilderness and savage life; the latter, civilization with all its arms. The conquests of the American are therefore gained by the plowshare; those of the Russian by the sword. The Anglo-American relies upon personal interest to accomplish his ends and gives free scope to the unguided strength and common sense of the people; the Russian centres all the authority of society in a single arm. The principal instrument of the former is freedom; of the latter, servitude. Their starting-point is different and their courses are not the same; yet each of them seems marked out by the will of Heaven to sway the destinies of half the globe.

IV

We have seen that Alexis de Tocqueville's interests ranged far into almost every aspect of American life. Yet in his own estimate, one theme in particular dominated all others: the growing tyranny of the majority, the ever-increasing and most formidable barriers raised by the majority around the free expression of opinion, and, as a result, the frightening oneness of American thinking, the absence of eccentricity and divergence from the norm.

A perfect liberty of the mind exists in America, said Tocqueville, just as long as the sovereign majority has yet to decide its course. But once the majority has made up its mind, then all contrary thought must cease, and all controversy must be abandoned, not at the risk of death or physical punishment, but rather at the more subtle and more intolerable pain of ostracism, of being shunned by one's fellows, of being rejected by society.

Throughout history kings and princely rulers had sought without success to control human thought, that most elusive and invisible power of all. Yet where absolute monarchs had failed, democracy succeeds, for the strength of the majority is unlimited and all-pervasive, and the doctrines of equality and majority rule have substituted for the tyranny of the few over the many the more absolute, imperious and widely accepted tyranny of the many over the few.

In contrast to the marked individualism of earlier American society, Tocqueville saw uniformity, conformity and a drab sameness as the characteristics of modern democracy. Originally, men sought freedom to break off the brutal chains of inequality fashioned by the monarchies and aristocracies of old. But "as the conditions of men become equal amongst a people, individuals seem of less, and society of greater, importance." Increasingly, then, men in democracies put a premium upon equality and sameness rather than upon difference, and soon they become intolerant of the very freedom to be different. Besides, in an equalitarian democracy, men are prone to be "lost in the crowd" of their fellows; they lose respect for their own freedom and individuality, and so become grossly indifferent to the free expressions of individual thought, taste and desire on the part of all others. In short, democracy and equality are great levelers. Thus they make it impossible for one man or a few men to oppress the many. But in turn they make it equally impossible for any one man to be free from the oppression of the many. In consequence, the democratic majority can become the greatest, most absolute tyranny of all.

* * * * * * * * * *

Today, of course, Tocqueville's concern for the growing tyranny of the majority strikes home with particular force. It is true that a half-century after *Democracy in America* first appeared, Lord Bryce wrote that Tocqueville's "tyranny of the majority does not strike one as a serious evil in the America of today . . . Faint are the traces which remain of that intolerance of heterodoxy in politics, religion or social views whereon he dilates." But in evaluating Lord Bryce's criticism, one suspects that because he lacked Tocqueville's brilliant and prophetic perceptivity, he simply couldn't fathom what real truth there was to the Frenchman's estimate. Besides, even as Bryce wrote in 1887, the thoroughly majority-oriented democracy that Tocqueville had foreseen and that we experience today had not as yet actually thrust its way through to the surface of American life. Now, however, it has, and modern, frontierless, industrial America—with its factory-made, standardized food, clothing, housing, communications and even amusements— has surely placed a premium upon sameness, undermined individualism and created to perfection what contemporary sociologists bemoan as pre-eminently an "age of conformity." With all of the tensions of cold and hot wars working towards a rather specious "unity of purpose," political non-conformity seems to have all but disappeared. And, generally speaking, the economic, social and political eccentricities that characterized the days of Washington and Jefferson seem to have been largely swallowed up in our age of mass democracy.

To be sure, that Tocqueville's dire predictions should in our times have come so much closer to realization is not at all strange, not even in terms of the very factors that he felt would mitigate the growing tyranny of the majority. For Tocqueville saw one such factor in an almost total absence of government intervention in Americans' everyday life. "Nothing," he wrote in the 1830's, "is more striking to a European traveller in the United States than the absence of what we term . . . government." Yet today one finds the mark of government everywhere.

Tocqueville also distinguished between centralized government and centralized administration. A central government, the means by which over-all policy is set for the nation, is necessary and virtually indispensable. But administration is the means by which such over-all policy is executed, and in Tocqueville's time it was still a separate, decentralized entity, its power placed primarily in state and local agencies which alone dealt with individuals. However, suggested Tocqueville, if the central power "after having established the general principles of government . . . descended to the details of their application; and if, having regulated the great interests of the country, it could descend to the circle of individual interests, freedom would soon be banished from the New World." And who today would deny that over the past half century our federal government has not only established the general principles of government, but also descended to the details of their application, has not only regulated the great interests of the country, but also descended to the circle of individual interests as well?

Then, too, when Tocqueville wrote further of the forces in America that mitigated the mass tyranny he feared, he purposefully singled out the independence of the press, the ease with which one might set up his own newspaper, the total absence of centralized press opinion. Yet today the American press is marked by a constantly declining number of independent publications, by the rise of great newspaper chains, and by a generally pervasive emphasis upon the manufacture of public opinion through the various means of *mass* communications.

Besides, the natural physical substructure of freedom in Tocqueville's time—an open frontier and the widest range of economic opportunity for the free individual—has almost com-

pletely disappeared in our own century. And quite clearly the
free exchange of ideas no longer has its roots deep even in our
physical environment as it did when Tocqueville wrote. As a
result, the questions raised in *Democracy in America* are even
more pressing and challenging today than they were when
Tocqueville and Beaumont first came to the New World to
search out "the image of democracy itself, with its inclinations,
its character, its prejudices, and its passions, in order to learn
what we have to fear or to hope from its progress."

    *   *   *   *   *   *   *   *   *

Alexis de Tocqueville's great work cannot fully be understood, of course, unless one realizes that the young Frenchman
never really despaired of democracy in America. He foresaw
an ever-growing tyranny of the majority, he rigorously and
lengthily analyzed the many factors in American civilization
that seemed to lead resolutely towards conformity and the
constriction of the open society, and he felt certain that if left
to their own devices, Americans would naturally veer away
from the individualism of their forefathers. Yet if conformity
seemed destined to be the "natural" lot of men in democratic
ages, then Tocqueville would make individualism, independence and personal freedom the product of "art" instead. If
for America the future seemed destined to sweep away Nature's own props to freedom, then Tocqueville was equally
determined that new props be constructed in their place.
Surely, he wrote, one shouldn't simply assume that freedom in
democracy is completely dependent upon the physical presence
of an open frontier:

> If those nations whose social condition is democratic
> could remain free only while they inhabit uncultivated re-
> gions, we must despair of the future destiny of the human
> race; for democracy is rapidly acquiring a more extended
> sway, and the wilds are gradually peopled with men.

Nor could one rightly abandon democracy, give up hope
for freedom within its confines, and turn instead to the re-
establishment of those older, more aristocratic patterns of
society and government in which freedom had traditionally
been more secure. ("Thus, the question is not how to reconstruct aristocratic society, but how to make liberty proceed
out of that democratic state of society in which God has placed
us.") Freedom *and* democracy must be man's future objective.
And however formidable the obstacles in his path, man's artistry *can* still make valid what is now a thoughtless and rather
magical equation of equality with freedom, of democracy (or

majority rule) with liberty. Such was Tocqueville's faith, for
had it been otherwise, he wrote,

> . . . I should not have written this book, but I should have
> confined myself to deploring in secret the destiny of mankind.
> I have sought to point out the dangers to which the principle
> of equality exposes the independence of man, because I
> firmly believe that these dangers are the most formidable as
> well as the least foreseen of all those which futurity holds
> in store; but I do not think that they are insurmountable.

Tocqueville, then, saw that "the very essence of democratic
government consists in the absolute sovereignty of the majority." And yet the manner in which democracies might surmount the dangers inherent in majority rule did not escape the
Frenchman. He noted the tools which free men might in their
artistry create to strengthen their ancient freedoms. And in our
own age of conformity, Tocqueville's suggested bulwarks to
freedom take on an even greater meaning:

An independent press, that alone provides the individual a
voice with which to appeal from oppression to the whole
nation, or to mankind itself.

Decentralization, which, to the extent that it is feasible, diminishes absolute authority. . . . And local self-government, as
well as social, economic and intellectual associations or groups,
which give free men a stake in their society, a sense of responsibility and self-importance that keeps them from being "lost in
the crowd" and that makes them more jealous of their liberties.

Forms, manners and traditions, which men in democratic
times generally hold in contempt, but which mold a protective
barrier about our freedoms, encase them in a social framework
at times even stronger than the wrathful will of the majority.
. . . And a forthright legal profession and judiciary to uphold
these forms, to nourish and to defend them.

Groups of citizens to guard always the rights and interests of
their individual fellows, constantly aware that their own freedom depends upon the extent to which they will defend that of
every other citizen.

These are but some of the devices that free men themselves
can contrive and perpetuate to preserve their liberties and
independence against the tyranny of the majority. In our
democratic times, the strongest possible drive towards such a
tyranny is inevitable, but our submission to it is not. And like
Pico and the Humanists of old, Tocqueville saw man's fate as
his own, his destiny awaiting his own creation:

> I am aware that many of my contemporaries maintain that
> nations are never their own masters here below, and that

they necessarily obey some insurmountable and unintelligent power, arising from anterior events, from their race, or
from the soil and climate of their country. Such principles
are false and cowardly; such principles can never produce
aught but feeble men and pusillanimous nations. Providence
had not created mankind entirely independent or entirely
free. It is true, that around every man a fatal circle is traced,
beyond which he cannot pass; but within the wide verge of
that circle he is powerful and free; as it is with men, so with
communities. The nations of our time cannot prevent the
condition of man from becoming equal; but it depends upon
themselves whether the principle of equality is to lead them
to servitude or freedom, to knowledge or barbarism, to prosperity or wretchedness.

With free will and wisdom, then, men may see the pitfalls of
the democratic ages that stretch before them. And then, rather
than submit to these pitfalls—the most extreme of which is
the subversion of freedom by the tyranny of the majority—
they may choose instead a wiser path, the path of freedom
and democracy.

* * * * * * * *

In abridging the two long volumes of *Democracy in America*, every effort has been made to retain not only the spirit and
essential meaning of Tocqueville's classic, but also the most
important descriptive and analytical passages as well. Dele-
tions and changes were made at all times with an eye first to
the needs and purposes of a general as well as academic
audience. Only then were the space requirements of an inexpensive paper-bound edition considered. Thus, though it was
not an easy task to pare and cut down this masterpiece of our
political and social literature, its best portions are presented
here, taken with some modifications from the original Henry
Reeve translation as revised by Frances Bowen.

For the most thorough and enlightening study of Alexis de
Tocqueville and his work, the reader is enthusiastically referred
to George Pierson's *Tocqueville and Beaumont in America*.

Richard D. Heffner

New York City
August 5th, 1955

AUTHOR'S INTRODUCTION

☆

AMONGST the novel objects that attracted my attention during my stay in the United States, nothing struck me more forcibly than the general equality of condition among the people. I readily discovered the prodigious influence which this primary fact exercises on the whole course of society; it gives a peculiar direction to public opinion, and a peculiar tenor to the laws; it imparts new maxims to the governing authorities, and peculiar habits to the governed.

I soon perceived that the influence of this fact extends far beyond the political character and the laws of the country, and that it has no less empire over civil society than over the government; it creates opinions, gives birth to new sentiments, founds novel customs, and modifies whatever it does not produce. The more I advanced in the study of American society, the more I perceived that this equality of condition is the fundamental fact from which all others seem to be derived, and the central point at which all my observations constantly terminated.

I then turned my thoughts to our own hemisphere, and thought that I discerned there something analogous to the spectacle which the New World presented to me. I observed that equality of condition, though it has not there reached the extreme limit which it seems to have attained in the United States, is constantly approaching it; and that the democracy which governs the American communities appears to be rapidly rising into power in Europe. Hence I conceived the idea of the book which is now before the reader.

It is evident to all alike that a great democratic revolution is going on amongst us; but all do not look at it in the same light. To some it appears to be novel but accidental, and, as such, they hope it may still be checked; to others it seems irresistible, because it is the most uniform, the most ancient, and the most permanent tendency which is to be found in history.

I look back for a moment on the situation of France seven hundred years ago, when the territory was divided amongst a small number of families, who were the owners of the soil and the rulers of the inhabitants; the right of governing descended with the family inheritance from generation to generation; force was the only means by which man could act on man; and landed property was the sole source of power. Soon, however, the political power of the clergy was founded, and began to increase: the clergy opened their ranks to all classes, to the poor and the rich, the vassal and the lord; through the Church, equality penetrated into the Government, and he who as a serf must have vegetated in perpetual bondage took his place as a priest in the midst of nobles, and not unfrequently above the heads of kings.

The different relations of men with each other became more complicated and numerous as society gradually became more stable and civilized. Hence the want of civil laws was felt; and the ministers of law soon rose from the obscurity of the tribunals and their dusty chambers, to appear at the court of the monarch, by the side of the feudal barons clothed in their ermine and their mail. Whilst the kings were ruining themselves by their great enterprises, and the nobles exhausting their resources by private wars, the lower orders were enriching themselves by commerce. The influence of money began to be perceptible in state affairs. The transactions of business opened a new road to power, and the financier rose to a station of political influence in which he was at once flattered and despised.

Gradually the diffusion of intelligence, and the increasing taste for literature and art, caused learning and talent to become a means of government; mental ability led to social power, and the man of letters took a part in the affairs of the state. The value attached to high birth declined just as fast as new avenues to power were discovered. In the eleventh century, nobility was beyond all price; in the thirteenth, it might be purchased. Nobility was first conferred by gift in 1270; and equality was thus introduced into the government by the aristocracy itself.

In the course of these seven hundred years, it sometimes happened that the nobles, in order to resist the authority of the crown, or to diminish the power of their rivals, granted some political influence to the common people. Or, more frequently, the king permitted the lower orders to have a share in the government, with the intention of depressing the aristocracy. In France, the kings have always been the most active and the most constant of levellers. When they were strong and ambitious, they spared no pains to raise the people to the level of the nobles; when they were temperate and feeble, they allowed the people to rise above themselves. Some assisted the democracy by their talents, others by their vices. Louis XI.

and Louis XIV. reduced all ranks beneath the throne to the
same degree of subjection; and, finally, Louis XV. descended,
himself and all his court, into the dust.

As soon as land began to be held on any other than a feudal
tenure, and personal property in its turn became able to confer
influence and power, every discovery in the arts, every improvement in commerce or manufactures, created so many
new elements of equality among men. Henceforward every
new invention, every new want which it occasioned, and every
new desire which craved satisfaction, was a step towards a
general levelling. The taste for luxury, the love of war, the empire of fashion, and the most superficial as well as the deepest
passions of the human heart, seemed to co-operate to enrich
the poor and to impoverish the rich.

From the time when the exercise of the intellect became
a source of strength and of wealth, we see that every addition
to science, every fresh truth, and every new idea became
a germ of power placed within the reach of the people. Poetry,
eloquence, and memory, the grace of the mind, the glow of
imagination, depth of thought, and all the gifts which Heaven
scatters at a venture, turned to the advantage of the democracy;
and even when they were in the possession of its adversaries,
they still served its cause by throwing into bold relief the
natural greatness of man. Its conquests spread, therefore, with
those of civilization and knowledge; and literature became an
arsenal open to all, where the poor and the weak daily resorted
for arms.

In running over the pages of our history for seven hundred
years, we shall scarcely find a single great event which has
not promoted equality of condition. The Crusades and the
English wars decimated the nobles and divided their possessions: the municipal corporations introduced democratic
liberty into the bosom of feudal monarchy; the invention of
fire-arms equalized the vassal and the noble on the field of
battle; the art of printing opened the same resources to the
minds of all classes; the post-office brought knowledge alike to
the door of the cottage and to the gate of the palace; and
Protestantism proclaimed that all men are alike able to find
the road to heaven. The discovery of America opened a thousand new paths to fortune, and led obscure adventurers to
wealth and power.

If, beginning with the eleventh century, we examine what
has happened in France from one half-century to another, we
shall not fail to perceive, at the end of each of these periods,
that a twofold revolution has taken place in the state of
society. The noble has gone down on the social ladder, and the

commoner has gone up; the one descends as the other rises. Every half-century brings them nearer to each other, and they will soon meet.

Nor is this peculiar to France. Whithersoever we turn our eyes, we perceive the same revolution going on throughout the Christian world. The various occurrences of national existence have everywhere turned to the advantage of democracy: all men have aided it by their exertions, both those who have intentionally labored in its cause, and those who have served it unwittingly; those who have fought for it, and those who have declared themselves its opponents, have all been driven along in the same track, have all labored to one end; some ignorantly and some unwillingly, all have been blind instruments in the hands of God.

The gradual development of the principle of equality is, therefore, a Providential fact. It has all the chief characteristics of such a fact: it is universal, it is durable, it constantly eludes all human interference, and all events as well as all men contribute to its progress.

Would it, then, be wise to imagine that a social movement, the causes of which lie so far back, can be checked by the efforts of one generation? Can it be believed that the democracy which has overthrown the feudal system, and vanquished kings, will retreat before tradesmen and capitalists? Will it stop now that it has grown so strong, and its adversaries so weak? Whither, then, are we tending? No one can say, for terms of comparison already fail us. The conditions of men are more equal in Christian countries at the present day than they have been at any previous time, or in any part of the world; so that the magnitude of what already has been done prevents us from foreseeing what is yet to be accomplished.

The whole book which is here offered to the public has been written under the impression of a kind of religious terror produced in the author's mind by the view of that irresistible revolution which has advanced for centuries in spite of every obstacle, and which is still advancing in the midst of the ruins it has caused. It is not necessary that God himself should speak in order that we may discover the unquestionable signs of his will. It is enough to ascertain what is the habitual course of nature and the constant tendency of events. I know, without a special revelation, that the planets move in the orbits traced by the Creator's hand.

If the men of our time should be convinced, by attentive observation and sincere reflection, that the gradual and progressive development of social equality is at once the past and the future of their history, this discovery alone would

confer the sacred character of a Divine decree upon the
change. To attempt to check democracy would be in that case
to resist the will of God; and the nations would then be constrained to make the best of the social lot awarded to them
by Providence.

The Christian nations of our day seem to me to present
a most alarming spectacle; the movement which impels them is
already so strong that it cannot be stopped, but it is not yet
so rapid that it cannot be guided. Their fate is still in their
own hands; yet a little while, and it may be so no longer.

The first of the duties which are at this time imposed upon
those who direct our affairs, is to educate the democracy; to
renovate, if possible, its religious belief; to purify its morals; to
regulate its movements; to substitute by degrees a knowledge
of business for its inexperience, and an acquaintance with its
true interests for its blind instincts; to adapt its government
to time and place, and to make it conform to the occurrences
and the men of the times. A new science of politics is needed
for a new world.

This, however, is what we think of least; placed in the
middle of a rapid stream, we obstinately fix our eyes on the
ruins which may still be described upon the shore we have left,
whilst the current hurries us away, and drags us backward
toward the gulf.

In no country in Europe has the great social revolution
which I have just described made such rapid progress as in
France; but it has always advanced without guidance. The
heads of the state have made no preparation for it, and it has
advanced without their consent or without their knowledge.
The most powerful, the most intelligent, and the most moral
classes of the nation have never attempted to take hold of it
in order to guide it. The democracy has consequently been
abandoned to its wild instincts, and it has grown up like those
children who have no parental guidance, who receive their
education in the public streets, and who are acquainted only
with the vices and wretchedness of society. Its existence was
seemingly unknown, when suddenly it acquired supreme
power. Every one then submitted to its caprices; it was wor-
shipped as the idol of strength; and when afterwards it was
enfeebled by its own excesses, the legislator conceived the rash
project of destroying it, instead of instructing it and correcting
its vices. No attempt was made to fit it to govern, but all
were bent on excluding it from the government.

The consequence has been, that the democratic revolution
has taken place in the body of society, without that con-
comitant change in the laws, ideas, customs, and manners,

which was necessary to render such a revolution beneficial. Thus we have a democracy, without anything to lessen its vices and bring out its natural advantages; and although we already perceive the evils it brings, we are ignorant of the benefits it may confer.

While the power of the crown, supported by the aristocracy, peaceably governed the nations of Europe, society, in the midst of its wretchedness, had several sources of happiness which can now scarcely be conceived or appreciated. The power of a part of his subjects was an insurmountable barrier to the tyranny of the prince; and the monarch, who felt the almost divine character which he enjoyed in the eyes of the multitude, derived a motive for the just use of his power from the respect which he inspired. The nobles, high as they were placed above the people, could not but take that calm and benevolent interest in their fate which the shepherd feels towards his flock; and without acknowledging the poor as their equals, they watched over the destiny of those whose welfare Providence had intrusted to their care. The people, never having conceived the idea of a social condition different from their own, and never expecting to become equal to their leaders, received benefits from them without discussing their rights. They became attached to them when they were clement and just, and submitted to their exactions without resistance or servility, as to the inevitable visitations of the Deity. Custom and the manners of the time, moreover, had established certain limits to oppression, and put a sort of legal restraint upon violence.

As the noble never suspected that any one would attempt to deprive him of the privileges which he believed to be legitimate, and as the serf looked upon his own inferiority as a consequence of the immutable order of nature, it is easy to imagine that some mutual exchange of good-will took place between two classes so differently gifted by fate. Inequality and wretchedness were then to be found in society; but the souls of neither rank of men were degraded. Men are not corrupted by the exercise of power, or debased by the habit of obedience; but by the exercise of a power which they believe to be illegitimate, and by obedience to a rule which they consider to be usurped and oppressive.

On the one side were wealth, strength, and leisure, accompanied by the refinements of luxury, the elegance of taste, the pleasures of wit, and the cultivation of the arts; on the other, were labor, clownishness, and ignorance. But in the midst of this coarse and ignorant multitude it was not uncommon to meet with energetic passions, generous sentiments, profound religious convictions, and wild virtues. The social state thus organized might boast of its stability, its power, and, above all, its glory.

But the scene is now changed. Gradually the distinctions of rank are done away; the barriers which once severed mankind are falling down; property is divided, power is shared by many, the light of intelligence spreads, and the capacities of all classes are equally cultivated. The State becomes democratic, and the empire of democracy is slowly and peaceably introduced into the institutions and the manners of the nation.

I can conceive of a society in which all men would feel an equal love and respect for the laws of which they consider themselves as the authors; in which the authority of the government would be respected as necessary, though not as divine; and in which the loyalty of the subject to the chief magistrate would not be a passion, but a quiet and rational persuasion. Every individual being in the possession of rights which he is sure to retain, a kind of manly confidence and reciprocal courtesy would arise between all classes, alike removed from pride and servility. The people, well acquainted with their own true interests, would understand that, in order to profit by the advantages of society, it is necessary to satisfy its requisitions. The voluntary association of the citizens might then take the place of the individual exertions of the nobles, and the community would be alike protected from anarchy and from oppression.

I admit that, in a democratic state thus constituted, society would not be stationary. But the impulses of the social body might there be regulated and made progressive. If there were less splendor than in the midst of an aristocracy, the contrast of misery would also be less frequent; the pleasures of enjoyment might be less excessive, but those of comfort would be more general; the sciences might be less perfectly cultivated, but ignorance would be less common; the impetuosity of the feelings would be repressed, and the habits of the nation softened; there would be more vices and fewer great crimes.

In the absence of enthusiasm and an ardent faith, great sacrifices may be obtained from the members of a commonwealth by an appeal to their understandings and their experience; each individual will feel the same necessity of union with his fellows to protect his own weakness; and as he knows that he can obtain their help only on condition of helping them, he will readily perceive that his personal interest is identified with the interests of the whole community. The nation, taken as a whole, will be less brilliant, less glorious, and perhaps less strong; but the majority of the citizens will enjoy a greater degree of prosperity, and the people will remain quiet, not because they despair of a change for the better, but because they are conscious that they are well off already. If all the consequences of this state of things were not good or useful, society would at least have appropriated all such as were useful and good; and having once and for ever renounced the social advantages of aristocracy, mankind would enter into possession of all the benefits which democracy can afford.

But here it may be asked what we have adopted in the place of those institutions, those ideas, and those customs of our forefathers which we have abandoned. The spell of royalty is broken, but it has not been succeeded by the majesty of the laws. The people have learned to despise all authority, but they still fear it; and fear now extorts more than was formerly paid from reverence and love. I perceive that we have destroyed those individual powers which were able, single-handed, to cope with tyranny; but it is the government that has inherited the privileges of which families, corporations, and individuals have been deprived; to the power of a small number of persons—which, if it was sometimes oppressive, was often conservative—has succeeded the weakness of the whole community.

The division of property has lessened the distance which separated the rich from the poor; but it would seem that the nearer they draw to each other, the greater is their mutual hatred, and the more vehement the envy and the dread with which they resist each other's claims to power; the idea of Right does not exist for either party, and Force affords to both the only argument for the present, and the only guaranty for the future.

The poor man retains the prejudices of his forefathers without their faith, and their ignorance without their virtues; he has adopted the doctrine of self-interest as the rule of his actions, without understanding the science which puts it to use; and his selfishness is no less blind than was formerly his devotedness to others. If society is tranquil, it is not because it is conscious of its strength and its well-being, but because it fears its weakness and its infirmities; a single effort may cost it its life. Everybody feels the evil, but no one has courage or energy enough to seek the cure. The desires, the repinings, the sorrows, and the joys of the present time lead to no visible or permanent result, like the passions of old men, which terminate in impotence.

We have, then, abandoned whatever advantages the old state of things afforded, without receiving any compensation from our present condition; we have destroyed an aristocracy, and we seem inclined to survey its ruins with complacency, and to fix our abode in the midst of them.

The phenomena which the intellectual world presents are not less deplorable. The democracy of France, hampered in its course or abandoned to its lawless passions, has overthrown whatever crossed its path, and has shaken all that it has not destroyed. Its empire has not been gradually introduced, or peaceably established, but it has constantly advanced in the midst of the disorders and the agitations of a conflict. In the heat of the struggle, each partisan is hurried beyond the natural limits of his opinions by the doctrines and the excesses of his opponents, until he loses sight of the end of his exertions, and holds a language which does not express his real sentiments or secret instincts. Hence arises the strange confusion which we are compelled to witness.

I can recall nothing in history more worthy of sorrow and pity, than the scenes which are passing under our eyes. It is as if the natural bond which unites the opinions of man to his tastes, and his actions to his principles, was now broken; the sympathy which has always been observed between the feelings and the ideas of mankind appears to be dissolved, and all the laws of moral analogy to be abolished.

Zealous Christians are still found amongst us, whose minds are nurtured on the thoughts which pertain to a future life, and who readily espouse the cause of human liberty as the source of all moral greatness. Christianity, which has declared that all men are equal in the sight of God, will not refuse to acknowledge that all citizens are equal in the eye of the law. But, by a singular concourse of events, religion has been for a time entangled with those institutions which democracy assails; and it is not unfrequently brought to reject the equality which it loves, and to curse that cause of liberty as a foe, whose efforts it might hallow by its alliance.

By the side of these religious men, I discern others whose looks are turned to earth rather than to heaven. These are the partisans of liberty, not only as the source of the noblest virtues, but more especially as the root of all solid advantages; and they sincerely desire to secure its authority, and to impart its blessings to mankind. It is natural that they should hasten to invoke the assistance of religion, for they must know that liberty cannot be established without morality, nor morality without faith. But they have seen religion in the ranks of their adversaries, and they inquire no further; some of them attack it openly, and the remainder are afraid to defend it.

In former ages, slavery was advocated by the venal and

slavish-minded, whilst the independent and the warm-hearted
were struggling without hope to save the liberties of mankind.
But men of high and generous characters are now to be met
with, whose opinions are at variance with their inclinations,
and who praise that servility which they have themselves never
known. Others, on the contrary, speak of liberty as if they
were able to feel its sanctity and its majesty, and loudly claim
for humanity those rights which they have always refused to
acknowledge.

There are virtuous and peaceful individuals whose pure
morality, quiet habits, opulence, and talents fit them to be the
leaders of the surrounding population. Their love of country is
sincere, and they are ready to make the greatest sacrifices for
its welfare. But civilization often finds them among its opponents; they confound its abuses with its benefits, and the idea of
evil is inseparable in their minds from that of novelty. Near
these I find others, whose object is to materialize mankind, to
hit upon what is expedient without heeding what is just, to
acquire knowledge without faith, and prosperity apart from
virtue; claiming to be the champions of modern civilization,
they place themselves arrogantly at its head, usurping a place
which is abandoned to them, and of which they are wholly
unworthy.

Where are we, then?

The religionists are the enemies of liberty, and the friends of
liberty attack religion; the high-minded and the noble advocate bondage, and the meanest and most servile preach independence; honest and enlightened citizens are opposed to all
progress, whilst men without patriotism and without principle
put themselves forward as the apostles of civilization and
intelligence. Has such been the fate of the centuries which
have preceded our own? and has man always inhabited a
world like the present, where all things are out of their natural
connections, where virtue is without genius, and genius without honor; where the love of order is confounded with a taste
for oppression, and the holy rites of freedom with a contempt
of law; where the light thrown by conscience on human
actions is dim, and where nothing seems to be any longer
forbidden or allowed, honorable or shameful, false or true?

I cannot believe that the Creator made man to leave him in
an endless struggle with the intellectual miseries which surround us. God destines a calmer and a more certain future to
the communities of Europe. I am ignorant of his designs, but
I shall not cease to believe in them because I cannot fathom
them, and I had rather mistrust my own capacity than his
justice.

There is a country in the world where the great social revolution which I am speaking of seems to have nearly reached its natural limits. It has been effected with ease and quietness; say rather that this country is reaping the fruits of the democratic revolution which we are undergoing, without having had the revolution itself.

The emigrants who colonized the shores of America in the beginning of the seventeenth century somehow separated the democratic principle from all the principles which it had to contend with in the old communities of Europe, and transplanted it alone to the New World. It has there been able to spread in perfect freedom, and peaceably to determine the character of the laws by influencing the manners of the country.

It appears to me beyond a doubt that, sooner or later, we shall arrive, like the Americans, at an almost complete equality of condition. But I do not conclude from this, that we shall ever be necessarily led to draw the same political consequences which the Americans have derived from a similar social organization. I am far from supposing that they have chosen the only form of government which a democracy may adopt; but as the generative cause of laws and manners in the two countries is the same, it is of immense interest for us to know what it has produced in each of them.

It is not, then, merely to satisfy a legitimate curiosity that I have examined America; my wish has been to find there instruction by which we may ourselves profit. Whoever should imagine that I have intended to write a panegyric would be strangely mistaken, and on reading this book, he will perceive that such was not my design: nor has it been my object to advocate any form of government in particular, for I am of opinion that absolute excellence is rarely to be found in any system of laws. I have not even pretended to judge whether the social revolution, which I believe to be irresistible, is advantageous or prejudicial to mankind. I have acknowledged this revolution as a fact already accomplished, or on the eve of its accomplishment; and I have selected the nation, from amongst those which have undergone it, in which its development has been the most peaceful and the most complete, in order to discern its natural consequences, and to find out, if possible, the means of rendering it profitable to mankind. I confess that, in America, I saw more than America; I sought there the image of democracy itself, with its inclinations, its character, its prejudices, and its passions, in order to learn what we have to fear or to hope from its progress.

In the first part of this work, I have attempted to show the direction given to the laws by the democracy of America, which is abandoned almost without restraint to its instinctive propensities; and to exhibit the course it prescribes to the government and the influence it exercises on affairs. I have sought to discover the evils and the advantages which it brings. I have examined the precautions used by the Americans to direct it, as well as those which they have not adopted, and I have undertaken to point out the causes which enable it to govern society. I do not know whether I have succeeded in making known what I saw in America, but I am certain that such has been my sincere desire, and that I have never, knowingly, moulded facts to ideas, instead of ideas to facts.

Whenever a point could be established by the aid of written documents, I have had recourse to the original text, and to the most authentic and approved works. . . . Whenever opinions, political customs, or remarks on the manners of the country were concerned, I have endeavored to consult the most enlightened men I met with. If the point in question was important or doubtful, I was not satisfied with one testimony, but I formed my opinion on the evidence of several witnesses. Here the reader must necessarily rely upon my word. I could frequently have quoted names which are either known to him, or which deserve to be so, in proof of what I advance; but I have carefully abstained from this practice. A stranger frequently hears important truths at the fireside of his host, which the latter would perhaps conceal from the ear of friendship; he consoles himself with his guest for the silence to which he is restricted, and the shortness of the traveller's stay takes away all fear of his indiscretion. I carefully noted every conversation of this nature as soon as it occurred, but these notes will never leave my writing-case. I had rather injure the success of my statements than add my name to the list of those strangers who repay the generous hospitality they have received by subsequent chagrin and annoyance.

I am aware that, notwithstanding my care, nothing will be easier than to criticise this book, if any one ever chooses to criticise it.

Those readers who may examine it closely will discover, I think, in the whole work, a dominant thought which binds, so to speak, its several parts together. But the diversity of the subjects I have had to treat is exceedingly great, and it will not be difficult to oppose an isolated fact of the body of facts which I cite, or an isolated idea to the body of ideas I put forth. I hope to be read in the spirit which has guided my labors, and that my book may be judged by the general impression it leaves, as I have formed my own judgment not on any single reason, but upon the mass of evidence.

It must not be forgotten that the author who wishes to be understood is obliged to push all his ideas to their utmost theoretical consequences, and often to the verge of what is false or impracticable; for if it be necessary sometimes to depart from the rules of logic in action, such is not the case in discourse, and a man finds it almost as difficult to be inconsistent in his language, as to be consistent in his conduct.

I conclude by myself pointing out what many readers will consider the principal defect of the work. This book is written to favor no particular views, and in composing it, I have entertained no design of serving or attacking any party. I have undertaken, not to see differently from others, but to look further than others, and whilst they are busied for the morrow only, I have turned my thoughts to the whole future.

PART ONE

✦

1. Origin of the Anglo-Americans.

AFTER the birth of a human being, his early years are obscurely spent in the toils or pleasures of childhood. As he grows up, the world receives him, when his manhood begins, and he enters into contact with his fellows. He is then studied for the first time, and it is imagined that the germ of the vices and the virtues of his maturer years is then formed. This, if I am not mistaken, is a great error. We must begin higher up; we must watch the infant in his mother's arms; we must see the first images which the external world casts upon the dark mirror of his mind, the first occurrences which he witnesses; we must hear the first words which awaken the sleeping powers of thought, and stand by his earliest efforts,—if we would understand the prejudices, the habits, and the passions which will rule his life. The entire man is, so to speak, to be seen in the cradle of the child.

The growth of nations presents something analogous to this; they all bear some marks of their origin. The circumstances which accompanied their birth and contributed to their development affect the whole term of their being. If we were able to go back to the elements of states, and to examine the oldest monuments of their history, I doubt not that we should discover in them the primal cause of the prejudices, the habits, the ruling passions, and, in short, of all that constitutes what is called the national character. We should there find the explanation of certain customs which now seem at variance with the prevailing manners; of such laws as conflict with established principles; and of such incoherent opinions as are here and there to be met with in society, like those fragments of broken chains which we sometimes see hanging from the vaults of an old edifice, and supporting nothing. This might explain the destinies of certain nations which seem borne on by an unknown force to ends of which they themselves are ignorant. But hitherto facts have been wanting to researches of this kind: the spirit of inquiry has only come upon communities in their latter days; and when they at length contemplated their origin, time had already obscured it, or ignorance and pride adorned it with truth-concealing fables.

America is the only country in which it has been possible to witness the natural and tranquil growth of society, and where the influence exercised on the future condition of states by their origin is clearly distinguishable. . . . America, consequently, exhibits in the broad light of day the phenomena which the ignorance or rudeness of earlier ages conceals from our researches. Near enough to the time when the states of America were founded, to be accurately acquainted with their elements, and sufficiently removed from that period to judge of some of their results, the men of our own day seem destined to see further than their predecessors into the series of human events. Providence has given us a torch which our forefathers did not possess, and has allowed us to discern fundamental causes in the history of the world which the obscurity of the past concealed from them. If we carefully examine the social and political state of America, after having studied its history, we shall remain perfectly convinced that not an opinion, not a custom, not a law, I may even say not an event, is upon record which the origin of that people will not explain. The readers of this book will find in the present chapter the germ of all that is to follow, and the key to almost the whole work.

The emigrants who came at different periods to occupy the territory now covered by the American Union differed from each other in many respects; their aim was not the same, and they governed themselves on different principles. These men had, however, certain features in common, and they were all placed in an analogous situation. The tie of language is, perhaps, the strongest and the most durable that can unite mankind. All the emigrants spoke the same tongue; they were all offsets from the same people. Born in a country which had been agitated for centuries by the struggles of faction, and in which all parties had been obliged in their turn to place themselves under the protection of the laws, their political education had been perfected in this rude school; and they were more conversant with the notions of right, and the principles of true freedom, than the greater part of their European contemporaries. At the period of the first emigrations, the township system, that fruitful germ of free institutions, was deeply rooted in the habits of the English; and with it the doctrine of the sovereignty of the people had been introduced into the bosom of the monarchy of the house of Tudor. . . .

Another remark, to which we shall hereafter have occasion

to recur, is applicable not only to the English, but to . . . all the Europeans who successively established themselves in the New World. All these European colonies contained the elements, if not the development, of a complete democracy. Two causes led to this result. It may be said generally, that on leaving the mother country the emigrants had, in general, no notion of superiority one over another. The happy and the powerful do not go into exile, and there are no surer guaranties of equality among men than poverty and misfortune. It happened, however, on several occasions, that persons of rank were driven to America by political and religious quarrels. Laws were made to establish a gradation of ranks; but it was soon found that the soil of America was opposed to a territorial aristocracy. To bring that refractory land into cultivation, the constant and interested exertions of the owner himself were necessary; and when the ground was prepared, its produce was found to be insufficient to enrich a proprietor and a farmer at the same time. The land was then naturally broken up into small portions, which the proprietor cultivated for himself. Land is the basis of an aristocracy, which clings to the soil that supports it; for it is not by privileges alone, nor by birth, but by landed property handed down from generation to generation, that an aristocracy is constituted. A nation may present immense fortunes and extreme wretchedness; but unless those fortunes are territorial, there is no true aristocracy, but simply the class of the rich and that of the poor.

All the British colonies had then a great degree of family likeness at the epoch of their settlement. All of them, from their beginning, seemed destined to witness the growth, not of the aristocratic liberty of their mother country, but of that freedom of the middle and lower orders of which the history of the world had as yet furnished no complete example. In this general uniformity, however, several striking differences were discernible, which it is necessary to point out. Two branches may be distinguished in the great Anglo-American family, which have hitherto grown up without entirely commingling; the one in the South, the other in the North.

Virginia received the first English colony; the emigrants took possession of it in 1607. The idea that mines of gold and silver are the sources of national wealth was at that time singularly prevalent in Europe; a fatal delusion, which has done more to impoverish the European nations who adopted it, and has cost more lives in America, than the united influence of war and bad laws. The men sent to Virginia were seekers of gold, adventurers without resources and without character, whose turbulent and restless spirit endangered the infant

colony, and rendered its progress uncertain. Artisans and
agriculturists arrived afterwards; and, although they were a
more moral and orderly race of men, they were hardly in any
respect above the level of the inferior classes in England. No
lofty views, no spiritual conception, presided over the foundation of these new settlements. The colony was scarcely established when slavery was introduced; this was the capital fact
which was to exercise an immense influence on the character,
the laws, and the whole future of the South. Slavery . . .
dishonors labor; it introduces idleness into society, and with
idleness, ignorance and pride, luxury and distress. It enervates
the powers of the mind, and benumbs the activity of man.
The influence of slavery, united to the English character,
explains the manners and the social condition of the Southern
States.

In the North, the same English character . . . received
totally different colors. Here . . . the two or three main ideas
which now constitute the basis of the social theory of the
United States were first combined. . . . They now extend
their influence . . . over the whole American world. The
civilization of New England has been like a beacon lit upon
a hill, which, after it has diffused its warmth immediately
around it, also tinges the distant horizon with its glow. . . .

The settlers who established themselves on the shores of
New England all belonged to the more independent classes of
their native country. Their union on the soil of America at
once presented the singular phenomenon of a society contain-
ing neither lords nor common people, and we may almost say,
neither rich nor poor. These men possessed, in proportion to
their number, a greater mass of intelligence than is to be found
in any European nation of our own time. All, perhaps without
a single exception, had received a good education, and many
of them were known in Europe for their talents and their
acquirements. The other colonies had been founded by adventurers without families; the emigrants of New England brought
with them the best elements of order and morality; they landed
on the desert coast accompanied by their wives and children.
But what especially distinguished them from all others was the
aim of their undertaking. They had not been obliged by
necessity to leave their country; the social position they abandoned was one to be regretted, and their means of subsistence
were certain. . . . In facing the inevitable sufferings of exile,
their object was the triumph of an idea.

The emigrants, or, as they deservedly styled themselves, the
Pilgrims, belonged to that English sect the austerity of whose
principles had acquired for them the name of Puritans. Puri-

tanism was not merely a religious doctrine, but it corresponded
in many points with the most absolute democratic and republican theories. It was this tendency which had aroused its most
dangerous adversaries. Persecuted by the government of the
mother country, and disgusted by the habits of a society which
the rigor of their own principles condemned, the Puritans went
forth to seek some rude and unfrequented part of the world,
where they could live according to their own opinions, and
worship God in freedom. . . . Puritanism . . . was scarcely
less a political than a religious doctrine. No sooner had the
emigrants landed on the barren coast . . . than it was their
first care to constitute a society, by subscribing the [Mayflower
Compact]:

"IN THE NAME OF GOD. AMEN. We, whose names are
underwritten, the loyal subjects of our dread Sovereign Lord
King James, &s. &c., Having undertaken for the glory of God,
and advancement of the Christian Faith, and the honour of
our King and country, a voyage to plant the first colony in the
northern parts of Virginia; Do by these presents solemnly and
mutually, in the presence of God and one another, covenant
and combine ourselves together into a civil body politick, for
our better ordering and preservation, and furtherance of the
ends aforesaid: and by virtue hereof do enact, constitute, and
frame such just and equal laws, ordinances, acts, constitutions,
and offices, from time to time, as shall be thought most meet
and convenient for the general good of the Colony: unto which
we promise all due submission and obedience . . ."

This happened in 1620, and from that time forwards the
emigration went on. The religious and political passions which
ravaged the British empire during the whole reign of Charles I.
drove fresh crowds of sectarians every year to the shores of
America. In England, the stronghold of Puritanism continued
to be in the middle classes; and it was from the middle classes
that most of the emigrants came. The population of New
England increased rapidly; and whilst the hierarchy of rank
despotically classed the inhabitants of the mother country, the
colony approximated more and more the novel spectacle of a
community homogeneous in all its parts. A democracy, more
perfect than antiquity had dared to dream of, started in full
size and panoply from the midst of an ancient feudal society.

The English government was not dissatisfied with a large
emigration which removed the elements of fresh discord and
further revolutions. On the contrary, it did everything to
encourage it, and seemed to have no anxiety about the destiny
of those who sought a shelter on the soil of America from
the rigor of their laws. It appeared as if New England was a

region given up to the dreams of fancy, and the unrestrained experiments of innovators. The English colonies (and this is one of the main causes of their prosperity) have always enjoyed more internal freedom and more political independence than the colonies of other nations; and this principle of liberty was nowhere more extensively applied than in the States of New England. . . .

The means used by the English government to people these new domains were of several kinds: the king sometimes appointed a governor of his own choice, who ruled a portion of the New World in the name and under the immediate orders of the crown; this is the colonial system adopted by the other countries of Europe. Sometimes, grants of certain tracts were made by the crown to an individual or to a company, in which case all the civil and political power fell into the hands of one or more persons, who, under the inspection and control of the crown, sold the lands and governed the inhabitants. Lastly, a third system consisted in allowing a certain number of emigrants to form themselves into a political society under the protection of the mother country, and to govern themselves in whatever was not contrary to her laws. This mode of colonization, so favorable to liberty, was adopted only in New England.

In 1628, a charter of this kind was granted by Charles I. to the emigrants who went to form the colony of Massachusetts. But, in general, charters were not given to the colonies of New England till their existence had become an established fact. Plymouth, Providence, New Haven, Connecticut, and Rhode Island were founded without the help, and almost without the knowledge, of the mother country. The new settlers did not derive their powers from the head of the empire, although they did not deny its supremacy; they constituted themselves into a society, and it was not till thirty or forty years afterwards, under Charles II., that their existence was legally recognized by a royal charter.

This frequently renders it difficult, in studying the earliest historical and legislative records of New England, to detect the link which connected the emigrants with the land of their forefathers. They continually exercised the rights of sovereignty; they named their magistrates, concluded peace or declared war, made police regulations, and enacted laws, as if their allegiance was due only to God. Nothing can be more curious, and at the same time more instructive, than the legislation of that period; it is there that the solution of the great social problem which the United States now present to the world is to be found. . . .

The chief care of the legislators . . . was the maintenance

of orderly conduct and good morals in the community: thus they constantly invaded the domain of conscience, and there was scarcely a sin which was not subject to magisterial censure. The reader is aware of the rigor with which these laws punished rape and adultery; intercourse between unmarried persons was likewise severely repressed. The judge was empowered to inflict either a pecuniary penalty, a whipping, or marriage, on the misdemeanants; and if the records of the old courts of New Haven may be believed, prosecutions of this kind were not unfrequent. We find a sentence, bearing date the 1st of May, 1660, inflicting a fine and reprimand on a young woman who was accused of using improper language, and of allowing herself to be kissed. The Code of 1650 abounds in preventive measures. It punishes idleness and drunkenness with severity. Innkeepers were forbidden to furnish more than a certain quantity of liquor to each consumer; and simple lying, whenever it may be injurious, is checked by a fine or a flogging. In other places, the legislator, entirely forgetting the great principles of religious toleration which he had himself demanded in Europe, makes attendance on divine service compulsory, and goes so far as to visit with severe punishment, and even with death, Christians who chose to worship God according to a ritual differing from his own. Sometimes, indeed, the zeal for regulation induces him to descend to the most frivolous particulars: thus a law is to be found in the same code which prohibits the use of tobacco. It must not be forgotten that these fantastical and vexatious laws were not imposed by authority, but that they were freely voted by all the persons interested in them, and that the manners of the community were even more austere and puritanical than the laws. . . .

These errors are no doubt discreditable to human reason; they attest the inferiority of our nature, which is incapable of laying firm hold upon what is true and just, and is often reduced to the alternative of two excesses. In strict connection with this penal legislation, which bears such striking marks of a narrow, sectarian spirit, and of those religious passions which had been warmed by persecution and were still fermenting among the people, a body of political laws is to be found, which, though written two hundred years ago, is still in advance of the liberties of our age.

The general principles which are the groundwork of modern constitutions—principles which, in the seventeenth century, were imperfectly known in Europe, and not completely triumphant even in Great Britain—were all recognized and established by the laws of New England: the intervention of the people in public affairs, the free voting of taxes, the responsibil-

ity of the agents of power, personal liberty, and trial by jury,
were all positively established without discussion. . . .

In the laws of . . . New England we find the germ and
gradual development of the township independence, which is
the life and mainspring of American liberty at the present day.
The political existence of the majority of the nations of Europe
commenced in the superior ranks of society, and was gradually
and imperfectly communicated to the different members of the
social body. In America, on the contrary, it may be said that
the township was organized before the county, the county before the State, the State before the Union.

In New England, townships were completely and definitely
constituted as early as 1650. The independence of the township
was the nucleus round which the local interests, passions,
rights, and duties collected and clung. It gave scope to the
activity of a real political life, thoroughly democratic and
republican. The colonies still recognized the supremacy of the
mother country; monarchy was still the law of the State; but
the republic was already established in every township. The
towns named their own magistrates of every kind, rated themselves, and levied their own taxes. In the New England town,
the law of representation was not adopted; but the affairs of
the community were discussed, as at Athens, in the market-
place, by a general assembly of the citizens.

In studying the laws which were promulgated at this early
era of the American republics, it is impossible not to be
struck by the remarkable acquaintance with the science of
government, and the advanced theory of legislation, which
they display. The ideas there formed of the duties of society
towards its members are evidently much loftier and more
comprehensive than those of European legislators at that time:
obligations were there imposed upon it which it elsewhere
slighted. In the States of New England, from the first, the condition of the poor was provided for; strict measures were
appointed to attend to them; records were established in every
town, in which the results of public deliberations, and the
births, deaths, and marriages of the citizens, were entered;
clerks were directed to keep these records; officers were
charged with the administration of vacant inheritances, and
with the arbitration of litigated landmarks; and many others
were created, whose chief functions were the maintenance of
public order in the community. The law enters into a thousand
various details to anticipate and satisfy a crowd of social wants
which are even now very inadequately felt in France.

But it is by the mandates relating to Public Education that
the original character of American civilization is at once placed

in the clearest light. "It being," says the law, "one chief project of that old deluder, Satan, to keep men from the knowledge of the Scripture by persuading them from the use of tongues, to the end that learning may not be buried in the graves of our forefathers, in church and commonwealth, the Lord assisting our endeavors." Here follow clauses establishing schools in every township, and obliging the inhabitants, under pain of heavy fines, to support them. Schools of a superior kind were founded in the same manner in the more populous districts. The municipal authorities were bound to enforce the sending of children to school by their parents; they were empowered to inflict fines upon all who refused compliance; and in cases of continued resistance, society assumed the place of the parent, took possession of the child, and deprived the father of those natural rights which he used to so bad a purpose. The reader will undoubtedly have remarked the preamble of these enactments: in America, religion is the road to knowledge, and the observance of the divine laws leads man to civil freedom.

If, after having cast a rapid glance over the state of American society in 1650, we turn to the condition of Europe, and more especially to that of the Continent, at the same period, we cannot fail to be struck with astonishment. On the continent of Europe, at the beginning of the seventeenth century, absolute monarchy had everywhere triumphed over the ruins of the oligarchical and feudal liberties of the Middle Ages. Never perhaps were the ideas of right more completely overlooked, than in the midst of the splendor and literature of Europe; never was there less political activity among the people; never were the principles of true freedom less widely circulated; and at that very time, those principles, which were scorned or unknown by the nations of Europe, were proclaimed in the deserts of the New World, and were accepted as the future creed of a great people. The boldest theories of the human mind were reduced to practice by a community so humble, that not a statesman condescended to attend to it; and a system of legislation without a precedent was produced offhand by the natural originality of men's imaginations. . . .

I have said enough to put the character of Anglo-American civilization in its true light. It is the result (and this should be constantly present to the mind) of two distinct elements, which in other places have been in frequent hostility, but which in America have been admirably incorporated and combined with one another. I allude to the spirit of Religion and the spirit of Liberty.

The settlers of New England were at the same time ardent

sectarians and daring innovators. Narrow as the limits of some
of their religious opinions were, they were free from all political prejudices. Hence arose two tendencies, distinct but not
opposite, which are everywhere discernible in the manners as
well as the laws of the country.

One would think that men who had sacrificed their friends,
their family, and their native land to a religious conviction
would be wholly absorbed in the pursuit of the treasure which
they had just purchased at so high a price. And yet we find
them seeking with nearly equal zeal for material wealth and
moral good,—for well-being and freedom on earth, and salvation in heaven. They moulded and altered at pleasure all political principles, and all human laws and institutions; they broke
down the barriers of the society in which they were born; they
disregarded the old principles which had governed the world
for ages; a career without bounds, a field without a horizon,
was opened before them: they precipitate themselves into it,
and traverse it in every direction. But, having reached the limits
of the political world, they stop of their own accord, and lay
aside with awe the use of their most formidable faculties; they
no longer doubt or innovate; they abstain from raising even
the veil of the sanctuary, and bow with submissive respect
before truths which they admit without discussion.

Thus, in the moral world, everything is classified, systema-
tized, foreseen, and decided beforehand; in the political world,
everything is agitated, disputed, and uncertain. In the one is a
passive though a voluntary obedience; in the other, an independence scornful of experience, and jealous of all authority.
These two tendencies, apparently so discrepant, are far from
conflicting; they advance together, and mutually support each
other. Religion perceives that civil liberty affords a noble exercise to the faculties of man, and that the political world is a
field prepared by the Creator for the efforts of mind. Free and
powerful in its own sphere, satisfied with the place reserved
for it, religion never more surely establishes its empire than
when it reigns in the hearts of men unsupported by aught
beside its native strength.

Liberty regards religion as its companion in all its battles
and its triumphs,—as the cradle of its infancy, and the divine
source of its claims. It considers religion as the safeguard of
morality, and morality as the best security of law, and the
surest pledge of the duration of freedom. . . .

2. Democratic Social Condition of the Anglo-Americans.

SOCIAL condition is commonly the result of circumstances, sometimes of laws, oftener still of these two causes united; but when once established, it may justly be considered as itself the source of almost all the laws, the usages, and the ideas which regulate the conduct of nations: whatever it does not produce, it modifies. If we would become acquainted with the legislation and the manners of a nation, therefore, we must begin by the study of its social condition.

The Striking Characteristic of the Social Condition of the Anglo-Americans Is Its Essential Democracy.

. . . The social condition of the Americans is eminently democratic; this was its character at the foundation of the colonies, and it is still more strongly marked at the present day. . . . Great equality existed among the emigrants who settled on the shores of New England. Even the germs of aristocracy were never planted in that part of the Union. The only influence which obtained there was that of intellect; the people were used to reverence certain names as the emblems of knowledge and virtue. . . .

This was the state of things to the east of the Hudson: to the southwest of that river, and as far as the Floridas, the case was different. In most of the States situated to the southwest of the Hudson some great English proprietors had settled, who had imported with them aristocratic principles and the English law of inheritance. I have explained the reasons why it was impossible ever to establish a powerful aristocracy in America; these reasons existed with less force to the southwest of the Hudson. In the South, one man, aided by slaves, could cultivate a great extent of country; it was therefore common to see rich landed proprietors. But their influence was not altogether aristocratic, as that term is understood in Europe, since they possessed no privileges; and the cultivation of their estates being carried on by slaves, they had no tenants depending on them, and consequently no patronage. Still, the great proprietors south of the Hudson constituted a superior class, having ideas and tastes of its own, and forming the centre of political action. This kind of aristocracy sympathized with the body of the people, whose passions and interests it easily embraced; but it was too weak and too short-lived to excite either love or hatred. This was the class which headed the insurrection in the South, and furnished the best leaders of the American Revolution.

At this period, society was shaken to its centre. The people, in whose name the struggle had taken place, conceived the desire of exercising the authority which it had acquired, its democratic tendencies were awakened; and having thrown off the yoke of the mother country, it aspired to independence of every kind. The influence of individuals gradually ceased to be felt, and custom and law united to produce the same result.

But the law of inheritance was the last step to equality. I am surprised that ancient and modern jurists have not attributed to this law a greater influence on human affairs. It is true that these laws belong to civil affairs; but they ought, nevertheless, to be placed at the head of all political institutions; for they exercise an incredible influence upon the social state of a people, whilst political laws only show what this state already is. They have, moreover, a sure and uniform manner of operating upon society, affecting, as it were, generations yet unborn. Through their means, man acquires a kind of preternatural power over the future lot of his fellow-creatures. When the legislator has once regulated the law of inheritance, he may rest from his labor. The machine once put in motion will go on for ages, and advance, as if self-guided, towards a point indicated beforehand. When framed in a particular manner, this law unites, draws together, and vests property and power in a few hands; it causes an aristocracy, so to speak, to spring out of the ground. If formed on opposite principles, its action is still more rapid; it divides, distributes, and disperses both property and power. Alarmed by the rapidity of its progress, those who despair of arresting its motion endeavor, at least, to obstruct it by difficulties and impediments. They vainly seek to counteract its effect by contrary efforts; but it shatters and reduces to powder every obstacle, until we can no longer see anything but a moving and impalpable cloud of dust, which signals the coming of the Democracy. . . .

In virtue of the law of partible inheritance, the death of every proprietor brings about a kind of revolution in the property; not only do his possessions change hands, but their very nature is altered, since they are parcelled into shares, which become smaller and smaller at each division. This is the direct, and as it were the physical, effect of the law. It follows, then, that, in countries where equality of inheritance is established by law, property, and especially landed property, must constantly

tend to division into smaller and smaller parts. . . . But the
law of equal division exercises its influence not merely upon
the property itself, but it affects the minds of the heirs, and
brings their passions into play. These indirect consequences
tend powerfully to the destruction of large fortunes, and especially of large domains.

Among nations whose law of descent is founded upon the
right of primogeniture, landed estates often pass from generation to generation without undergoing division,—the consequence of which is, that family feeling is to a certain degree
incorporated with the estate. The family represents the estate,
the estate the family,—whose name, together with its origin,
its glory, its power, and its virtues, is thus perpetuated in an
imperishable memorial of the past and a sure pledge of the
future. When the equal partition of property is established by
law, the intimate connection is destroyed between family feeling and the preservation of the paternal estate; the property
ceases to represent the family; for, as it must inevitably be
divided after one or two generations, it has evidently a constant tendency to diminish, and must in the end be completely
dispersed. The sons of the great landed proprietor, if they are
few in number, or if fortune befriends them, may indeed entertain the hope of being as wealthy as their father, but not of
possessing the same property that he did; their riches must be
composed of other elements than his. Now, as soon as you
divest the land-owner of that interest in the preservation of
his estate which he derives from association, from tradition,
and from family pride, you may be certain that, sooner or
later, he will dispose of it; for there is a strong pecuniary
interest in favor of selling, as floating capital produces higher
interest than real property, and is more readily available to
gratify the passions of the moment.

Great landed estates which have once been divided never
come together again; for the small proprietor draws from his
land a better revenue, in proportion, than the large owner does
from his; and of course, he sells it at a higher rate. The calcula-
tions of gain, therefore, which decide the rich man to sell his
domain, will still more powerfully influence him against buying
small estates to unite them into a large one. What is called
family pride is often founded upon an illusion of self-love. A
man wishes to perpetuate and immortalize himself, as it were,
in his great-grandchildren. Where family pride ceases to act,
individual selfishness comes into play. When the idea of family
becomes vague, indeterminate, and uncertain, a man thinks of
his present convenience; he provides for the establishment of
his next succeeding generation, and no more. Either a man

gives up the idea of perpetuating his family, or at any rate, he
seeks to accomplish it by other means than by a landed estate.

Thus, not only does the law of partible inheritance render it
difficult for families to preserve their ancestral domains entire,
but it deprives them of the inclination to attempt it, and compels them in some measure to co-operate with the law in their
own extinction. . . . By both these means, the law succeeds
in striking at the root of landed property, and dispersing rapidly both families and fortunes. Most certainly it is not for us,
Frenchmen of the nineteenth century, who daily witness the
political and social changes which the law of partition is bringing to pass, to question its influence. It is perpetually conspicuous in our country, overthrowing the walls of our dwellings,
and removing the landmarks of our fields. But although it has
produced great effects in France, much still remains for it to
do. Our recollections, opinions, and habits present powerful
obstacles to its progress.

In the United States, it has nearly completed its work of
destruction, and there we can best study its results. The English laws concerning the transmission of property were abolished in almost all the States at the time of the Revolution.
The law of entail was so modified as not materially to interrupt
the free circulation of property. The first generation having
passed away, estates began to be parcelled out; and the change
became more and more rapid with the progress of time. And
now, after a lapse of a little more than sixty years, the aspect
of society is totally altered; the families of the great landed
proprietors are almost all commingled with the general mass.
. . . The sons of these opulent citizens have become mer-
chants, lawyers, or physicians. Most of them have lapsed
into obscurity. The last trace of hereditary ranks and distinctions is destroyed,—the law of partition has reduced all to one
level.

I do not mean that there is any lack of wealthy individuals
in the United States; I know of no country, indeed, where the
love of money has taken stronger hold on the affections of men,
and where a profounder contempt is expressed for the theory
of the permanent equality of property. But wealth circulates
with inconceivable rapidity, and experience shows that it is
rare to find two succeeding generations in the full enjoyment
of it.

This picture, which may, perhaps, be thought to be over-
charged, still gives a very imperfect idea of what is taking place
in the new States of the West and Southwest. At the end of the
last century, a few bold adventurers began to penetrate into
the valley of the Mississippi; and the mass of the population

very soon began to move in that direction: communities
unheard of till then suddenly appeared in the desert. States
whose names were not in existence a few years before, claimed
their place in the American Union; and in the Western settlements we may behold democracy arrived at its utmost limits.
In these States, founded off-hand, and as it were by chance,
the inhabitants are but of yesterday. Scarcely known to one
another, the nearest neighbors are ignorant of each other's
history. In this part of the American continent, therefore, the
population has escaped the influence not only of great names
and great wealth, but even of the natural aristocracy of knowledge and virtue. None are there able to wield that respectable
power which men willingly grant to the remembrance of a
life spent in doing good before their eyes. The new States of the
West are already inhabited; but society has no existence among
them.

It is not only the fortunes of men which are equal in
America; even their acquirements partake in some degree of
the same uniformity. I do not believe that there is a country in
the world where, in proportion to the population, there are so
few ignorant, and at the same time so few learned, individuals.
Primary instruction is within the reach of everybody; superior
instruction is scarcely to be obtained by any. This is not surprising; it is, in fact, the necessary consequence of what we
have advanced above. Almost all the Americans are in easy
circumstances, and can, therefore, obtain the first elements of
human knowledge.

In America, there are but few wealthy persons; nearly all
Americans have to take a profession. Now, every profession
requires an apprenticeship. The Americans can devote to general education only the early years of life. At fifteen, they enter
upon their calling, and thus their education generally ends at
the age when ours begins. Whatever is done afterwards is
with a view to some special and lucrative object; a science is
taken up as a matter of business, and the only branch of it
which is attended to is such as admits of an immediate practical application.

In America, most of the rich men were formerly poor; most
of those who now enjoy leisure were absorbed in business
during their youth; the consequence of which is, that when
they might have had a taste for study, they had no time for it,
and when the time is at their disposal, they have no longer the
inclination. There is no class, then, in America, in which the
taste for intellectual pleasures is transmitted with hereditary
fortune and leisure, and by which the labors of the intellect are
held in honor. Accordingly, there is an equal want of the desire

and the power of application to these objects. A middling
standard is fixed in America for human knowledge. All approach as near to it as they can; some as they rise, others as
they descend. Of course, a multitude of persons are to be found
who entertain the same number of ideas on religion, history,
science, political economy, legislation, and government. The
gifts of intellect proceed directly from God, and man cannot
prevent their unequal distribution. But it is at least a consequence of what we have just said, that although the capacities
of men are different, as the Creator intended they should be,
Americans find the means of putting them to use are equal.

In America, the aristocratic element has always been feeble
from its birth; and if at the present day it is not actually
destroyed, it is at any rate so completely disabled, that we can
scarcely assign to it any degree of influence on the course of
affairs. The democratic principle, on the contrary, has gained
so much strength by time, by events, and by legislation, as to
have become not only predominant, but all-powerful. There
is no family or corporate authority, and it is rare to find even
the influence of individual character enjoy any durability.
America, then, exhibits in her social state an extraordinary
phenomenon. Men are there seen on a greater equality in
point of fortune and intellect, or, in other words, more equal in
their strength, than in any other country of the world, or in any
age of which history has preserved the remembrance.

Political Consequences of Social Democracy.

The political consequences of such a social condition as this
are easily deducible. It is impossible to believe that equality
will not eventually find its way into the political world, as it
does everywhere else. To conceive of men remaining forever
unequal upon a single point, yet equal on all others, is impossible; they must come in the end to be equal upon all.

Now I know of only two methods of establishing equality
in the political world; every citizen must be put in possession
of his rights, or rights must be granted to no one. For nations
which are arrived at the same stage of social existence as the
Anglo-Americans, it is, therefore, very difficult to discover a
medium between the sovereignty of all and the absolute power
of one man: and it would be vain to deny that the social condition which I have been describing is just as liable to one of
these consequences as to the other. There is, in fact, a manly
and lawful passion for equality which incites men to wish all to
be powerful and honored. This passion tends to elevate the
humble to the rank of the great; but there exists also in the

human heart a depraved taste for equality, which impels the weak to attempt to lower the powerful to their own level, and reduces men to prefer equality in slavery to inequality with freedom. Not that those nations whose social condition is democratic naturally despise liberty; on the contrary, they have an instinctive love of it. But liberty is not the chief and constant object of their desires; equality is their idol: they make rapid and sudden efforts to obtain liberty, and, if they miss their aim, resign themselves to their disappointment; but nothing can satisfy them without equality, and they would rather perish than lose it.

On the other hand, in a state where the citizens are all nearly on an equality, it becomes difficult for them to preserve their independence against the aggressions of power. No one among them being strong enough to engage in the struggle alone with advantage, nothing but a general combination can protect their liberty. Now, such a union is not always possible. From the same social position, then, nations may derive one or the other of two great political results; these results are extremely different from each other, but they both proceed from the same cause. The Anglo-Americans are the first nation who, having been exposed to this formidable alternative, have been happy enough to escape the dominion of absolute power. They have been allowed by their circumstances, their origin, their intelligence, and especially by their morals, to establish and maintain the sovereignty of the people.

3. The Sovereignty of the People in America.

WHENEVER the political laws of the United States are to be discussed, it is with the doctrine of the sovereignty of the people that we must begin.

The principle of the sovereignty of the people, which is always to be found, more or less, at the bottom of almost all human institutions, generally remains there concealed from view. It is obeyed without being recognized, or if for a moment it be brought to light, it is hastily cast back into the gloom of the sanctuary.

"The will of the nation" is one of those phrases which have been most largely abused by the wily and the despotic of every age. Some have seen the expression of it in the purchased suffrages of a few of the satellites of power; others, in the votes of a timid or an interested minority; and some have even discovered it in the silence of a people, on the supposition that the fact of submission established the right to command.

In America, the principle of the sovereignty of the people is not either barren or concealed, as it is with some other nations; it is recognized by the customs and proclaimed by the laws; it spreads freely, and arrives without impediment at its most remote consequences. If there be a country in the world where the doctrine of the sovereignty of the people can be fairly appreciated, where it can be studied in its application to the affairs of society, and where its dangers and its advantages may be judged, that country is assuredly America.

I have already observed that, from their origin, the sovereignty of the people was the fundamental principle of most of the British colonies in America. It was far, however, from then exercising as much influence on the government of society as it now does. Two obstacles—the one external, the other internal—checked its invasive progress.

It could not ostensibly disclose itself in the laws of colonies which were still constrained to obey the mother country; it was therefore obliged to rule secretly in the provincial assemblies, and especially in the townships.

American society at that time was not yet prepared to adopt it with all its consequences. Intelligence in New England, and wealth in the country to the south of the Hudson, (as I have shown in the preceding chapter,) long exercised a sort of aristocratic influence, which tended to keep the exercise of social power in the hands of a few. Not all the public functionaries were chosen by popular vote, nor were all the citizens voters. The electoral franchise was everywhere somewhat restricted, and made dependent on a certain qualification, which was very low in the North, and more considerable in the South.

The American Revolution broke out, and the doctrine of the sovereignty of the people came out of the townships, and took possession of the State. Every class was enlisted in its cause; battles were fought and victories obtained for it; it became the law of laws.

A change almost as rapid was effected in the interior of society, where the law of inheritance completed the abolition of local influences.

As soon as this effect of the laws and of the Revolution became apparent to every eye, victory was irrevocably pronounced in favor of the democratic cause. All power was, in fact, in its hands, and resistance was no longer possible. The higher orders submitted without a murmur and without a struggle to an evil which was thenceforth inevitable. The ordinary fate of falling powers awaited them: each of their members followed his own interest; and as it was impossible to wring the power from the hands of a people whom they did not detest sufficiently to brave, their only aim was to secure its good-will at any price. The most democratic laws were consequently voted by the very men whose interests they impaired: and thus, although the higher classes did not excite the passions of the people against their order, they themselves accelerated the triumph of the new state of things; so that, by a singular change, the democratic impulse was found to be most irresistible in the very States where the aristocracy had the firmest hold. The State of Maryland, which had been founded by men of rank, was the first to proclaim universal suffrage, and to introduce the most democratic forms into the whole of its government.

When a nation begins to modify the elective qualification, it may easily be foreseen that, sooner or later, that qualification will be entirely abolished. There is no more invariable rule in the history of society: the further electoral rights are extended, the greater is the need of extending them; for after each concession the strength of the democracy increases, and its demands increase with its strength. The ambition of those who are below the appointed rate is irritated in exact proportion to the great number of those who are above it. The exception at last becomes the rule, concession follows concession, and no stop can be made short of universal suffrage.

At the present day the principle of the sovereignty of the people has acquired, in the United States, all the practical development which the imagination can conceive. It is unencumbered by those fictions which are thrown over it in other countries, and it appears in every possible form, according to the exigency of the occasion. Sometimes the laws are made by the people in a body, as at Athens; and sometimes its representatives, chosen by universal suffrage, transact business in its name, and under its immediate supervision.

In some countries, a power exists which, though it is in a degree foreign to the social body, directs it, and forces it to pursue a certain track. In others, the ruling force is divided, being partly within and partly without the ranks of the people. But nothing of the kind is to be seen in the United States; there society governs itself for itself. All power centres in its bosom; and scarcely an individual is to be met with who would venture to conceive, or, still less, to express, the idea of seeking it elsewhere. The nation participates in the making of its laws by the choice of its legislators, and in the execution of them by the choice of the agents of the executive government; it may almost be said to govern itself, so feeble and so restricted is the

share left to the administration, so little do the authorities
forget their popular origin and the power from which they
emanate. The people reign in the American political world as
the Deity does in the universe. They are the cause and the
aim of all things; everything comes from them, and everything is absorbed in them.

4. Local Government.

. . . THE principle of the sovereignty of the people governs
the whole political system of the Anglo-Americans. Every page
of this book will afford new applications of the same doctrine.
In the nations by which the sovereignty of the people is recognized, every individual has an equal share of power, and participates equally in the government of the state. Why, then,
does he obey the government, and what are the natural limits
of this obedience? Every individual is always supposed to be
as well informed, as virtuous, and as strong as any of his
fellow-citizens. He obeys the government, not because he is
inferior to those who conduct it, or because he is less capable
than any other of governing himself; but because he acknowledges the utility of an association with his fellow-men, and he
knows that no such association can exist without a regulating
force. He is a subject in all that concerns the duties of citizens
to each other; he is free, and responsible to God alone, for all
that concerns himself. Hence arises the maxim, that every one
is the best and sole judge of his own private interest, and that
society has no right to control a man's actions, unless they are
prejudicial to the common weal, or unless the common weal
demands his help. This doctrine is universally admitted in the
United States. I shall hereafter examine the general influence
which it exercises on the ordinary actions of life: I am now
speaking of the municipal bodies.

The township, taken as a whole, and in relation to the central government, is only an individual, like any other to whom
the theory I have just described is applicable. Municipal independence in the United States is, therefore, a natural consequence of this very principle of the sovereignty of the people.
All the American republics recognize it more or less; but circumstances have peculiarly favored its growth in New England.

In this part of the Union, political life had its origin in
the townships; and it may almost be said that each of them
originally formed an independent nation. When the kings of

England afterwards asserted their supremacy, they were content to assume the central power of the state. They left the townships where they were before; and although they are now subject to the state, they were not at first, or were hardly so. They did not receive their powers from the central authority, but, on the contrary, they gave up a portion of their independence to the state. This is an important distinction, and one which the reader must constantly recollect. The townships are generally subordinate to the state only in those interests which I shall term *social*, as they are common to all the others. They are independent in all that concerns themselves alone; and amongst the inhabitants of New England, I believe that not a man is to be found who would acknowledge that the state has any right to interfere in their town affairs. The towns of New England buy and sell, prosecute or are indicted, augment or diminish their rates, and no administrative authority ever thinks of offering any opposition.

There are certain social duties, however, which they are bound to fulfil. If the State is in need of money, a town cannot withhold the supplies; if the State projects a road, the township cannot refuse to let it cross its territory; if a police regulation is made by the State, it must be enforced by the town; if a uniform system of public instruction is enacted, every town is bound to establish the schools which the law ordains. When I come to speak of the administration of the law in the United States I shall point out how, and by what means, the townships are compelled to obey in these different cases: I here merely show the existence of the obligation. Strict as this obligation is, the government of the State imposes it in principle only, and in its performance the township resumes all its independent rights. Thus, taxes are voted by the State, but they are levied and collected by the township; the establishment of a school is obligatory, but the township builds, pays, and superintends it. In France, the state collector receives the local imposts; in America, the town collector receives the taxes of the State. Thus the French government lends its agents to the *commune;* in America, the township lends its agents to the government. This alone shows how widely the two nations differ.

Spirit of the Townships of New England.

In America, not only do municipal bodies exist, but they are kept alive and supported, by town spirit. The township of New England possesses two advantages, which strongly excite the interest of mankind,—namely, independence and authority.

Its sphere is limited, indeed; but within that sphere, its action is unrestrained. This independence alone gives it a real importance, which its extent and population would not insure.

It is to be remembered, too, that the affections of men generally turn towards power. Patriotism is not durable in a conquered nation. The New-Englander is attached to his township, not so much because he was born in it, but because it is a free and strong community, of which he is a member, and which deserves the care spent in managing it. In Europe, the absence of local public spirit is a frequent subject of regret to those who are in power; every one agrees that there is no surer guaranty of order and tranquillity, and yet nothing is more difficult to create. If the municipal bodies were made powerful and independent, it is feared that they would become too strong, and expose the state to anarchy. Yet, without power and independence, a town may contain good subjects, but it can have no active citizens. Another important fact is, that the township of New England is so constituted as to excite the warmest of human affections, without arousing the ambitious passions of the heart of man. The officers of the county are not elected, and their authority is very limited. Even the State is only a second-rate community whose tranquil and obscure administration offers no inducement sufficient to draw men away from the home of their interests into the turmoil of public affairs. The Federal Government confers power and honor on the men who conduct it; but these individuals can never be very numerous. The high station of the Presidency can only be reached at an advanced period of life; and the other Federal functionaries of a high class are generally men who have been favored by good luck, or have been distinguished in some other career. Such cannot be the permanent aim of the ambitious. But the township, at the centre of the ordinary relations of life, serves as a field for the desire of public esteem, the want of exciting interest, and the taste for authority and popularity; and the passions which commonly embroil society change their character, when they find a vent so near the domestic hearth and the family circle.

In the American townships, power has been disseminated with admirable skill, for the purpose of interesting the greatest possible number of persons in the common weal. Independently of the voters, who are from time to time called into action, the power is divided among innumerable functionaries and officers, who all, in their several spheres, represent the powerful community in whose name they act. The local administration thus affords an unfailing source of profit and interest to a vast number of individuals.

The American system, which divides the local authority among so many citizens, does not scruple to multiply the functions of the town officers. For in the United States, it is believed, and with truth, that patriotism is a kind of devotion which is strengthened by ritual observance. In this manner, the activity of the township is continually perceptible; it is daily manifested in the fulfilment of a duty, or the exercise of a right; and a constant though gentle motion is thus kept up in society, which animates without disturbing it. The American attaches himself to his little community for the same reason that the mountaineer clings to his hills, because the characteristic features of his country are there more distinctly marked; it has a more striking physiognomy.

The existence of the townships of New England is, in general, a happy one. Their government is suited to their tastes, and chosen by themselves. In the midst of the profound peace and general comfort which reign in America, the commotions of municipal life are unfrequent. The conduct of local business is easy. The political education of the people has long been complete; say rather that it was complete, when the people first set foot upon the soil. In New England, no tradition exists of a distinction of ranks; no portion of the community is tempted to oppress the remainder; and the wrongs which may injure isolated individuals are forgotten in the general contentment which prevails. If the government has faults, (and it would no doubt be easy to point out some,) they do not attract notice, for the government really emanates from those it governs, and whether it acts ill or well, this fact casts the protecting spell of a parental pride over its demerits. Besides, they have nothing wherewith to compare it. England formerly governed the mass of the colonies; but the people was always sovereign in the township, where its rule is not only an ancient, but a primitive state.

The native of New England is attached to his township because it is independent and free: this co-operation in its affairs insures his attachment to its interest; the well-being it affords him secures his affection; and its welfare is the aim of his ambition and of his future exertions. He takes a part in every occurrence in the place; he practises the art of government in the small sphere within his reach; he accustoms himself to those forms without which liberty can only advance by revolutions; he imbibes their spirit; he acquires a taste for order, comprehends the balance of powers, and collects clear practical notions on the nature of his duties and the extent of his rights. . . .

5. Decentralization in America—Its Effects.

NOTHING is more striking to a European traveller in the United States, than the absence of what we term the Government, or the Administration. Written laws exist in America, and one sees the daily execution of them; but although everything moves regularly, the mover can nowhere be discovered. The hand which directs the social machine is invisible. Nevertheless, as all persons must have recourse to certain grammatical forms, which are the foundation of human language, in order to express their thoughts; so all communities are obliged to secure their existence by submitting to a certain amount of authority, without which they fall into anarchy. This authority may be distributed in several ways, but it must always exist somewhere.

There are two methods of diminishing the force of authority in a nation. The first is to weaken the supreme power in its very principle, by forbidding or preventing society from acting in its own defence under certain circumstances. To weaken authority in this manner is the European way of establishing freedom.

The second manner of diminishing the influences of authority does not consist in stripping society of some of its rights, nor in paralyzing its escorts, but in distributing the exercise of its powers among various hands, and in multiplying functionaries, to each of whom is given the degree of power necessary for him to perform his duty. There may be nations whom this distribution of social powers might lead to anarchy; but in itself, it is not anarchical. The authority thus divided is, indeed, rendered less irresistible and less perilous, but it is not destroyed.

The Revolution of the United States was the result of a mature and reflecting preference of freedom, and not of a vague or ill-defined craving for independence. It contracted no alliance with the turbulent passions of anarchy; but its course was marked, on the contrary, by a love of order and law.

It was never assumed in the United States, that the citizen of a free country has a right to do whatever he pleases; on the contrary, more social obligations were there imposed upon him than anywhere else. No idea was ever entertained of attacking the principle or contesting the rights of society;

but the exercise of its authority was divided, in order that the office might be powerful and the officer insignificant, and that the community should be at once regulated and free. In no country in the world does the law hold so absolute a language as in America; and in no country is the right of applying it vested in so many hands. The administrative power in the United States presents nothing either centralized or hierarchical in its constitution; this accounts for its passing unperceived. The power exists, but its representative is nowhere to be seen. . . .

Centralization is a word in general and daily use, without any precise meaning being attached to it. Nevertheless, there exist two distinct kinds of centralization, which it is necessary to discriminate with accuracy.

Certain interests are common to all parts of a nation, such as the enactment of its general laws, and the maintenance of its foreign relations. Other interests are peculiar to certain parts of the nation; such, for instance, as the business of the several townships. When the power which directs the former or general interests is concentrated in one place or in the same persons, it constitutes a centralized government. To concentrate in like manner into one place the direction of the latter or local interests, constitutes what may be termed a centralized administration.

Upon some points, these two kinds of centralization coincide; but by classifying the objects which fall more particularly within the province of each, they may easily be distinguished.

It is evident that a centralized government acquires immense power when united to centralized administration. Thus combined, it accustoms men to set their own will habitually and completely aside; to submit, not only for once, or upon one point, but in every respect, and at all times. Not only, therefore, does this union of power subdue them compulsorily, but it affects their ordinary habits; it isolates them, and then influences each separately.

These two kinds of centralization mutually assist and attract each other; but they must not be supposed to be inseparable. It is impossible to imagine a more completely centralized government than that which existed in France under Louis XIV.; when the same individual was the author and the interpreter of the laws, and the representative of France at home and abroad, he was justified in asserting that he constituted the state. Nevertheless, the administration was much less centralized under Louis XIV. than it is at the present day.

In England, the centralization of the government is carried

to great perfection; the state has the compact vigor of one man, and its will puts immense masses in motion, and turns its whole power where it pleases. But England, which has done so great things for the last fifty years, has never centralized its administration. Indeed, I cannot conceive that a nation can live and prosper without a powerful centralization of government. But I am of opinion that a centralized administration is fit only to enervate the nations in which it exists, by incessantly diminishing their local spirit. Although such an administration can bring together at a given moment, on a given point, all the disposable resources of a people, it injures the renewal of those resources. It may insure a victory in the hour of strife, but it gradually relaxes the sinews of strength. It may help admirably the transient greatness of a man, but not the durable prosperity of a nation.

Observe, that whenever it is said that a state cannot act because it is not centralized, it is the centralization of the government which is spoken of. It is frequently asserted, and we assent to the proposition, that the German empire has never been able to bring all its powers into action. But the reason was, that the state was never able to enforce obedience to its general laws; the several members of that great body always claimed the right, or found the means, of refusing their co-operation to the representatives of the common authority, even in the affairs which concerned the mass of the people; in other words, there was no centralization of government. The same remark is applicable to the Middle Ages; the cause of all the miseries of feudal society was, that the control, not only of administration, but of government, was divided amongst a thousand hands, and broken up in a thousand different ways. The want of a centralized government prevented the nations of Europe from advancing with energy in any straightforward course.

We have shown that, in the United States, there is no centralized administration, and no hierarchy of public functionaries. Local authority has been carried farther than any European nation could endure without great inconvenience, and it has even produced some disadvantageous consequences in America. But in the United States, the centralization of the government is perfect; and it would be easy to prove that the national power is more concentrated there than it has ever been in the old nations of Europe. Not only is there but one legislative body in each State,—not only does there exist but one source of political authority,—but numerous assemblies in districts or counties have not, in general, been multiplied, lest they should be tempted to leave their administrative duties and interfere with the government. In America, the legislature of each State is supreme; nothing can impede its authority,—neither privileges, nor local immunities, nor personal influence, nor even the empire of reason, since it represents that majority which claims to be the sole organ of reason. Its own determination is, therefore, the only limit to its action. In juxtaposition with it, and under its immediate control, is the representative of the executive power, whose duty it is to constrain the refractory to submit by superior force. The only symptom of weakness lies in certain details of the action of the government. The American republics have no standing armies to intimidate a discontented minority; but as no minority has as yet been reduced to declare open war, the necessity of an army has not been felt. The State usually employs the officers of the township or the county to deal with the citizens. Thus, for instance, in New England, the town assessor fixes the rate of taxes; the town collector receives them; the town treasurer transmits the amount to the public treasury; and the disputes which may arise are brought before the ordinary courts of justice. This method of collecting taxes is slow as well as inconvenient, and it would prove a perpetual hindrance to a government whose pecuniary demands were large. It is desirable that, in whatever materially affects its existence, the government should be served by officers of its own, appointed by itself, removable at its pleasure, and accustomed to rapid methods of proceeding. But it will always be easy for the central government, organized as it is in America, to introduce more energetic and efficacious modes of action according to its wants.

The want of a centralized government will not, then, as has often been asserted, prove the destruction of the republics of the New World; for from the American governments being not sufficiently centralized, I shall prove hereafter that they are too much so. The legislative bodies daily encroach upon the authority of the government, and their tendency, like that of the French Convention, is to appropriate it entirely to themselves. The social power thus centralized is constantly changing hands, because it is subordinate to the power of the people. It often forgets the maxims of wisdom and foresight in the consciousness of its strength. Hence arises its danger. Its vigor, and not its impotence, will probably be the cause of its ultimate destruction.

The system of decentralized administration produces several different effects in America. The Americans seem to me to have outstepped the limits of sound policy, in isolating the administration of the government: for order, even in secondary affairs, is a matter of national importance. As the State has no administrative functionaries of its own, stationed on different points of its territory, to whom it can give a common impulse, the consequence is, that it rarely attempts to issue any general police regulations. The want of these regulations is severely felt, and is frequently observed by Europeans. The appearance of disorder which prevails on the surface leads him at first to imagine that society is in a state of anarchy; nor does he perceive his mistake till he has gone deeper into the subject. Certain undertakings are of importance to the whole State; but they cannot be put in execution, because there is no State administration to direct them. Abandoned to the exertions of the towns or counties, under the care of elected and temporary agents, they lead to no result, or at least to no durable benefit.

The partisans of centralization in Europe are wont to maintain that the government can administer the affairs of each locality better than the citizens could do it for themselves: this may be true, when the central power is enlightened, and the local authorities are ignorant; when it is alert, and they are slow; when it is accustomed to act, and they to obey. Indeed, it is evident that this double tendency must augment with the increase of centralization, and that the readiness of the one and the incapacity of the others must become more and more prominent. But I deny that it is so, when the people are as enlightened, as awake to their interests, and as accustomed to reflect on them, as the Americans are. I am persuaded, on the contrary, that, in this case, the collective strength of the citizens will always conduce more efficaciously to the public welfare than the authority of the government. I know it is difficult to point out with certainty the means of arousing a sleeping population, and of giving it passions and knowledge which it does not possess; it is, I am well aware, an arduous task to persuade men to busy themselves about their own affairs. It would frequently be easier to interest them in the punctilios of court etiquette, than in the repairs of their common dwelling. But whenever a central administration affects completely to supersede the persons most interested, I believe that it is either misled, or desirous to mislead. However enlightened and skilful a central power may be, it cannot of itself embrace all the details of the life of a great nation. Such vigilance exceeds the powers of man. And when it attempts unaided to create and set in motion so many complicated springs, it must submit to a very imperfect result, or exhaust itself in bootless efforts.

Centralization easily succeeds, indeed, in subjecting the ex-

ternal actions of men to a certain uniformity, which we come
at last to love for its own sake, independently of the objects
to which it is applied, like those devotees who worship the
statue, and forget the deity it represents. Centralization imparts without difficulty an admirable regularity to the routine
of business; provides skilfully for the details of the social
police; represses small disorders and petty misdemeanors;
maintains society in a *status quo* alike secure from improve-
and decline; and perpetuates a drowsy regularity in the conduct
of affairs, which the heads of the administration are wont to
call good order and public tranquillity; in short, it excels in
prevention, but not in action. Its force deserts it, when society
is to be profoundly moved, or accelerated in its course; and if
once the co-operation of private citizens is necessary to the
furtherance of its measures, the secret of its impotence is disclosed. Even whilst the centralized power, in its despair, in-
vokes the assistance of the citizens, it says to them: "You
shall act just as I please, as much as I please, and in the direction which I please. You are to take charge of the details, without aspiring to guide the system; you are to work in darkness; and afterwards you may judge my work by its results."
These are not the conditions on which the alliance of the
human will is to be obtained; it must be free in its gait, and
responsible for its acts, or (such as the constitution of man)
the citizen had rather remain a passive spectator, than a dependent actor, in schemes with which he is unacquainted.

It is undeniable, that the want of those uniform regulations which control the conduct of every inhabitant of France,
is not unfrequently felt in the United States. Gross instances
of social indifference and neglect are to be met with; and
from time to time, disgraceful blemishes are seen, in complete
contrast with the surrounding civilization. Useful undertakings, which cannot succeed without perpetual attention and
rigorous exactitude, are frequently abandoned; for in America,
as well as in other countries, the people proceed by sudden
impulses and momentary exertions. The European, accustomed to find a functionary always at hand to interfere with
all he undertakes, reconciles himself with difficulty to the
complex mechanism of the administration of the townships.
In general, it may be affirmed that the lesser details of the
police, which render life easy and comfortable, are neglected in America, but that the essential guaranties of man in
society are as strong there as elsewhere. In America, the power
which conducts the administration is far less regular, less
enlightened, and less skilful, but a hundred-fold greater, than
in Europe. In no country in the world, do the citizens make

such exertions for the common weal. I know of no people who
have established schools so numerous and efficacious, places
of public worship better suited to the wants of the inhabitants,
or roads kept in better repair. Uniformity or permanence
of design, the minute arrangement of details, and the perfection of administrative system, must not be sought for in the
United States: what we find there is, the presence of a power
which, if it is somewhat wild, is at least robust, and an existence checkered with accidents, indeed, but full of anima-
tion and effort.

Granting, for an instant, that the villages and counties of
the United States would be more usefully governed by a central authority, which they had never seen, than by functionaries taken from among them,—admitting, for the sake of
argument, that there would be more security in America, and
the resources of society would be better employed there, if the
whole administration centred in a single arm,—still the
political advantages which the Americans derive from their
decentralized system would induce me to prefer it to the contrary plan. It profits me but little, after all, that a vigilant
authority always protects the tranquillity of my pleasures,
and constantly averts all dangers from my path, without my
care or concern, if this same authority is the absolute master
of my liberty and my life, and if it so monopolizes movement
and life, that when it languishes everything languishes around
it, that when it sleeps everything must sleep, and that when it
dies the state itself must perish.

There are countries in Europe, where the natives consider
themselves as a kind of settlers, indifferent to the fate of the
spot which they inhabit. The greatest changes are effected there
without their concurrence, and (unless chance may have apprised them of the event) without their knowledge; nay, more,
the condition of his village, the police of his street, the repairs of the church or the parsonage, do not concern him;
for he looks upon all these things as unconnected with himself,
and as the property of a powerful stranger whom he calls the
government. He has only a life-interest in these possessions,
without the spirit of ownership or any ideas of improvement.
This want of interest in his own affairs goes so far, that if his
own safety or that of his children is at last endangered, instead of trying to avert the peril, he will fold his arms, and
wait till the whole nation comes to his aid. This man, who has
so completely sacrificed his own free will, does not, more than
any other person, love obedience; he cowers, it is true, before the pettiest officer; but he braves the law with the spirit of

a conquered foe, as soon as its superior force is withdrawn: he perpetually oscillates between servitude and license.

When a nation has arrived at this state, it must either change its customs and its laws, or perish; for the source of public virtues is dried up; and though it may contain subjects, it has no citizens. Such communities are a natural prey to foreign conquests; and if they do not wholly disappear from the scene, it is only because they are surrounded by other nations similar or inferior to themselves; it is because they still have no indefinable instinct of patriotism; and an involuntary pride in the name of their country, or a vague reminiscence of its bygone fame, suffices to give them an impulse of self-preservation.

Nor can the prodigious exertions made by certain nations to defend a country in which they had lived, so to speak, as strangers, be adduced in favor of such a system; for it will be found that, in these cases, their main incitement was religion. The permanence, the glory, or the prosperity of the nation were become parts of their faith; and in defending their country, they defended also that Holy City of which they were all citizens. The Turkish tribes have never taken an active share in the conduct of their affairs; but they accomplished stupendous enterprises, as long as the victories of the Sultan were triumphs of the Mohammedan faith. In the present age, they are in rapid decay, because their religion is departing, and despotism only remains. Montesquieu, who attributed to absolute power an authority peculiar to itself, did it, as I conceive, an undeserved honor; for despotism, taken by itself, can maintain nothing durable. On close inspection, we shall find that religion, and not fear, has ever been the cause of the long-lived prosperity of an absolute government. Do what you may, there is no true power among men except in the free union of their will; and patriotism or religion are the only two motives in the world which can long urge all the people towards the same end.

Laws cannot rekindle an extinguished faith; but men may be interested by the laws in the fate of their country. It depends upon the laws to awaken and direct the vague impulse of patriotism, which never abandons the human heart; and if it be connected with the thoughts, the passions, and the daily habits of life, it may be consolidated into a durable and rational sentiment. Let it not be said that it is too late to make the experiment; for nations do not grow old as men do, and every fresh generation is a new people ready for the care of the legislator.

It is not the *administrative*, but the *political* effects of decentralization, that I most admire in America. In the United

States, the interests of the country are everywhere kept in view; they are an object of solicitude to the people of the whole Union, and every citizen is as warmly attached to them as if they were his own. He takes pride in the glory of his nation; he boasts of its success, to which he conceives himself to have contributed; and he rejoices in the general prosperity by which he profits. The feeling he entertains toward the state is analogous to that which unites him to his family, and it is by a kind of selfishness that he interests himself in the welfare of his country.

To the European, a public officer represents a superior force: to an American, he represents a right. In America, then, it may be said that no one renders obedience to man, but to justice and to law. If the opinion which the citizen entertains of himself is exaggerated, it is at least salutary; he unhesitatingly confides in his own powers, which appear to him to be all-sufficient. When a private individual meditates an undertaking, however directly connected it may be with the welfare of society, he never thinks of soliciting the co-operation of the government; but he publishes his plan, offers to execute it, courts the assistance of other individuals, and struggles manfully against all obstacles. Undoubtedly he is often less successful than the state might have been in his position; but in the end, the sum of these private undertakings far exceeds all that the government could have done.

As the administrative authority is within the reach of the citizens, whom in some degree it represents, it excites neither their jealousy nor hatred: as its resources are limited, every one feels that he must not rely solely on its aid. Thus, when the administration thinks fit to act within its own limits, it is not abandoned to itself, as in Europe; the duties of private citizens are not supposed to have lapsed because the state has come into action; but every one is ready, on the contrary, to guide and support it. This action of individuals, joined to that of the public authorities, frequently accomplishes what the most energetic centralized administration would be unable to do.

It would be easy to adduce several facts in proof of what I advance, but I had rather give only one, with which I am best acquainted. In America, the means which the authorities have at their disposal for the discovery of crimes and the arrest of criminals are few. A state police does not exist, and passports are unknown. The criminal police of the United States cannot be compared to that of France; the magistrates and public agents are not numerous; they do not always initiate the measures for arresting the guilty; and the examinations of prisoners are rapid and oral. Yet I believe that in no country does crime more rarely elude punishment. The reason is, that every one conceives himself to be interested in furnishing evidence of the crime, and in seizing the delinquent. During my stay in the United States, I witnessed the spontaneous formation of committees in a country for the pursuit and prosecution of a man who had committed a great crime. In Europe, a criminal is an unhappy man who is struggling for his life against the agents of power, whilst the people are merely a spectator of the conflict: in America, he is looked upon as an enemy of the human race, and the whole of mankind is against him.

I believe that provincial institutions are useful to all nations, but nowhere do they appear to me to be more necessary than amongst a democratic people. In an aristocracy, order can always be maintained in the midst of liberty; and as the rulers have a great deal to lose, order is to them a matter of great interest. In like manner, an aristocracy protects the people from the excesses of despotism, because it always possesses an organized power ready to resist a despot. But a democracy without provincial institutions has no security against these evils. How can a populace, unaccustomed to freedom in small concerns, learn to use it temperately in great affairs? What resistance can be offered to tyranny in a country where each individual is weak, and where the citizens are not united by any common interest? Those who dread the license of the mob, and those who fear absolute power, ought alike to desire the gradual development of provincial liberties.

I am also convinced, that democratic nations are most likely to fall beneath the yoke of a centralized administration, for several reasons, amongst which is the following.

The constant tendency of these nations is to concentrate all the strength of the government in the hands of the only power which directly represents the people; because, beyond the people, nothing is to be perceived but a mass of equal individuals. But when the same power already has all the attributes of government, it can scarcely refrain from penetrating into the details of the administration, and an opportunity of doing so is sure to present itself in the long run, as was the case in France. In the French Revolution, there were two impulses in opposite directions, which must never be confounded; the one was favorable to liberty, the other to despotism. Under the ancient monarchy, the king was the sole author of the laws; and below the power of the sovereign, certain vestiges of provincial institutions, half destroyed, were still distinguishable. These provincial institutions were incoherent, ill arranged, and

frequently absurd; in the hands of the aristocracy, they had
sometimes been converted into instruments of oppression. The
Revolution declared itself the enemy at once of royalty and
of provincial institutions; it conformed in indiscriminate
hatred all that had preceded it,—despotic power and the
checks of its abuses; and its tendency was at once to repub-
licanize and to centralize. This double character of the French
Revolution is a fact which has been adroitly handled by the
friends of absolute power. Can they be accused of laboring in
the cause of despotism, when they are defending that centralized administration which was one of the great innovations of
the Revolution? In this manner, popularity may be united
with hostility to the rights of the people, and the secret slave
of tyranny may be the professed lover of freedom.

I have visited the two nations in which the system of provincial liberty has been most perfectly established, and I
have listened to the opinions of different parties in those countries. In America, I met with men who secretly aspired to
destroy the democratic institutions of the Union in England,
I found others who openly attacked the aristocracy; but I found
no one who did not regard provincial independence as a great
good. In both countries, I heard a thousand different causes
assigned for the evils of the state; but the local system was
never mentioned amongst them. I heard citizens attribute the
power and prosperity of their country to a multitude of reasons; but they *all* placed the advantages of local institutions in
the foremost rank.

Am I to suppose that when men, who are naturally so
divided on religious opinions and on political theories, agree
on one point, (and that one which they can best judge, as it is
one of which they have daily experience,) they are all in error?
The only nations which deny the utility of provincial liberties
are those which have fewest of them; in other words, those
only censure the institution who do not know it.

6. *Judicial Power in the United States, and Its Influence on Political Society.*

I HAVE thought it right to devote a separate chapter to the
judicial authorities of the United States, lest their great
political importance should be lessened in the reader's eyes
by a merely incidental mention of them. Confederations have
existed in other countries beside America; I have seen repub-

lics elsewhere than upon the shores of the New World alone: the representative system of government has been adopted in several states of Europe; but I am not aware that any nation of the globe has hitherto organized a judicial power in the same manner as the Americans. The judicial organization of the United States is the institution which a stranger has the greatest difficulty in understanding. He hears the authority of a judge invoked in the political occurrences of every day, and he naturally concludes that, in the United States, the judges are important political functionaries: nevertheless, when he examines the nature of the tribunals, they offer at the first glance nothing which is contrary to the usual habits and privileges of those bodies; and the magistrates seem to him to interfere in public affairs only by chance, but by a chance which recurs every day. . . .

The first characteristic of judicial power in all nations is the duty of arbitration. But rights must be contested in order to warrant the interference of a tribunal; and an action must be brought before the decision of a judge can be had. As long, therefore, as a law is uncontested, the judicial authority is not called upon to discuss it, and it may exist without being perceived. When a judge in a given case attacks a law relating to that case, he extends the circle of his customary duties, without, however, stepping beyond it, since he is in some measure obliged to decide upon the law in order to decide the case. But if he pronounces upon a law without proceeding from a case, he clearly steps beyond his sphere, and invades that of the legislative authority.

The second characteristic of judicial power is, that it pronounces on special cases, and not upon general principles. If a judge, in deciding a particular point, destroys a general principle by passing a judgment which tends to reject all the inferences from that principle, and consequently to annul it, he remains within the ordinary limits of his functions. But if he directly attacks a general principle without having a particular case in view, he leaves the circle in which all nations have agreed to confine his authority; he assumes a more important, and perhaps a more useful influence, than that of the magistrate; but he ceases to represent the judicial power.

The third characteristic of the judicial power is, that it can only act when it is called upon, or when, in legal phrase, it has taken cognizance of an affair. This characteristic is less general than the other two; but, notwithstanding the exceptions, I think it may be regarded as essential; the judicial power is, by its nature, devoid of action; it must be put in motion in order to produce a result. When it is called upon to repress a crime, it punishes the criminal; when a wrong is to be redressed, it is ready to redress it; when an act requires interpretation, it is prepared to interpret it; but it does not pursue criminals, hunt out wrongs, or examine evidence of its own accord. A judicial functionary who should take the initiative, and usurp the censureship of the laws, would in some measure do violence to the passive nature of his authority.

The Americans have retained these three distinguishing characteristics of the judicial power: an American judge can only pronounce a decision when litigation has arisen, he is conversant only with special cases, and he cannot act until the cause has been duly brought before the court. His position is, therefore, perfectly similar to that of the magistrates of other nations; and yet he is invested with immense political power. How comes that about? If the sphere of his authority and his means of action are the same as those of other judges, whence does he derive a power which they do not possess? The cause of this difference lies in the simple fact, that the Americans have acknowledged the right of the judges to found their decisions on the *Constitution* rather than on the *laws*. In other words, they have not permitted them to apply such laws as may appear to them to be unconstitutional.

I am aware that a similar right has been sometimes claimed —but claimed in vain—by courts of justice in other countries; but in America it is recognized by all the authorities; and not a party, not so much as an individual, is found to contest it. This fact can be explained only by the principles of the American constitutions. In France, the constitution is—or, at least, is supposed to be—immutable; and the received theory is, that no power has the right of changing any part of it. In England, the constitution may change continually; or rather, it does not in reality exist; the Parliament is at once a legislative and a constituent assembly. The political theories of America are more simple and more rational. An American constitution is not supposed to be immutable, as in France; nor is it susceptible of modification by the ordinary powers of society, as in England. It constitutes a detached whole, which, as it represents the will of the whole people, is no less binding on the legislator than on the private citizen, but which may be altered by the will of the people in predetermined cases, according to established rules. In America, the constitution may therefore vary; but as long as it exists, it is the origin of all authority, and the sole vehicle of the predominating force. . . .

In the United States, the constitution governs the legislator as much as the private citizen: as it is the first of laws, it cannot be modified by a law; and it is therefore just that the tribunals should obey the constitution in preference to any law. This condition belongs to the very essence of the judicature; for to select that legal obligation by which he is most strictly bound, is in some sort the natural right of every magistrate.

In France, the constitution is also the first of laws, and the judges have the same right to take it as the ground of their decisions; but were they to exercise this right, they must perforce encroach on rights more sacred than their own, namely, on those of society, in whose name they are acting. In this case, reasons of state clearly prevail over ordinary motives. In America, where the nation can always reduce its magistrates to obedience by changing its constitution, no danger of this kind is to be feared. Upon this point, therefore, the political and the logical reason agree, and the people as well as the judges preserve their privileges.

Whenever a law which the judge holds to be unconstitutional is invoked in a tribunal of the United States, he may refuse to admit it as a rule; this power is the only one which is peculiar to the American magistrate, but it gives rise to immense political influence. In truth, few laws can escape the searching analysis of the judicial power for any length of time, for there are few which are not prejudicial to some private interest or other, and none which may not be brought before a court of justice by the choice of parties, or by the necessity of the case. But as soon as a judge has refused to apply any given law in a case, that law immediately loses a portion of its moral force. Those to whom it is prejudicial learn that means exist of overcoming its authority; and similar suits are multiplied, until it becomes powerless. The alternative, then, is, that the people must alter the constitution, or the legislature must repeal the law. The political power which the Americans have intrusted to their courts of justice is therefore immense; but the evils of this power are considerably diminished by the impossibility of attacking the laws except through the courts of justice. If the judge had been empowered to contest the law on the ground of theoretical generalities,—if he were able to take the initiative, and to censure the legislator,—he would play a prominent political part; and as the champion or the antagonist of a party, he would have brought the hostile passions of the nation into the conflict. But when a judge contests a law in an obscure debate on some particular case, the importance of his attack is concealed from public notice; his decision bears upon the interest of an individual, and the law is slighted only incidentally. Moreover, although it is censured, it is not abolished; its moral force may be diminished, but its authority is not taken away; and its final destruction can be accomplished only by the reiterated attacks of judicial functionaries. It will be seen, also, that by leaving it to private interest to censure the law, and by intimately uniting the trial of the law with the trial of an individual, legislation is protected from wanton assaults, and from the daily aggressions of party spirit. The errors of the legislator are exposed only to meet a real want; and it is always a positive and appreciable fact which must serve as the basis of a prosecution.

I am inclined to believe this practice of the American courts to be at once most favorable to liberty and to public order. If the judge could only attack the legislator openly and directly, he would sometimes be afraid to oppose him; and at other times, party spirit might encourage him to brave it at every turn. The laws would consequently be attacked when the power from which they emanated was weak, and obeyed when it was strong;—that is to say, when it would be useful to respect them, they would often be contested; and when it would be easy to convert them into an instrument of oppression, they would be respected. But the American judge is brought into the political arena independently of his own will. He only judges the law because he is obliged to judge a case. The political question which he is called upon to resolve is connected with the interests of the parties, and he cannot refuse to decide it without a denial of justice. He performs his functions as a citizen, by fulfilling the precise duties which belong to his profession as a magistrate. It is true that, upon this system, the judicial censorship of the courts of justice over the legislature cannot extend to all laws indiscriminately, inasmuch as some of them can never give rise to that precise species of contest which is termed a lawsuit; and even when such a contest is possible, it may happen that no one cares to bring it before a court of justice. The Americans have often felt this inconvenience; but they have left the remedy incomplete, lest they should give it an efficacy which might in some cases prove dangerous. Within these limits, the power vested in the American courts of justice, of pronouncing a statute to be unconstitutional, forms one of the most powerful barriers which has ever been devised against the tyranny of political assemblies.

It is hardly necessary to say that, in a free country like America, all the citizens have the right of indicting public functionaries before the ordinary tribunals, and that all the judges have the power of convicting public officers. The right granted to the courts of justice of punishing the agents of the executive government, when they violate the laws, is so natural a one, that it cannot be looked upon as an extraordinary privilege. Nor do the springs of government appear to me to be weakened in the United States, by rendering all public officers responsible to the tribunals. The Americans seem, on the contrary, to have increased by this means that respect which is due to the authorities, and at the same time, to have made these authorities more careful not to offend. I was struck by the small number of political trials which occur in the United States; but I had no difficulty in accounting for this circumstance. A prosecution, of whatever nature it may be, is always a difficult and expensive undertaking. It is easy to attack a public man in the journals, but the motives for bringing him before the tribunals must be serious. A solid ground of complaint must exist, before any one thinks of prosecuting a public officer, and these officers are careful not to furnish such grounds of complaint, when they are afraid of being prosecuted.

This does not depend upon the republican form of American institutions, for the same thing happens in England. These two nations do not regard the impeachment of the principal officers of state as the guaranty of their independence. But they hold that it is rather by minor prosecutions, which the humblest citizen can institute at any time, that liberty is protected, and not by those great judicial procedures, which are rarely employed until it is too late.

In the Middle Ages, when it was very difficult to reach offenders, the judges inflicted frightful punishments on the few who were arrested; but this did not diminish the number of crimes. It has since been discovered that, when justice is more certain and more mild, it is more efficacious. The English and the Americans hold that tyranny and oppression are to be treated like any other crime, by lessening the penalty and facilitating conviction. . . .

7. Aspects of the Federal Constitution.

. . . THE thirteen Colonies, which simultaneously threw off the yoke of England towards the end of the last century, had, as I have already said, the same religion, the same language, the same customs, and almost the same laws; they were struggling against a common enemy; and these reasons were sufficiently strong to unite them one to another, and to consolidate them into one nation. But as each of them had always had a separate existence, and a government within its reach, separate interests and peculiar customs had sprung up, which

were opposed to such a compact and intimate union as would
have absorbed the individual importance of each in the general
importance of all. Hence arose two opposite tendencies,—
the one prompting the Anglo-Americans to unite, the other to
divide, their strength.

As long as the war with the mother country lasted, the
principle of union was kept alive by necessity; and although
the laws which constituted it were defective, the common tie
subsisted in spite of their imperfections. But no sooner was
peace concluded, than the faults of this legislation became
manifest, and the state seemed to be suddenly dissolved. Each
Colony became an independent republic, and assumed an
absolute sovereignty. The Federal government, condemned to
impotence by its Constitution, and no longer sustained by the
presence of a common danger, witnessed the outrages offered
to its flag by the great nations of Europe, whilst it was scarcely
able to maintain its ground against the Indian tribes, and to
pay the interest of the debt which had been contracted during
the war of independence. It was already on the verge of
destruction, when it officially proclaimed its inability to conduct the government, and appealed to the constituent authority.

If America ever approached (for however brief a time)
that lofty pinnacle of glory to which the proud imagination of
its inhabitants is wont to point, it was at this solemn moment,
when the national power abdicated, as it were, its authority.
All ages have furnished the spectacle of a people struggling
with energy to win its independence; and the efforts of the
Americans in throwing off the English yoke have been considerably exaggerated. Separated from their enemies by three
thousand miles of ocean, and backed by a powerful ally, the
United States owed their victory much more to their geographical position than to the valor of their armies or the patriotism
of their citizens. It would be ridiculous to compare the American war to the wars of the French Revolution, or the efforts of
the Americans to those of the French, when France, attacked
by the whole of Europe, without money, without credit, without allies, threw forward a twentieth part of her population to
meet her enemies, and with one hand carried the torch of
revolution beyond the frontiers, whilst she stifled with the other
a flame that was devouring the country within. But it is new
in the history of society, to see a great people turn a calm and
scrutinizing eye upon itself, when apprised by the legislature
that the wheels of its government are stopped,—to see it
carefully examine the extent of the evil, and patiently wait
two whole years until a remedy is discovered, to which it

voluntarily submitted without its costing a tear or a drop of blood from mankind.

When the inadequacy of the first constitution was discovered, America had the double advantage of that calm which had succeeded the effervescence of the Revolution, and of the aid of those great men whom the Revolution had created. The assembly which accepted the task of composing the second constitution was small; but George Washington was its President, and it contained the finest minds and the noblest characters which had ever appeared in the New World. This national Convention, after long and mature deliberation, offered to the acceptance of the people the body of general laws which still rules the Union. All the States adopted it successively. The new Federal government commenced its functions in 1789, after an interregnum of two years. The Revolution of America terminated precisely when that of France began.

The first question which awaited the Americans was, so to divide the sovereignty that each of the different States which composed the Union should continue to govern itself in all that concerned its internal prosperity, whilst the entire nation, represented by the Union, should continue to form a compact body, and to provide for all general exigencies. The problem was a complex and difficult one. It was as impossible to determine beforehand, with any degree of accuracy, the share of authority which each of the two governments was to enjoy, as to foresee all the incidents in the life of a nation.

The obligations and the claims of the Federal government were simple and easily definable, because the Union had been formed with the express purpose of meeting certain great general wants; but the claims and obligations of the individual States, on the other hand, were complicated and various, because their government had penetrated into all the details of social life. The attributes of the Federal government were therefore carefully defined, and all that was not included among them was declared to remain to the governments of the several States. Thus the government of the States remained the rule, and that of the Confederation was the exception.

But as it was foreseen that, in practice, questions might arise as to the exact limits of this exceptional authority, and it would be dangerous to submit these questions to the decision of the ordinary courts of justice, established in the different States by the States themselves, a high Federal court was created, one of whose duties was to maintain the balance of power between the two rival governments, as it had been established by the Constitution.

The people in themselves are only individuals; and the spe-

cial reason why they need to be united under one government
is, that they may appear to advantage before foreigners. The
exclusive right of making peace and war, of concluding treaties
of commerce, raising armies, and equipping fleets, was therefore granted to the Union. The necessity of a national government was less imperiously felt in the conduct of the internal
affairs of society; but there are certain general interests which
can only be attended to with advantage by a general authority.
The Union was invested with the power of controlling the
monetary system, carrying the mails, and opening the great
roads which were to unite the different parts of the country.
The independence of the government of each State in its
sphere was recognized; yet the Federal government was author-
ized to interfere in the internal affairs of the States in a few
predetermined cases, in which an indiscreet use of their independence might compromise the safety of the whole Union.
Thus, whilst the power of modifying and changing their legislation at pleasure was preserved to each of the confederate
republics, they are forbidden to enact *ex-post-facto* laws, or to
grant any titles of nobility. Lastly, as it was necessary that the
Federal government should be able to fulfil its engagements, it
has an unlimited power of levying taxes.

In examining the division of powers, as established by the
Federal Constitution, remarking on the one hand the portion
of sovereignty which has been reserved to the several States,
and on the other, the share of power which has been given to
the Union, it is evident that the Federal legislators entertained
very clear and accurate notions respecting the centralization of
government. The United States form not only a republic, but a
confederation; yet the national authority is more centralized
there than it was in several of the absolute monarchies of
Europe. . . .

Executive Power.

If the executive government is feebler in America than in
France, the cause is perhaps more attributable to the circumstances than to the laws of the country.

It is chiefly in its foreign relations that the executive power
of a nation finds occasion to exert its skill and its strength. If
the existence of the Union were perpetually threatened, if its
chief interests were in daily connection with those of other
powerful nations, the executive government would assume an
increased importance in proportion to the measures expected
of it, and to those which it would execute. The President of
the United States, it is true, is the commander-in-chief of the

army, but the army is composed of only six thousand men; he commands the fleet, but the fleet reckons but few sail; he conducts the foreign relations of the Union, but the United States are a nation without neighbors. Separated from the rest of the world by the ocean, and too weak as yet to aim at the dominion of the seas, they have no enemies, and their interests rarely come into contact with those of any other nation of the globe. This proves that the practical operation of the government must not be judged by the theory of its constitution. The President of the United States possesses almost royal prerogatives, which he has no opportunity of exercising, and the privileges which he can at present use are very circumscribed. The laws allow him to be strong, but circumstances keep him weak. . . .

Advantages of the Federal System in General, and Its Special Utility in America.

In small states, the watchfulness of society penetrates into every part, and the spirit of improvement enters into the smallest details; the ambition of the people being necessarily checked by its weakness, all the efforts and resources of the citizens are turned to the internal well-being of the community, and are not likely to evaporate in the fleeting breath of glory. The powers of every individual being generally limited, his desires are proportionally small. Mediocrity of fortune makes the various conditions of life nearly equal, and the manners of the inhabitants are orderly and simple. Thus, all things considered, and allowance being made for the various degrees of morality and enlightenment, we shall generally find in small nations more persons in easy circumstances, more contentment and tranquillity, than in large ones.

When tyranny is established in the bosom of a small state, it is more galling than elsewhere, because, acting in a narrower circle, everything in that circle is affected by it. It supplies the place of those great designs which it cannot entertain, by a violent or exasperating interference in a multitude of minute details; and it leaves the political world, to which it properly belongs, to meddle with the arrangements of private life. Tastes as well as actions are to be regulated; and the families of the citizens, as well as the state, are to be governed. This invasion of rights occurs, however, but seldom, freedom being in truth the natural state of small communities. The temptations which the government offers to ambition are too weak, and the resources of private individuals are too slender, for the sovereign power easily to fall into the grasp of a single man;

and should such an event occur, the subjects of the state can easily unite and overthrow the tyrant and the tyranny at once by a common effort. Small nations have therefore ever been the cradle of political liberty; and the fact that many of them have lost their liberty by becoming larger, shows that their freedom was more a consequence of their small size than of the character of the people.

The history of the world affords no instance of a great nation retaining the form of republican government for a long series of years. . . . All the passions which are most fatal to republican institutions increase with an increasing territory, whilst the virtues which favor them do not augment in the same proportion. The ambition of private citizens increases with the power of the state; the strength of parties, with the importance of the ends they have in view; but the love of country, which ought to check these destructive agencies, is not stronger in a large than in a small republic. It might, indeed, be easily proved that it is less powerful and less developed. Great wealth and extreme poverty, capital cities of large size, a lax morality, selfishness and antagonism of interests, are the dangers which almost invariably arise from the magnitude of states. Several of these evils scarcely injure a monarchy, and some of them even contribute to its strength and duration. In monarchical states, the government has its peculiar strength; it may use, but it does not depend on, the community; and the more numerous the people, the stronger is the prince. But the only security which a republican government possesses against these evils lies in the support of the majority. This support is not, however, proportionably greater in a large republic than in a small one; and thus, whilst the means of attack perpetually increase, both in number and influence, the power of resistance remains the same; or it may rather be said to diminish, since the inclinations and interests of the people are more diversified by the increase of the population, and the difficulty of forming a compact majority is constantly augmented. It has been observed, moreover, that the intensity of human passions is heightened not only by the importance of the end which they propose to attain, but by the multitude of individuals who are animated by them at the same time. Every one has had occasion to remark, that his emotions in the midst of a sympathizing crowd are far greater than those which he would have felt in solitude. In great republics, political passions become irresistible, not only because they aim at gigantic objects, but because they are felt and shared by millions of men at the same time.

It may, therefore, be asserted as a general proposition,

that nothing is more opposed to the well-being and the freedom of men than vast empires. Nevertheless, it is important to acknowledge the peculiar advantages of great states. For the very reason that the desire of power is more intense in these communities than amongst ordinary men, the love of glory is also more developed in the hearts of certain citizens, who regard the applause of a great people as a reward worthy of their exertions, and an elevating encouragement to man. If we would learn why great nations contribute more powerfully to the increase of knowledge and the advance of civilization than small states, we shall discover an adequate cause in the more rapid and energetic circulation of ideas, and in those great cities which are the intellectual centres where all the rays of human genius are reflected and combined. To this it may be added, that most important discoveries demand a use of national power which the government of a small state is unable to make: in great nations, the government has more enlarged ideas, and is more completely disengaged from the routine of precedent and the selfishness of local feeling; its designs are conceived with more talent, and executed with more boldness.

In time of peace, the well-being of small nations is undoubtedly more general and complete; but they are apt to suffer more acutely from the calamities of war than those great empires whose distant frontiers may long avert the presence of the danger from the mass of the people, who are therefore more frequently afflicted than ruined by the contest.

But in this matter, as in many others, the decisive argument is the necessity of the case. If none but small nations existed, I do not doubt that mankind would be more happy and more free; but the existence of great nations is unavoidable.

Political strength thus becomes a condition of national prosperity. It profits a state but little to be affluent and free, if it is perpetually exposed to be pillaged or subjugated; its manufactures and commerce are of small advantage, if another nation has the empire of the seas and gives the law in all the markets of the globe. Small nations are often miserable, not because they are small, but because they are weak; and great empires prosper, less because they are great, than because they are strong. Physical strength is therefore one of the first conditions of the happiness, and even of the existence, of nations. Hence it occurs, that, unless very peculiar circumstances intervene, small nations are always united to large empires in the end, either by force or by their own consent. I know not a more deplorable condition than that of a people unable to defend itself or to provide for its own wants.

The Federal system was created with the intention of com-

bining the different advantages which result from the magnitude and the littleness of nations; and a glance at the United
States of America discovers the advantages which they have
derived from its adoption.

In great centralized nations, the legislator is obliged to give
a character of uniformity to the laws, which does not always
suit the diversity of customs and of districts; as he takes no
cognizance of special cases, he can only proceed upon general
principles; and the population are obliged to conform to the
exigencies of the legislation, since the legislation cannot adapt
itself to the exigencies and the customs of the population;
which is a great cause of trouble and misery. This disadvan-
tage does not exist in confederations; Congress regulates the
principal measures of the national government; and all the
details of the administration are reserved to the provincial
legislatures. One can hardly imagine how much this division of
sovereignty contributes to the well-being of each of the States
which compose the Union. In these small communities, which
are never agitated by the desire of aggrandizement or the care
of self-defence, all public authority and private energy are
turned towards internal improvements. The central government of each State, which is in immediate juxtaposition to the
citizens, is daily apprised of the wants which arise in society;
and new projects are proposed every year, which are discussed
at town-meetings or by the legislature, and which are transmitted by the press to stimulate the zeal and to excite the
interest of the citizens. This spirit of improvement is constantly
alive in the American republics, without compromising their
tranquillity; the ambition of power yields to the less refined and
less dangerous desire for well-being. It is generally believed in
America, that the existence and the permanence of the republican form of government in the New World depend upon the
existence and the duration of the Federal system; and it is not
unusual to attribute a large share of the misfortunes which
have befallen the new States of South America to the injudi-
cious erection of great republics, instead of a divided and
confederate sovereignty.

It is incontestably true, that the tastes and the habits of
republican government in the United States were first created
in the townships and the provincial assemblies. In a small State,
like that of Connecticut, for instance, where cutting a canal or
laying down a road is a great political question, where the State
has no army to pay and no wars to carry on, and where much
wealth or much honor cannot be given to the rulers, no form
of government can be more natural or more appropriate than a
republic. But it is this same republican spirit, it is these

manners and customs of a free people, which have been created and nurtured in the different States, which must be afterwards applied to the country at large. The public spirit of the Union is, so to speak, nothing more than an aggregate or summary of the patriotic zeal of the separate provinces. Every citizen of the United States transports, so to speak, his attachment to his little republic into the common store of American patriotism. In defending the Union, he defends the increasing prosperity of his own State or county, the right of conducting its affairs, and the hope of causing measures of improvement to be adopted in it which may be favorable to his own interests; and these are motives which are wont to stir men more than the general interests of the country and the glory of the nation.

On the other hand, if the temper and the manners of the inhabitants especially fitted them to promote the welfare of a great republic, the federal system renders their task less difficult. The confederation of all the American States presents none of the ordinary inconveniences resulting from great agglomerations of men. The Union is a great republic in extent, but the paucity of objects for which its government acts assimilates it to a small State. Its acts are important, but they are rare. As the sovereignty of the Union is limited and incomplete, its exercise is not dangerous to liberty; for it does not excite those insatiable desires of fame and power which have proved so fatal to great republics. As there is no common centre to the country, great capital cities, colossal wealth, abject poverty, and sudden revolutions are alike unknown; and political passion, instead of spreading over the land like a fire on the prairies, spends its strength against the interests and the individual passions of every State.

Nevertheless, tangible objects and ideas circulate throughout the Union as freely as in a country inhabited by one people. Nothing checks the spirit of enterprise. The government invites the aid of all who have talents or knowledge to serve it. Inside of the frontiers of the Union, profound peace prevails, as within the heart of some great empire; abroad, it ranks with the most powerful nations of the earth: two thousand miles of coast are open to the commerce of the world; and as it holds the keys of a New World, its flag is respected in the most remote seas. The Union is happy and free as a small people, and glorious and strong as a great nation. . . .

The Impact of War.

. . . The most important occurrence in the life of a nation is the breaking out of a war. In war, a people act as one

man against foreign nations, in defence of their very existence.
The skill of the government, the good sense of the community,
and the natural fondness which men almost always entertain
for their country, may be enough, as long as the only object is
to maintain peace in the interior of the state, and to favor its
internal prosperity; but that the nation may carry on a great
war, the people must make more numerous and painful sacrifices; and to suppose that a great number of men will, of
their own accord, submit to these exigencies, is to betray an
ignorance of human nature. All the nations which have been
obliged to sustain a long and serious warfare have consequently
been led to augment the power of their government. Those
who have not succeeded in this attempt have been subjugated.
A long war almost always reduces nations to the wretched
alternative of being abandoned to ruin by defeat, or to despotism by success. War therefore renders the weakness of a
government most apparent and most alarming; and I have
shown that the inherent defect of federal governments is that
of being weak.

The federal system not only has no centralized administration, and nothing which resembles one, but the central government itself is imperfectly organized, which is always a
great cause of weakness when the nation is opposed to other
countries which are themselves governed by a single authority. . . .

How happens it, then, that the American Union, with all
the relative perfection of its laws, is not dissolved by the
occurrence of a great war? It is because it has no great wars to
fear. Placed in the centre of an immense continent, which
offers a boundless field for human industry, the Union is
almost as much insulated from the world as if all its frontiers
were girt by the ocean. Canada contains only a million of
inhabitants, and its population is divided into two inimical
nations. The rigor of the climate limits the extension of its
territory, and shuts up its ports during the six months of winter.
From Canada to the Gulf of Mexico a few savage tribes are to
be met with, which retire, perishing in their retreat, before
six thousand soldiers. To the south, the Union has a point of
contact with the empire of Mexico; and it is thence that
serious hostilities may one day be expected to arise. But for a
long while to come, the uncivilized state of the Mexican people,
the depravity of their morals, and their extreme poverty, will
prevent that country from ranking high amongst nations. As
for the powers of Europe, they are too distant to be formidable.

The great advantage of the United States does not, then,
consist in a Federal Constitution which allows them to carry

on great wars, but in a geographical position which renders such wars extremely improbable.

No one can be more inclined than I am to appreciate the advantages of the Federal system, which I hold to be one of the combinations most favorable to the prosperity and freedom of man. I envy the lot of those nations which have been able to adopt it; but I cannot believe that any confederate people could maintain a long or an equal contest with a nation of similar strength in which the government is centralized. A people which should divide its sovereignty into fractional parts, in the presence of the great military monarchies of Europe, would, in my opinion, by that very act abdicate its power, and perhaps its existence and its name. But such is the admirable position of the New World, that man has no other enemy than himself; and that, in order to be happy and to be free, he has only to determine that he will be so.

8. Political Parties.

. . . In America, the people appoint the legislative and the executive power, and furnish the jurors who punish all infractions of the laws. The institutions are democratic, not only in their principle, but in all their consequences; and the people elect their representatives *directly*, and for the most part *annually*, in order to insure their dependence. The people are, therefore, the real directing power; and although the form of government is representative, it is evident that the opinions, the prejudices, the interests, and even the passions of the people are hindered by no permanent obstacles from exercising a perpetual influence on the daily conduct of affairs. In the United States, the majority governs in the name of the people, as is the case in all countries in which the people are supreme. This majority is principally composed of peaceable citizens, who, either by inclination or by interest, sincerely wish the welfare of their country. But they are surrounded by the incessant agitation of parties, who attempt to gain their co-operation and support.

A great distinction must be made between parties. Some countries are so large that the different populations which inhabit them, although united under the same government, have contradictory interests; and they may consequently be in a perpetual state of opposition. In this case, the different fractions of the people may more properly be considered as

distinct nations than as mere parties; and if a civil war breaks
out, the struggle is carried on by rival states rather than by
factions in the same state. But when the citizens entertain
different opinions upon subjects which affect the whole country
alike,—such, for instance, as the principles upon which the
government is to be conducted,—then distinctions arise which
may correctly be styled parties. Parties are a necessary evil in
free governments; but they have not at all times the same
character and the same propensities. . . .

America has had great parties, but has them no longer; and
if her happiness is thereby considerably increased, her morality
has suffered. When the war of independence was terminated,
and the foundations of the new government were to be laid
down, the nation was divided between two opinions,—two
opinions which are as old as the world, and which are perpetually to be met with, under different forms and various names,
in all free communities,—the one tending to limit, the other to
extend indefinitely, the power of the people. The conflict
between these two opinions never assumed that degree of
violence in America which it has frequently displayed elsewhere. Both parties of the Americans were agreed upon the
most essential points; and neither of them had to destroy an
old constitution, or to overthrow the structure of society, in
order to triumph. In neither of them, consequently, were a
great number of private interests affected by success or defeat:
but moral principles of a high order, such as the love of
equality and of independence, were concerned in the struggle,
and these sufficed to kindle violent passions.

The party which desired to limit the power of the people,
endeavored to apply its doctrines more especially to the Constitution of the Union, whence it derived its name of *Federal*.
The other party, which affected to be exclusively attached to
the cause of liberty, took that of *Republican*. America is the
land of democracy, and the Federalists, therefore, were always
in a minority; but they reckoned on their side almost all the
great men whom the war of independence had produced, and
their moral power was very considerable. Their cause was,
moreover, favored by circumstances. The ruin of the first
Confederation had impressed the people with a dread of
anarchy, and the Federalists profited by this transient disposition of the multitude. For ten or twelve years, they were at the
head of affairs, and they were able to apply some, though not
all, of their principles; for the hostile current was becoming
from day to day too violent to be checked. In 1801, the
Republicans got possession of the government: Thomas Jefferson was elected President; and he increased the influence of

their party by the weight of his great name, the brilliancy of his talents, and his immense popularity.

The means by which the Federalists had maintained their position were artificial, and their resources were temporary: it was by the virtues or the talents of their leaders, as well as by fortunate circumstances, that they had risen to power. When the Republicans attained that station in their turn, their opponents were overwhelmed by utter defeat. An immense majority declared itself against the retiring party, and the Federalists found themselves in so small a minority, that they at once despaired of future success. From that moment, the Republican or Democratic party has proceeded from conquest to conquest, until it has acquired absolute supremacy in the country. The Federalists, perceiving that they were vanquished without resource, and isolated in the midst of the nation, fell into two divisions, of which one joined the victorious Republicans, and the other laid down their banners and changed their name. Many years have elapsed since they wholly ceased to exist as a party.

The accession of the Federalists to power was, in my opinion, one of the most fortunate incidents which accompanied the formation of the great American Union: they resisted the inevitable propensities of their country and their age. But whether their theories were good or bad, they had the fault of being inapplicable, as a whole, to the society which they wished to govern, and that which occurred under the auspices of Jefferson must therefore have taken place sooner or later. But their government at least gave the new republic time to acquire a certain stability, and afterwards to support without inconvenience the rapid growth of the very doctrines which they had combated. A considerable number of their principles, moreover, were embodied at last in the political creed of their opponents; and the Federal Constitution, which subsists at the present day, is a lasting monument of their patriotism and their wisdom.

Great political parties, then, are not to be met with in the United States at the present time. . . .

In the absence of great parties, the United States swarm with lesser controversies; and public opinion is divided into a thousand minute shades of difference upon questions of detail. The pains which are taken to create parties are inconceivable, and at the present day it is no easy task. In the United States, there is no religious animosity, because all religion is respected, and no sect is predominant; there is no jealousy of rank, because the people are everything, and none can contest their authority; lastly, there is no public misery to serve as a means

of agitation, because the physical position of the country opens
so wide a field to industry, that man only needs to be let alone
to be able to accomplish prodigies. Nevertheless, ambitious
men will succeed in creating parties, since it is difficult to eject
a person from authority upon the mere ground that his place is
coveted by others. All the skill of the actors in the political
world lies in the art of creating parties. A political aspirant in
the United States begins by discerning his own interest, and
discovering those other interests which may be collected
around, and amalgamated with it. He then contrives to find
out some doctrine or principle which may suit the purposes
of this new association, and which he adopts in order to
bring forward his party and secure its popularity: just as the
imprimatur of the king was in former days printed upon the
title-page of a volume, and was thus incorporated with a book
to which it in no wise belonged. This being done, the new
party is ushered into the political world.

All the domestic controversies of the Americans at first
appear to a stranger to be incomprehensible or puerile, and he
is at a loss whether to pity a people who take such arrant
trifles in good earnest, or to envy that happiness which enables
a community to discuss them. But when he comes to study the
secret propensities which govern the factions of America, he
easily perceives that the greater part of them are more or less
connected with one or the other of those two great divisions
which have always existed in free communities. The deeper
we penetrate into the inmost thought of these parties the more
do we perceive that the object of the one is to limit, and that of
the other to extend, the authority of the people. I do not assert
that the ostensible purpose, or even that the secret aim, of
American parties is to promote the rule of aristocracy or
democracy in the country; but I affirm that aristocratic or
democratic passions may easily be detected at the bottom of
all parties, and that, although they escape a superficial observation, they are the main point and soul of every faction in
the United States. . . .

It sometimes happens, in a people amongst whom various
opinions prevail, that the balance of parties is lost, and one of
them obtains an irresistible preponderance, overpowers all
obstacles, annihilates its opponents, and appropriates all the
resources of society to its own use. The vanquished despair of
success, hide their heads, and are silent. The nation seems to be
governed by a single principle, universal stillness prevails, and
the prevailing party assumes the credit of having restored peace
and unanimity to the country. But under this apparent unanim-

ity still exist profound differences of opinion, and real opposition.

This is what occurred in America; when the democratic party got the upper hand, it took exclusive possession of the conduct of affairs, and from that time, the laws and the customs of society have been adapted to its caprices. At the present day, the more affluent classes of society have no influence in political affairs; and wealth, far from conferring a right, is rather a cause of unpopularity than a means of attaining power. The rich abandon the lists, through unwillingness to contend, and frequently to contend in vain, against the poorer classes of their fellow-citizens. As they cannot occupy in public a position equivalent to what they hold in private life, they abandon the former, and give themselves up to the latter; and they constitute a private society in the state, which has its own tastes and pleasures. They submit to the state of things as an irremediable evil, but they are careful not to show that they are galled by its continuance; one often hears them laud the advantages of a republican government and democratic institutions when they are in public. Next to hating their enemies, men are most inclined to flatter them. . . .

But beneath this artificial enthusiasm, and these obsequious attentions to the preponderating power, it is easy to perceive that the rich have a hearty dislike of the democratic institutions of their country. The people form a power which they at once fear and despise. If the maladministration of the democracy ever brings about a revolutionary crisis, and monarchical institutions ever become practicable in the United States, the truth of what I advance will become obvious.

The two chief weapons which parties use in order to obtain success are the *newspapers* and public *associations*.

9. *Liberty of the Press in the United States.*

THE influence of the liberty of the press does not affect political opinions alone, but extends to all the opinions of men, and modifies customs as well as laws. . . . I confess that I do not entertain that firm and complete attachment to the liberty of the press which is wont to be excited by things that are supremely good in their very nature. I approve of it from a consideration more of the evils it prevents, than of the advantages it insures. If any one could point out an intermediate and yet a tenable position between the complete independence and the entire servitude of opinion, I should, perhaps, be inclined to adopt it; but the difficulty is, to discover this intermediate position. Intending to correct the licentiousness of the press, and to restore the use of orderly language, you first try the offender by a jury; but if the jury acquits him, the opinion which was that of a single individual becomes the opinion of the whole country. Too much and too little has therefore been done; go farther, then. You bring the delinquent before permanent magistrates; but even here, the cause must be heard before it can be decided; and the very principles which no book would have ventured to avow are blazoned forth in the pleadings, and what was obscurely hinted at in a single composition is thus repeated in a multitude of other publications. The language is only the expression, and (if I may so speak) the body, of the thought, but it is not the thought itself. Tribunals may condemn the body, but the sense, the spirit, of the work is too subtile for their authority. Too much has still been done to recede, too little to attain your end; you must go still farther. Establish a censorship of the press. But the tongue of the public speaker will still make itself heard, and your purpose is not yet accomplished; you have only increased the mischief. Thought is not, like physical strength, dependent upon the number of its agents; nor can authors be counted like the troops which compose an army. On the contrary, the authority of a principle is often increased by the small number of men by whom it is expressed. The words of one strong-minded man, addressed to the passions of a listening assembly, have more power than the vociferations of a thousand orators; and if it be allowed to speak freely in any one public place, the consequence is the same as if free speaking was allowed in every village. The liberty of speech must therefore be destroyed, as well as the liberty of the press. And now you have succeeded, everybody is reduced to silence. But your object was to repress the abuses of liberty, and you are brought to the feet of a despot. You have been led from the extreme of independence to the extreme of servitude, without finding a single tenable position on the way at which you could stop. . . .

The small influence of the American journals is attributable to several reasons, amongst which are the following.

The liberty of writing, like all other liberty, is most formidable when it is a novelty; for a people who have never been accustomed to hear state affairs discussed before them, place implicit confidence in the first tribune who presents himself. The Anglo-Americans have enjoyed this liberty ever since the foundation of the Colonies; moreover, the press cannot create human passions, however skilfully it may kindle them where

they exist. In America, political life is active, varied, even
agitated, but is rarely affected by those deep passions which
are excited only when material interests are impaired: and in
the United States, these interests are prosperous. A glance at a
French and an American newspaper is sufficient to show the
difference which exists in this respect between the two nations.
In France, the space allotted to commercial advertisements is
very limited, and the news-intelligence is not considerable; but
the essential part of the journal is the discussion of the politics
of the day. In America, three quarters of the enormous sheet
are filled with advertisements, and the remainder is frequently
occupied by political intelligence or trivial anecdotes: it is only
from time to time, that one finds a corner devoted to passionate
discussions, like those which the journalists of France every
day give to their readers.

It has been demonstrated by observation, and discovered by
the sure instinct even of the pettiest despots, that the influence
of a power is increased in proportion as its direction is centralized. In France, the press combines a two-fold centralization; almost all its power is centred in the same spot, and, so
to speak, in the same hands; for its organs are far from numerous. The influence of a public press thus constituted, upon a
sceptical nation, must be almost unbounded. It is an enemy
with whom a government may sign an occasional truce, but
which it is difficult to resist for any length of time.

Neither of these kinds of centralization exists in America.
The United States have no metropolis; the intelligence and the
power of the people are disseminated through all the parts of
this vast country, and instead of radiating from a common
point, they cross each other in every direction; the Americans
have nowhere established any central direction of opinion, any
more than of the conduct of affairs. This difference arises from
local circumstances, and not from human power; but it is
owing to the laws of the Union that there are no licenses to
be granted to printers, no securities demanded from editors,
as in France, and no stamp duty, as in France and England.
The consequence is, that nothing is easier than to set up a
newspaper, as a small number of subscribers suffices to de-
fray the expenses.

Hence the number of periodical and semi-periodical publications in the United States is almost incredibly large.
The most enlightened Americans attribute the little influence of the press to this excessive dissemination of its
power; and it is an axiom of political science in that country, that the only way to neutralize the effect of the public
journals is to multiply their number. I cannot see how a

truth which is so self-evident should not already have been more generally admitted in Europe. I can see why the persons who hope to bring about revolutions by means of the press, should be desirous of confining it to a few powerful organs; but it is inconceivable that the official partisans of the existing state of things, and the natural supporters of the laws, should attempt to diminish the influence of the press by concentrating its power. The governments of Europe seem to treat the press with the courtesy which the knights of old showed to their opponents; having found from their own experience that centralization is a powerful weapon, they have furnished their enemies with it, in order doubtless to have more glory for overcoming them.

In America, there is scarcely a hamlet which has not its newspaper. It may readily be imagined, that neither discipline nor unity of action can be established among so many combatants; and each one consequently fights under his own standard. All the political journals of the United States are, indeed, arrayed on the side of the administration or against it; but they attack and defend it in a thousand different ways. They cannot form those great currents of opinion which sweep away the strongest dikes. This division of the influence of the press produces other consequences scarcely less remarkable. The facility with which newspapers can be established produces a multitude of them; but as the competition prevents any considerable profit, persons of much capacity are rarely led to engage in these undertakings. Such is the number of the public prints, that, even if they were a source of wealth, writers of ability could not be found to direct them all. The journalists of the United States are generally in a very humble position, with a scanty education and a vulgar turn of mind. The will of the majority is the most general of laws, and it establishes certain habits to which every one must then conform; the aggregate of these common habits is what is called the class-spirit (*esprit de corps*) of each profession; thus there is the class-spirit of the bar, of the court, &c. The class-spirit of the French journalists consists in a violent, but frequently an eloquent and lofty, manner of discussing the great interests of the state: and the exceptions to this mode of writing are only occasional. The characteristics of the American journalist consist in an open and coarse appeal to the passions of his readers; he abandons principles to assail the characters of individuals, to track them into private life, and disclose all their weaknesses and vices. . . .

But although the press is limited to these resources, its influence in America is immense. It causes political life to cir-

culate through all the parts of that vast territory. Its eye is
constantly open to detect the secret springs of political designs,
and to summon the leaders of all parties in turn to the bar of
public opinion. It rallies the interests of the community round
certain principles, and draws up the creed of every party; for
it affords a means of intercourse between those who hear and
address each other, without ever coming into immediate contact. When many organs of the press adopt the same line of
conduct, their influence in the long run becomes irresistible;
and public opinion, perpetually assailed from the same side,
eventually yields to the attack. In the United States, each
separate journal exercises but little authority; but the power
of the periodical press is second only to that of the people. . . .

10. *Political Associations in the United States.*

IN no country in the world has the principle of association
been more successfully used, or applied to a greater multitude
of objects, than in America. Besides the permanent associations, which are established by law, under the names of townships, cities, and counties, a vast number of others are formed
and maintained by the agency of private individuals.

The citizen of the United States is taught from infancy to
rely upon his own exertions, in order to resist the evils and
the difficulties of life; he looks upon the social authority with
an eye of mistrust and anxiety, and he claims its assistance
only when he is unable to do without it. This habit may be
traced even in the schools, where the children in their games
are wont to submit to rules which they have themselves established, and to punish misdemeanors which they have themselves defined. The same spirit pervades every act of social life.
If a stoppage occurs in a thoroughfare, and the circulation of
vehicles is hindered, the neighbors immediately form themselves into a deliberative body; and this extemporaneous assembly gives rise to an executive power, which remedies the
inconvenience before anybody has thought of recurring to a
pre-existing authority superior to that of the persons immediately concerned. If some public pleasure is concerned, an
association is formed to give more splendor and regularity to
the entertainment. Societies are formed to resist evils which
are exclusively of a moral nature, as to diminish the vice of
intemperance. In the United States, associations are established to promote the public safety, commerce, industry,

morality, and religion. There is no end which the human will despairs of attaining through the combined power of individuals united into a society. . . .

An association consists simply in the public assent which a number of individuals give to certain doctrines; and in the engagement which they contract to promote in a certain manner the spread of those doctrines. The right of associating with such views is very analogous to the liberty of unlicensed printing; but societies thus formed possess more authority than the press. When an opinion is represented by a society, it necessarily assumes a more exact and explicit form. It numbers its partisans, and compromises them in its cause: they, on the other hand, become acquainted with each other, and their zeal is increased by their number. An association unites into one channel the efforts of diverging minds, and urges them vigorously towards the one end which it clearly points out.

The second degree in the exercise of the right of association is the power of meeting. When an association is allowed to establish centres of action at certain important points in the country, its activity is increased, and its influence extended. Men have the opportunity of seeing each other; means of execution are combined; and opinions are maintained with a warmth and energy which written language can never attain. Lastly, in the exercise of the right of political association, there is a third degree: the partisans of an opinion may unite in electoral bodies, and choose delegates to represent them in a central assembly. This is, properly speaking, the application of the representative system to a party.

Thus, in the first instance, a society is formed between individuals professing the same opinion, and the tie which keeps it together is of a purely intellectual nature. In the second case, small assemblies are formed, which represent only a fraction of the party. Lastly, in the third case, they constitute, as it were, a separate nation in the midst of the nation, a government within the government. Their delegates, like the real delegates of the majority, represent the whole collective force of their party; and, like them, also, have an appearance of nationality and all the moral power which results from it. It is true that they have not the right, like the others, of making the laws; but they have the power of attacking those which are in force, and of drawing up beforehand those which ought to be enacted.

If, among a people who are imperfectly accustomed to the exercise of freedom, or are exposed to violent political passions, by the side of the majority who make the laws be placed a minority who only deliberate and get laws ready for adoption, I cannot but believe that public tranquillity would there incur very great risks. There is doubtless a wide difference between proving that one law is in itself better than another, and proving that the former ought to be substituted for the latter. But the imagination of the multitude is very apt to overlook this difference, which is so apparent to the minds of thinking men. It sometimes happens that a nation is divided into two nearly equal parties, each of which affects to represent the majority. If, near the directing power, another power be established, which exercises almost as much moral authority as the former, we are not to believe that it will long be content to speak without acting; or that it will always be restrained by the abstract consideration that associations are meant to direct opinions, but not to enforce them,—to suggest, but not to make, the laws.

The more I consider the independence of the press in its principal consequences, the more am I convinced that, in the modern world, it is the chief, and, so to speak, the constitutive element of liberty. A nation which is determined to remain free is therefore right in demanding, at any price, the exercise of this independence. But the *unlimited* liberty of political association cannot be entirely assimilated to the liberty of the press. The one is at the same time less necessary, and more dangerous, than the other. A nation may confine it within certain limits without forfeiting any part of its self-directing power; and it may sometimes be obliged to do so, in order to maintain its own authority. . . .

It must be acknowledged that the unrestrained liberty of political association has not hitherto produced, in the United States, the fatal results which might perhaps be expected from it elsewhere. The right of association was imported from England, and it has always existed in America; the exercise of this privilege is now incorporated with the manners and customs of the people. At the present time, the liberty of association has become a necessary guaranty against the tyranny of the majority. In the United States, as soon as a party has become dominant, all public authority passes into its hands: its private supporters occupy all the offices, and have all the force of the administration at their disposal. As the most distinguished members of the opposite party cannot surmount the barrier which excludes them from power, they must establish themselves outside of it, and oppose the whole moral authority of the minority to the physical power which domineers over it. Thus a dangerous expedient is used to obviate a still more formidable danger.

The omnipotence of the majority appears to me to be so full of peril to the American republics, that the dangerous means used to bridle it seem to be more advantageous than prejudicial. And here I will express an opinion which may remind the reader of what I said when speaking of the freedom of townships. There are no countries in which associations are more needed, to prevent the despotism of faction or the arbitrary power of a prince, than those which are democratically constituted. In aristocratic nations, the body of the nobles and the wealthy are in themselves natural associations, which check the abuses of power. In countries where such associations do not exist, if private individuals cannot create an artificial and temporary substitute for them, I can see no permanent protection against the most galling tyranny; and a great people may be oppressed with impunity by a small faction, or by a single individual. . . .

It cannot be denied that the unrestrained liberty of association for political purposes is the privilege which a people is longest in learning how to exercise. If it does not throw the nation into anarchy, it perpetually augments the chances of that calamity. On one point, however, this perilous liberty offers a security against dangers of another kind; in countries where associations are free, secret societies are unknown. In America, there are factions, but no conspiracies.

The most natural privilege of man, next to the right of acting for himself, is that of combining his exertions with those of his fellow-creatures, and of acting in common with them. The right of association therefore appears to me almost as inalienable in its nature as the right of personal liberty. No legislator can attack it without impairing the foundations of society. Nevertheless, if the liberty of association is only a source of advantage and prosperity to some nations, it may be perverted or carried to excess by others, and from an element of life may be changed into a cause of destruction. A comparison of the different methods which associations pursue, in those countries in which liberty is well understood, and in those where liberty degenerates into license, may be useful both to governments and to parties.

Most Europeans look upon association as a weapon which is to be hastily fashioned, and immediately tried in the conflict. A society is formed for discussion, but the idea of impending action prevails in the minds of all those who constitute it. It is, in fact, an army; and the time given to speech serves to reckon up the strength and to animate the courage of the host, after which they march against the enemy. Resources which lie within the bounds of law may suggest themselves,

to the persons who compose it, as means, but never as the
only means, of success.

Such, however, is not the manner in which the right of
association is understood in the United States. In America,
the citizens who form the minority associate, in order, first, to
show their numerical strength, and so to diminish the moral
power of the majority; and, secondly, to stimulate competition, and thus to discover those arguments which are most
fitted to act upon the majority: for they always entertain
hopes of drawing over the majority to their own side, and then
disposing of the supreme power in its name. Political associations in the United States are therefore peaceable in their
intentions, and strictly legal in the means which they employ; and they assert with perfect truth, that they aim at success only by lawful expedients.

The difference which exists in this respect between Americans and Europeans depends on several causes. In Europe,
there are parties which differ so much from the majority, that
they can never hope to acquire its support, and yet they think
they are strong enough in themselves to contend against it.
When a party of this kind forms an association, its object is,
not to convince, but to fight. In America, the individuals
who hold opinions much opposed to the majority can do nothing against it; and all other parties hope to win it over to
their own principles. The exercise of the right of association becomes dangerous, then, in proportion as great parties
find themselves wholly unable to acquire the majority. In a
country like the United States, in which the differences of opinion are mere differences of hue, the right of association may
remain unrestrained without evil consequences. Our inexperience of liberty leads us to regard the liberty of association
only as a right of attacking the government. The first notion
which presents itself to a party, as well as to an individual,
when it has acquired a consciousness of its own strength, is
that of violence: the notion of persuasion arises at a later
period, and is derived from experience. The English, who are
divided into parties which differ essentially from each other,
rarely abuse the right of association, because they have long
been accustomed to exercise it. In France, the passion for
war is so intense, there is no undertaking so mad, or so injurious to the welfare of the state, that a man does not consider
himself honored in defending it at the risk of his life.

But perhaps the most powerful of the causes which tend
to mitigate the violence of political associations in the United
States is universal suffrage. In countries in which universal
suffrage exists, the majority is never doubtful, because neither

party can reasonably pretend to represent that portion of the community which has not voted. The associations know as well as the nation at large, that they do not represent the majority. This results, indeed, from the very fact of their existence; for if they did represent the preponderating power, they would change the law instead of soliciting its reform. The consequence of this is, that the moral influence of the government which they attack is much increased, and their own power is much enfeebled.

In Europe, there are few associations which do not affect to represent the majority, or which do not believe that they represent it. This conviction or this pretension tends to augment their force amazingly, and contributes no less to legalize their measures. Violence may seem to be excusable, in defence of the cause of oppressed right. Thus it is, in the vast complication of human laws, that extreme liberty sometimes corrects the abuses of liberty, and that extreme democracy obviates the dangers of democracy. In Europe, associations consider themselves, in some degree, as the legislative and executive council of the people, which is unable to speak for itself; moved by this belief, they act and they command. In America, where they represent in the eyes of all only a minority of the nation, they argue and petition.

The means which associations in Europe employ, are in accordance with the end which they propose to obtain. As the principal aim of these bodies is to act, and not to debate, to fight rather than to convince, they are naturally led to adopt an organization which is not civic and peaceful, but partakes of the habits and maxims of military life. They centralize, also, the direction of their forces as much as possible, and intrust the power of the whole party to a small number of leaders.

The members of these associations respond to a watchword, like soldiers on duty; they profess the doctrine of passive obedience; say rather, that in uniting together they at once abjure the exercise of their own judgment and free will: and the tyrannical control which these societies exercise, is often far more insupportable than the authority possessed over society by the government which they attack. Their moral force is much diminished by these proceedings, and they lose the sacred character which always attaches to a struggle of the oppressed against their oppressors. He who in given cases consents to obey his fellows with servility, and who submits his will, and even his thoughts, to their control, how can he pretend that he wishes to be free?

The Americans have also established a government in their associations, but it is invariably borrowed from the forms of the civil administration. The independence of each individual is formally recognized; as in society, all the members advance at the same time towards the same end; but they are not all obliged to follow the same track. No one abjures the exercise of his reason and free will; but every one exerts that reason and will to promote a common undertaking. . . .

11. Advantages of Democracy in the United States.

. . . THE defects and weaknesses of a democratic government may readily be discovered; they are demonstrated by flagrant instances, whilst its salutary influence is insensible, and, so to speak, occult. A glance suffices to detect its faults, but its good qualities can be discerned only by long observation. The laws of the American democracy are frequently defective or incomplete; they sometimes attack vested rights, or sanction others which are dangerous to the community; and even if they were good, their frequency would still be a great evil. How comes it, then, that the American republics prosper and continue? . . .

Democratic laws generally tend to promote the welfare of the greatest possible number; for they emanate from the majority of the citizens, who are subject to error, but who cannot have an interest opposed to their own advantage. The laws of an aristocracy tend, on the contrary, to concentrate wealth and power in the hands of the minority; because an aristocracy, by its very nature, constitutes a minority. It may therefore be asserted, as a general proposition, that the purpose of a democracy in its legislation is more useful to humanity than that of an aristocracy. This is, however, the sum total of its advantages.

Aristocracies are infinitely more expert in the science of legislation than democracies ever can be. They are possessed of a self-control which protects them from the errors of temporary excitement; and they form far-reaching designs, which they know how to mature till a favorable opportunity arrives. Aristocratic government proceeds with the dexterity of art; it understands how to make the collective force of all its laws converge at the same time to a given point. Such is not the case with democracies, whose laws are almost always ineffective or inopportune. The means of democracy are therefore more imperfect than those of aristocracy, and the measures

which it unwittingly adopts are frequently opposed to its
own cause; but the object it has in view is more useful. . . .

An analogous observation may be made respecting public
officers. It is easy to perceive that the American democracy
frequently errs in the choice of the individuals to whom it in-
trusts the power of the administration. . . . The men who
are intrusted with the direction of public affairs in the United
States are frequently inferior, both in capacity and morality,
to those whom an aristocracy would raise to power. But their
interest is identified and confounded with that of the majority
of their fellow-citizens. They may frequently be faithless, and
frequently mistaken; but they will never systematically adopt
a line of conduct hostile to the majority; and they cannot give
a dangerous or exclusive tendency to the government.

The maladministration of a democratic magistrate, moreover, is an isolated fact, which has influence only during the
short period for which he is elected. Corruption and incapacity
do not act as common interests, which may connect men
permanently with one another. A corrupt or incapable magistrate will not concert his measures with another magistrate,
simply because the latter is as corrupt and incapable as himself; and these two men will never unite their endeavors to
promote the corruption and inaptitude of their remote posterity. The ambition and the manœuvres of the one will serve,
on the contrary, to unmask the other. The vices of a magistrate,
in democratic states, are usually wholly personal. . . .

In the United States, where the public officers have no
class-interests to promote, the general and constant influence
of the government is beneficial, although the individuals who
conduct it are frequently unskilled, and sometimes contemptible. There is, indeed, a secret tendency in democratic
institutions, which makes the exertions of the citizens subservient to the prosperity of the community, in spite of their
vices and mistakes; whilst in aristocratic institutions, there is a
secret bias, which, notwithstanding the talents and virtues
of those who conduct the government, leads them to contribute
to the evils which oppress their fellow-creatures. In aristocratic
governments, public men may frequently do harm without intending it; and in democratic states, they bring about good
results which they never thought of.

Public Spirit.

There is one sort of patriotic attachment, which principally
arises from that instinctive, disinterested, and undefinable feeling which connects the affections of man with his birthplace.

This natural fondness is united with a taste for ancient customs, and a reverence for traditions of the past; those who cherish it love their country as they love the mansion of their fathers. They love the tranquillity which it affords them; they cling to the peaceful habits which they have contracted within its bosom; they are attached to the reminiscences which it awakens; and they are even pleased by living there in a state of obedience. This patriotism is sometimes stimulated by religious enthusiasm, and then it is capable of making prodigious efforts. It is in itself a kind of religion: it does not reason, but it acts from the impulse of faith and sentiment. In some nations, the monarch is regarded as a personification of the country; and, the fervor of patriotism being converted into the fervor of loyalty, they take a sympathetic pride in his conquests, and glory in his power. There was a time, under the ancient monarchy, when the French felt a sort of satisfaction in the sense of their dependence upon the arbitrary will of their king; and they were wont to say with pride, "We live under the most powerful king in the world." But, like all instinctive passions, this kind of patriotism incites great transient exertions, but no continuity of effort. It may save the state in critical circumstances, but often allows it to decline in times of peace. Whilst the manners of a people are simple, and its faith unshaken,—whilst society is steadily based upon traditional institutions, whose legitimacy has never been contested,—this instinctive patriotism is wont to endure.

But there is another species of attachment to country, which is more rational than the one we have been describing. It is, perhaps, less generous and less ardent, but it is more fruitful and more lasting: it springs from knowledge; it is nurtured by the laws; it grows by the exercise of civil rights; and, in the end, it is confounded with the personal interests of the citizen. A man comprehends the influence which the well-being of his country has upon his own; he is aware that the laws permit him to contribute to that prosperity, and he labors to promote it, at first because it benefits him, and secondly because it is in part his own work.

But epochs sometimes occur in the life of a nation, when the old customs of a people are changed, public morality is destroyed, religious belief shaken, and the spell of tradition broken, whilst the diffusion of knowledge is yet imperfect, and the civil rights of the community are ill secured, or confined within narrow limits. The country then assumes a dim and dubious shape in the eyes of the citizens; they no longer behold it in the soil which they inhabit, for that soil is to them an inanimate clod; nor in the usages of their forefathers, which they have learned to regard as a debasing yoke; nor in religion, for of that they doubt; nor in the laws, which do not originate in their own authority; nor in the legislator, whom they fear and despise. The country is lost to their senses; they can neither discover it under its own nor under borrowed features, and they retire into a narrow and unenlightened selfishness. They are emancipated from prejudice, without having acknowledged the empire of reason; they have neither the instinctive patriotism of a monarchy, nor the reflecting patriotism of a republic; but they have stopped between the two in the midst of confusion and distress.

In this predicament, to retreat is impossible; for a people cannot recover the sentiments of their youth, any more than a man can return to the innocent tastes of childhood: such things may be regretted, but they cannot be renewed. They must go forward, and accelerate the union of private with public interests, since the period of disinterested patriotism is gone by forever.

I am certainly far from affirming, that, in order to obtain this result, the exercise of political rights should be immediately granted to all men. But I maintain that the most powerful, and perhaps the only, means which we still possess of interesting men in the welfare of their country, is to make them partakers in the government. At the present time, civic zeal seems to me to be inseparable from the exercise of political rights; and I think that the number of citizens will be found to augment or decrease in Europe in proportion as those rights are extended.

How happens it that in the United States, where the inhabitants arrived but as yesterday upon the soil which they now occupy, and brought neither customs nor traditions with them there; where they met each other for the first time with no previous acquaintance; where, in short, the instinctive love of country can scarcely exist;—how happens it that every one takes as zealous an interest in the affairs of his township, his county, and the whole State, as if they were his own? It is because every one, in his sphere, takes an active part in the government of society. The lower orders in the United States understand the influence exercised by the general prosperity upon their own welfare; simple as this observation is, it is too rarely made by the people. Besides, they are wont to regard this prosperity as the fruit of their own exertions. The citizen looks upon the fortune of the public as his own, and he labors for the good of the State, not merely from a sense of pride or duty, but from what I venture to term cupidity.

It is unnecessary to study the institutions and the history

of the Americans in order to know the truth of this remark,
for their manners render it sufficiently evident. As the American participates in all that is done in his country, he thinks
himself obliged to defend whatever may be censured in it;
for it is not only his country which is then attacked, it is
himself. The consequence is, that his national pride resorts
to a thousand artifices, and descends to all the petty tricks of
personal vanity.

Nothing is more embarrassing, in the ordinary intercourse
of life, than this irritable patriotism of the Americans. A
stranger may be well inclined to praise many of the institutions of their country, but he begs permission to blame some
things in it,—a permission which is inexorably refused. America is therefore a free country, in which, lest anybody should
be hurt by your remarks, you are not allowed to speak freely
of private individuals, or of the state; of the citizens, or of the
authorities; of public or of private undertakings; or, in short,
of anything at all, except, perhaps, the climate and the soil;
and even then, Americans will be found ready to defend both,
as if they had concurred in producing them.

In our times, we must choose between the patriotism of all
and the government of a few; for the social force and activity
which the first confers are irreconcilable with the pledges of
tranquillity which are given by the second.

Notion of Rights.

After the general idea of virtue, I know no higher principle
than that of right; or rather these two ideas are united in one.
The idea of right is simply that of virtue introduced into the
political world. It was the idea of right which enabled men
to define anarchy and tyranny; and which taught them how
to be independent without arrogance, and to obey without
servility. The man who submits to violence is debased by his
compliance; but when he submits to that right of authority
which he acknowledges in a fellow-creature, he rises in some
measure above the person who gives the command. There are
no great men without virtue; and there are no great nations,—
it may almost be added, there would be no society,—without
respect for right; for what is a union of rational and intelligent beings who are held together only by the bond of
force? . . .

The government of the democracy brings the notion of
political rights to the level of the humblest citizens, just as
the dissemination of wealth brings the notion of property
within the reach of all men; to my mind, this is one of its

greatest advantages. I do not say it is easy to teach men
how to exercise political rights; but I maintain that, when
it is possible, the effects which result from it are highly important; and I add, that, if there ever was a time at which
such an attempt ought to be made, that time is now. Do
you not see that religious belief is shaken, and the divine
notion of right is declining?—that morality is debased, and
the notion of moral right is therefore fading away? Argument is substituted for faith, and calculation for the impulses
of sentiment. If, in the midst of this general disruption, you
do not succeed in connecting the notion of right with that of
private interest, which is the only immutable point in the
human heart, what means will you have of governing the
world except by fear? When I am told that the laws are weak
and the people are turbulent, that passions are excited and
the authority of virtue is paralyzed, and therefore no measures must be taken to increase the rights of the democracy,
I reply, that, for these very reasons, some measures of the
kind ought to be taken; and I believe that governments are
still more interested in taking them than society at large, for
governments may perish, but society cannot die.

But I do not wish to exaggerate the example which America furnishes. There the people were invested with political
rights at a time when they could not be abused, for the inhabitants were few in number, and simple in their manners.
As they have increased, the Americans have not augmented
the power of the democracy; they have rather extended its
domain.

It cannot be doubted that the moment at which political
rights are granted to a people that had before been without
them is a very critical one,—that the measure, though often
necessary, is always dangerous. A child may kill before he is
aware of the value of life; and he may deprive another person
of his property, before he is aware that his own may be taken
from him. The lower orders, when first they are invested
with political rights, stand, in relation to those rights, in the
same position as the child does to the whole of nature; and
the celebrated adage may then be applied to them, *Homo
puer robustus*. This truth may be perceived even in America.
The States in which the citizens have enjoyed their rights
longest, are those in which they make the best use of them.

It cannot be repeated too often, that nothing is more fertile in prodigies than the art of being free; but there is nothing
more arduous than the apprenticeship of liberty. It is not so
with despotism: despotism often promises to make amends
for a thousand previous ills; it supports the right, it protects

the oppressed, and it maintains public order. The nation is lulled by the temporary prosperity which it produces, until it is roused to a sense of its misery. Liberty, on the contrary, is generally established with difficulty in the midst of storms; it is perfected by civil discord; and its benefits cannot be appreciated until it is already old.

Respect for the Law.

It is not always feasible to consult the whole people, either directly or indirectly, in the formation of the law; but it cannot be denied that, when this is possible, the authority of the law is much augmented. This popular origin, which impairs the excellence and the wisdom of legislation, contributes much to increase its power. There is an amazing strength in the expression of the will of a whole people; and when it declares itself, even the imagination of those who would wish to contest it is overawed. The truth of this fact is well known by parties; and they consequently strive to make out a majority whenever they can. If they have not the greater number of voters on their side, they assert that the true majority abstained from voting; and if they are foiled even there, they have recourse to those who had no right to vote.

In the United States, except slaves, servants, and paupers supported by the townships, there is no class of persons who do not exercise the elective franchise, and who do not indirectly contribute to make the laws. Those who wish to attack the laws must consequently either change the opinion of the nation, or trample upon its decision.

A second reason, which is still more direct and weighty, may be adduced: in the United States, every one is personally interested in enforcing the obedience of the whole community to the law; for as the minority may shortly rally the majority to its principles, it is interested in professing that respect for the decrees of the legislator which it may soon have occasion to claim for its own. However irksome an enactment may be, the citizen of the United States complies with it, not only because it is the work of the majority, but because it is his own, and he regards it as a contract to which he is himself a party.

In the United States, then, that numerous and turbulent multitude does not exist, who, regarding the law as their natural enemy, look upon it with fear and distrust. It is impossible, on the contrary, not to perceive that all classes display the utmost reliance upon the legislation of their country, and are attached to it by a kind of parental affection.

I am wrong, however, in saying all classes; for as, in America, the European scale of authority is inverted, the wealthy are there placed in a position analogous to that of the poor in the Old World, and it is the opulent classes who frequently look upon the law with suspicion. I have already observed that the advantage of democracy is not, as has been sometimes asserted, that it protects the interests of all, but simply that it protects those of the majority. In the United States, where the poor rule, the rich have always something to fear from the abuse of their power. This natural anxiety of the rich may produce a secret dissatisfaction; but society is not disturbed by it, for the same reason which withholds the confidence of the rich from the legislative authority, makes them obey its mandates: their wealth, which prevents them from making the law, prevents them from withstanding it. Amongst civilized nations, only those who have nothing to lose ever revolt; and if the laws of a democracy are not always worthy of respect, they are always respected; for those who usually infringe the laws cannot fail to obey those which they have themselves made, and by which they are benefited, whilst the citizens who might be interested in the infraction of them are induced, by their character and station, to submit to the decisions of the legislature, whatever they may be. Besides, the people in America obey the law, not only because it is their work, but because it may be changed if it be harmful; a law is observed because, first, it is a self-imposed evil, and, secondly, it is an evil of transient duration.

Political Activity Which Pervades The United States.

. . . It is not impossible to conceive the surprising liberty which the Americans enjoy; some idea may likewise be formed of their extreme equality; but the political activity which pervades the United States must be seen in order to be understood. No sooner do you set foot upon American ground, than you are stunned by a kind of tumult; a confused clamor is heard on every side; and a thousand simultaneous voices demand the satisfaction of their social wants. Everything is in motion around you; here, the people of one quarter of a town are met to decide upon the building of a church; there, the election of a representative is going on; a little further, the delegates of a district are posting to the town in order to consult some local improvements; in another place, the laborers of a village quit their ploughs to deliberate upon the project of a road or a public school. Meetings are called for the sole purpose of declaring their disap-

probation of the conduct of the government; whilst in other
assemblies, citizens salute the authorities of the day as the
fathers of their country. Societies are formed which regard
drunkenness as the principal cause of the evils of the state,
and solemnly bind themselves to give an example of temperance. The great political agitation of American legislative
bodies, which is the only one that attracts the attention of
foreigners, is a mere episode, or a sort of continuation, of
that universal movement which originates in the lowest classes
of the people, and extends successively to all the ranks of
society. It is impossible to spend more effort in the pursuit of
happiness.

The cares of politics engross a prominent place in the occupations of a citizen in the United States; and almost the
only pleasure which an American knows is to take a part
in the government, and to discuss its measures. This feeling
pervades the most trifling habits of life; even the women
frequently attend public meetings, and listen to political
harangues as a recreation from their household labors. De-
bating clubs are, to a certain extent, a substitute for theatrical
entertainments: an American cannot converse, but he can
discuss; and his talk falls into a dissertation. He speaks to you
as if he was addressing a meeting; and if he should chance to
become warm in the discussion, he will say "Gentlemen" to
the person with whom he is conversing.

In some countries, the inhabitants seem unwilling to avail
themselves of the political privileges which the law gives them;
it would seem that they set too high a value upon their time
to spend it on the interests of the community; and they shut
themselves up in a narrow selfishness, marked out by four
sunk fences and a quickset hedge. But if an American were
condemned to confine his activity to his own affairs, he would
be robbed of one half of his existence; he would feel an immense void in the life which he is accustomed to lead, and
his wretchedness would be unbearable. I am persuaded, that,
if ever a despotism should be established in America, it will
be more difficult to overcome the habits which freedom has
formed, than to conquer the love of freedom itself.

This ceaseless agitation which democratic government has
introduced into the political world, influences all social intercourse. I am not sure that, upon the whole, this is not the
greatest advantage of democracy; and I am less inclined to
applaud it for what it does, than for what it causes to be
done. It is incontestable that the people frequently conduct
public business very ill; but it is impossible that the lower
orders should take a part in public business without extend-

ing the circle of their ideas, and quitting the ordinary routine of their thoughts. The humblest individual who co-operates in the government of society acquires a certain degree of self-respect; and as he possesses authority, he can command the services of minds more enlightened than his own. He is canvassed by a multitude of applicants, and, in seeking to deceive him in a thousand ways, they really enlighten him. He takes a part in political undertakings which he did not originate, but which give him a taste for undertakings of the kind. New improvements are daily pointed out to him in the common property, and this gives him the desire of improving that property which is his own. He is perhaps neither happier nor better than those who came before him, but he is better informed and more active. I have no doubt that the democratic institutions of the United States, joined to the physical constitution of the country, are the cause (not the direct, as is so often asserted, but the indirect cause) of the prodigious commercial activity of the inhabitants. It is not created by the laws, but the people learn how to promote it by the experience derived from legislation.

When the opponents of democracy assert that a single man performs what he undertakes better than the government of all, it appears to me that they are right. The government of an individual, supposing an equality of knowledge on either side, is more consistent, more persevering, more uniform, and more accurate in details, than that of a multitude, and it selects with more discrimination the men whom it employs. If any deny this, they have never seen a democratic government, or have judged upon partial evidence. It is true that, even when local circumstances and the dispositions of the people allow democratic institutions to exist, they do not display a regular and methodical system of government. Democratic liberty is far from accomplishing all its projects with the skill of an adroit despotism. It frequently abandons them before they have borne their fruits, or risks them when the consequences may be dangerous; but in the end, it produces more than any absolute government; if it does fewer things well, it does a greater number of things. Under its sway, the grandeur is not in what the public administration does, but in what is done without it or outside of it. Democracy does not give the people the most skilful government, but it produces what the ablest governments are frequently unable to create; namely, an all-pervading and restless activity, a superabundant force, and an energy which is inseparable from it, and which may, however unfavorable circumstances may be, produce wonders. These are the true advantages of democracy.

In the present age, when the destinies of Christendom seem to be in suspense, some hasten to assail democracy as a hostile power, whilst it is yet growing; and others already adore this new deity which is springing forth from chaos. But both parties are imperfectly acquainted with the object of their hatred or their worship; they strike in the dark, and distribute their blows at random.

We must first understand what is wanted of society and its government. Do you wish to give a certain elevation to the human mind, and teach it to regard the things of this world with generous feelings, to inspire men with a scorn of mere temporal advantages, to form and nourish strong convictions, and keep alive the spirit of honorable devotedness? Is it your object to refine the habits, embellish the manners, and cultivate the arts, to promote the love of poetry, beauty, and glory? Would you constitute a people fitted to act powerfully upon all other nations, and prepared for those high enterprises which, whatever be their results, will leave a name forever famous in history? If you believe such to be the principal object of society, avoid the government of the democracy, for it would not lead you with certainty to the goal.

But if you hold it expedient to divert the moral and intellectual activity of man to the production of comfort, and the promotion of general well-being; if a clear understanding be more profitable to man than genius; if your object be not to stimulate the virtues of heroism, but the habits of peace; if you had rather witness vices than crimes, and are content to meet with fewer noble deeds, provided offences be diminished in the same proportion; if, instead of living in the midst of a brilliant society, you are contented to have prosperity around you; if, in short, you are of opinion that the principal object of a government is not to confer the greatest possible power and glory upon the body of the nation, but to insure the greatest enjoyment, and to avoid the most misery, to each of the individuals who comprise it,—if such be your desire, then equalize the conditions of men, and establish democratic institutions.

But if the time be past at which such a choice was possible, and if some power superior to that of man already hurries us, without consulting our wishes, towards one or the other of these two governments, let us endeavor to make the best of that which is allotted to us, and, by finding out both its good and its evil tendencies, be able to foster the former and repress the latter to the utmost.

12. Unlimited Power of the Majority in the United States and Its Consequences.

THE very essence of democratic government consists in the absolute sovereignty of the majority; for there is nothing in democratic states which is capable of resisting it. Most of the American constitutions have sought to increase this natural strength of the majority by artificial means.

The legislature is, of all political institutions, the one which is most easily swayed by the will of the majority. The Americans determined that the members of the legislature should be elected by the people *directly,* and for a *very brief term,* in order to subject them, not only to the general convictions, but even to the daily passions, of their constituents. The members of both houses are taken from the same classes in society, and nominated in the same manner; so that the movements of the legislative bodies are almost as rapid, and quite as irresistible, as those of a single assembly. It is to a legislature thus constituted, that almost all the authority of the government has been intrusted.

At the same time that the law increased the strength of those authorities which of themselves were strong, it enfeebled more and more those which were naturally weak. It deprived the representatives of the executive power of all stability and independence; and, by subjecting them completely to the caprices of the legislature, it robbed them of the slender influence which the nature of a democratic government might have allowed them to exercise. In several States, the judicial power was also submitted to the election of the majority; and in all of them, its existence was made to depend on the pleasure of the legislative authority, since the representatives were empowered annually to regulate the stipend of the judges.

Custom has done even more than law. A proceeding is becoming more and more general in the United States, which will, in the end, do away with the guaranties of representative government: it frequently happens that the voters, in electing a delegate, point out a certain line of conduct to him, and impose upon him certain positive obligations which he is pledged to fulfil. With the exception of the tumult, this comes to the same thing as if the majority itself held its deliberations in the market-place.

Several other circumstances concur to render the power

of the majority in America not only preponderant, but irresistible. The moral authority of the majority is partly based upon the notion, that there is more intelligence and wisdom in a number of men united than in a single individual, and that the number of the legislators is more important than their quality. The theory of equality is thus applied to the intellects of men; and human pride is thus assailed in its last retreat by a doctrine which the minority hesitate to admit, and to which they will but slowly assent. Like all other powers, and perhaps more than any other, the authority of the many requires the sanction of time in order to appear legitimate. At first, it enforces obedience by constraint; and its laws are not *respected* until they have been long maintained.

The right of governing society, which the majority supposes itself to derive from its superior intelligence, was introduced into the United States by the first settlers; and this idea, which of itself would be sufficient to create a free nation, has now been amalgamated with the manners of the people and the minor incidents of social life.

The French, under the old monarchy, held it for a maxim that the king could do no wrong; and if he did do wrong, the blame was imputed to his advisers. This notion made obedience very easy; it enabled the subject to complain of the law, without ceasing to love and honor the lawgiver. The Americans entertain the same opinion with respect to the majority.

The moral power of the majority is founded upon yet another principle, which is, that the interests of the many are to be preferred to those of the few. It will readily be perceived that the respect here professed for the rights of the greater number must naturally increase or diminish according to the state of parties. When a nation is divided into several great irreconcilable interests, the privilege of the majority is often overlooked, because it is intolerable to comply with its demands.

If there existed in America a class of citizens whom the legislating majority sought to deprive of exclusive privileges which they had possessed for ages, and to bring down from an elevated station to the level of the multitude, it is probable that the minority would be less ready to submit to its laws. But as the United States were colonized by men holding equal rank, there is as yet no natural or permanent disagreement between the interests of its different inhabitants.

There are communities in which the members of the minority can never hope to draw over the majority to their side, because they must then give up the very point which is at issue between them. Thus, an aristocracy can never become a majority whilst it retains its exclusive privileges, and it cannot cede its privileges without ceasing to be an aristocracy.

In the United States, political questions cannot be taken up in so general and absolute a manner; and all parties are willing to recognize the rights of the majority, because they all hope at some time to be able to exercise them to their own advantage. The majority, therefore, in that country, exercise a prodigious actual authority, and a power of opinion which is nearly as great; no obstacles exist which can impede or even retard its progress, so as to make it heed the complaints of those whom it crushes upon its path. This state of things is harmful in itself, and dangerous for the future. . . .

Tyranny of the Majority.

I hold it to be an impious and detestable maxim, that, politically speaking, the people have a right to do anything; and yet I have asserted that all authority originates in the will of the majority. Am I, then, in contradiction with myself?

A general law, which bears the name of justice, has been made and sanctioned, not only by a majority of this or that people, but by a majority of mankind. The rights of every people are therefore confined within the limits of what is just. A nation may be considered as a jury which is empowered to represent society at large, and to apply justice, which is its law. Ought such a jury, which represents society, to have more power than the society itself, whose laws it executes?

When I refuse to obey an unjust law, I do not contest the right of the majority to command, but I simply appeal from the sovereignty of the people to the sovereignty of mankind. Some have not feared to assert that a people can never outstep the boundaries of justice and reason in those affairs which are peculiarly its own; and that consequently full power may be given to the majority by which they are represented. But this is the language of a slave.

A majority taken collectively is only an individual, whose opinions, and frequently whose interests, are opposed to those of another individual, who is styled a minority. If it be admitted that a man possessing absolute power may misuse that power by wronging his adversaries, why should not a majority be liable to the same reproach? Men do not change their characters by uniting with each other; nor does their patience in the presence of obstacles increase with their strength. For my own part, I cannot believe it; the power to do everything, which I should refuse to one of my equals, I will never grant to any number of them.

I do not think, for the sake of preserving liberty, it is possible to combine several principles in the same government so as really to oppose them to one another. The form of government which is usually termed *mixed* has always appeared to me a mere chimera. Accurately speaking, there is no such thing as a *mixed government*, in the sense usually given to that word, because, in all communities, some one principle of action may be discovered which preponderates over the others. England, in the last century,—which has been especially cited as an example of this sort of government,— was essentially an aristocratic state, although it comprised some great elements of democracy; for the laws and customs of the country were such that the aristocracy could not but preponderate in the long run, and direct public affairs according to its own will. The error arose from seeing the interests of the nobles perpetually contending with those of the people, without considering the issue of the contest, which was really the important point. When a community actually has a mixed government,—that is to say, when it is equally divided between adverse principles,—it must either experience a revolution, or fall into anarchy.

I am therefore of opinion, that social power superior to all others must always be placed somewhere; but I think that liberty is endangered when this power finds no obstacle which can retard its course, and give it time to moderate its own vehemence.

Unlimited power is in itself a bad and dangerous thing. Human beings are not competent to exercise it with discretion. God alone can be omnipotent, because his wisdom and his justice are always equal to his power. There is no power on earth so worthy of honor in itself, or clothed with rights so sacred, that I would admit its uncontrolled and all-predominant authority. When I see that the right and the means of absolute command are conferred on any power whatever, be it called a people or a king, an aristocracy or a democracy, a monarchy or a republic, I say there is the germ of tyranny, and I seek to live elsewhere, under other laws.

In my opinion, the main evil of the present democratic institutions of the United States does not arise, as is often asserted in Europe, from their weakness, but from their irresistible strength. I am not so much alarmed at the excessive liberty which reigns in that country, as at the inadequate securities which one finds there against tyranny.

When an individual or a party is wronged in the United States, to whom can he apply for redress? If to public opinion, public opinion constitutes the majority; if to the legislature, it represents the majority, and implicitly obeys it; if to the executive power, it is appointed by the majority, and serves as a passive tool in its hands. The public force consists of the majority under arms; the jury is the majority invested with the right of hearing judicial cases; and in certain States, even the judges are elected by the majority. However iniquitous or absurd the measure of which you complain, you must submit to it as well as you can.

If, on the other hand, a legislative power could be so constituted as to represent the majority without necessarily being the slave of its passions, an executive so as to retain a proper share of authority, and a judiciary so as to remain independent of the other two powers, a government would be formed which would still be democratic, without incurring hardly any risk of tyranny.

I do not say that there is a frequent use of tyranny in America, at the present day; but I maintain that there is no sure barrier against it, and that the causes which mitigate the government there are to be found in the circumstances and the manners of the country, more than in its laws.

Effects of the Omnipotence of the Majority upon the Arbitrary Authority of American Public Officers.

A distinction must be drawn between tyranny and arbitrary power. Tyranny may be exercised by means of the law itself, and in that case it is not arbitrary; arbitrary power may be exercised for the public good, in which case it is not tyrannical. Tyranny usually employs arbitrary means, but, if necessary, it can do without them.

In the United States, the omnipotence of the majority, which is favorable to the legal despotism of the legislature, likewise favors the arbitrary authority of the magistrate. The majority has absolute power both to make the law and to watch over its execution; and as it has equal authority over those who are in power, and the community at large, it considers public officers as its passive agents, and readily confides to them the task of carrying out its designs. The details of their office, and the privileges which they are to enjoy, are rarely defined beforehand. It treats them as a master does his servants, since they are always at work in his sight, and he can direct or reprimand them at any instant.

In general, the American functionaries are far more independent within the sphere which is prescribed to them than the French civil officers. Sometimes, even, they are allowed by the popular authority to exceed those bounds; and as they are protected by the opinion, and backed by the power, of the majority, they dare do things which even a European, accustomed as he is to arbitrary power, is astonished at. By this means, habits are formed in the heart of a free country which may some day prove fatal to its liberties.

Power Exercised by the Majority in America upon Opinion.

It is in the examination of the exercise of thought in the United States, that we clearly perceive how far the power of the majority surpasses all the powers with which we are acquainted in Europe. Thought is an invisible and subtle power, that mocks all the efforts of tyranny. At the present time, the most absolute monarchs in Europe cannot prevent certain opinions hostile to their authority from circulating in secret through their dominions, and even in their courts. It is not so in America; as long as the majority is still undecided, discussion is carried on; but as soon as its decision is irrevocably pronounced, every one is silent, and the friends as well as the opponents of the measure unite in assenting to its propriety. The reason of this is perfectly clear: no monarch is so absolute as to combine all the powers of society in his own hands, and to conquer all opposition, as a majority is able to do, which has the right both of making and of executing the laws.

The authority of a king is physical, and controls the actions of men without subduing their will. But the majority possesses a power which is physical and moral at the same time, which acts upon the will as much as upon the actions, and represses not only all contest, but all controversy.

I know of no country in which there is so little independence of mind and real freedom of discussion as in America. In any constitutional state in Europe, every sort of religious and political theory may be freely preached and disseminated; for there is no country in Europe so subdued by any single authority, as not to protect the man who raises his voice in the cause of truth from the consequences of his hardihood. If he is unfortunate enough to live under an absolute government, the people are often upon his side; if he inhabits a free country, he can, if necessary, find a shelter behind the throne. The aristocratic part of society supports him in some countries, and the democracy in others. But in a nation where democratic institutions exist, organized like those of the United States, there is but one authority, one element of strength and success, with nothing beyond it.

In America, the majority raises formidable barriers around the liberty of opinion: within these barriers, an author may write what he pleases; but woe to him if he goes beyond them. Not that he is in danger of an *auto-da-fé*, but he is exposed to continued obloquy and persecution. His political career is closed forever, since he has offended the only authority which is able to open it. Every sort of compensation, even that of celebrity, is refused to him. Before publishing his opinions, he imagined that he held them in common with others; but no sooner has he declared them, than he is loudly censured by his opponents, whilst those who think like him, without having the courage to speak out, abandon him in silence. He yields at length, overcome by the daily effort which he has to make, and subsides into silence, as if he felt remorse for having spoken the truth.

Fetters and headsmen were the coarse instruments which tyranny formerly employed; but the civilization of our age has perfected despotism itself, though it seemed to have nothing to learn. Monarchs had, so to speak, materialized oppression: the democratic republics of the present day have rendered it as entirely an affair of the mind, as the will which it is intended to coerce. Under the absolute sway of one man, the body was attacked in order to subdue the soul; but the soul escaped the blows which were directed against it, and rose proudly superior. Such is not the course adopted by tyranny in democratic republics; there the body is left free, and the soul is enslaved. The master no longer says, "You shall think as I do, or you shall die"; but he says, "You are free to think differently from me, and to retain your life, your property, and all that you possess; but you are henceforth a stranger among your people. You may retain your civil rights, but they will be useless to you, for you will never be chosen by your fellow-citizens, if you solicit their votes; and they will affect to scorn you, if you ask for their esteem. You will remain among men, but you will be deprived of the rights of mankind. Your fellow-creatures will shun you like an impure being; and even those who believe in your innocence will abandon you, lest they should be shunned in their turn. Go in peace! I have given you your life, but it is an existence worse than death."

Absolute monarchies had dishonored despotism; let us beware lest democratic republics should reinstate it, and render it less odious and degrading in the eyes of the many, by making it still more onerous to the few.

Works have been published in the proudest nations of the Old World, expressly intended to censure the vices and the follies of the times: Labruyère inhabited the palace of Louis XIV., when he composed his chapter upon the Great, and

Molière criticised the courtiers in the pieces which were acted before the court. But the ruling power in the United States is not to be made game of. The smallest reproach irritates its sensibility, and the slightest joke which has any foundation in truth renders it indignant; from the forms of its language up to the solid virtues of its character, everything must be made the subject of encomium. No writer, whatever be his eminence, can escape paying this tribute of adulation to his fellow-citizens. The majority lives in the perpetual utterance of self-applause; and there are certain truths which the Americans can only learn from strangers or from experience.

If America has not as yet had any great writers, the reason is given in these facts; there can be no literary genius without freedom of opinion, and freedom of opinion does not exist in America. The Inquisition has never been able to prevent a vast number of anti-religious books from circulating in Spain. The empire of the majority succeeds much better in the United States, since it actually removes any wish to publish them. Unbelievers are to be met with in America, but there is no public organ of infidelity. Attempts have been made by some governments to protect morality by prohibiting licentious books. In the United States, no one is punished for this sort of books, but no one is induced to write them; not because all the citizens are immaculate in conduct, but because the majority of the community is decent and orderly.

In this case the use of the power is unquestionably good; and I am discussing the nature of the power itself. This irresistible authority is a constant fact, and its judicious exercise is only an accident.

Effects of the Tyranny of the Majority upon the National Character of the Americans.

The tendencies which I have just mentioned are as yet but slightly perceptible in political society; but they already exercise an unfavorable influence upon the national character of the Americans. I attribute the small number of distinguished men in political life to the ever-increasing despotism of the majority in the United States.

When the American Revolution broke out, they arose in great numbers; for public opinion then served, not to tyrannize over, but to direct the exertions of individuals. Those celebrated men, sharing the agitation of mind common at that period, had a grandeur peculiar to themselves, which was reflected back upon the nation, but was by no means borrowed from it.

In absolute governments, the great nobles who are nearest to the throne flatter the passions of the sovereign, and voluntarily truckle to his caprices. But the mass of the nation does not degrade itself by servitude; it often submits from weakness, from habit, or from ignorance, and sometimes from loyalty. Some nations have been known to sacrifice their own desires to those of the sovereign with pleasure and pride, thus exhibiting a sort of independence of mind in the very act of submission. These nations are miserable, but they are not degraded. There is a great difference between doing what one does not approve, and feigning to approve what one does; the one is the weakness of a feeble person, the other befits the temper of a lackey.

In free countries, where every one is more or less called upon to give his opinion on affairs of state,—in democratic republics, where public life is incessantly mingled with domestic affairs, where the sovereign authority is accessible on every side, and where its attention can always be attracted by vociferation,—more persons are to be met with who speculate upon its weaknesses, and live upon ministering to its passions, than in absolute monarchies. Not because men are naturally worse in these states than elsewhere, but the temptation is stronger and of easier access at the same time. The result is a more extensive debasement of character.

Democratic republics extend the practice of currying favor with the many, and introduce it into all classes at once: this is the most serious reproach that can be addressed to them. This is especially true in democratic states organized like the American republics, where the power of the majority is so absolute and irresistible that one must give up his rights as a citizen, and almost abjure his qualities as a man, if he intends to stray from the track which it prescribes.

In that immense crowd which throngs the avenues to power in the United States, I found very few men who displayed that manly candor and masculine independence of opinion which frequently distinguished the Americans in former times, and which constitutes the leading feature in distinguished characters wheresoever they may be found. It seems, at first sight, as if all the minds of the Americans were formed upon one model, so accurately do they follow the same route. A stranger does, indeed, sometimes meet with Americans who dissent from the rigor of these formularies,—with men who deplore the defects of the laws, the mutability and the ignorance of democracy, —who even go so far as to observe the evil tendencies which impair the national character, and to point out such remedies as it might be possible to apply; but no one is there to hear them except yourself, and you, to whom these secret reflections are confided, are a stranger and a bird of passage. They are very ready to communicate truths which are useless to you, but they hold a different language in public. . . .

The Greatest Dangers of the American Republics Proceed from the Omnipotence of the Majority.

Governments usually perish from impotence or from tyranny. In the former case, their power escapes from them; it is wrested from their grasp in the latter. Many observers who have witnessed the anarchy of democratic states, have imagined that the government of those states was naturally weak and impotent. The truth is, that, when war is once begun between parties, the government loses its control over society. But I do not think that a democratic power is naturally without force or resources; say, rather, that it is almost always by the abuse of its force, and the misemployment of its resources, that it becomes a failure. Anarchy is almost always produced by its tyranny or its mistakes, but not by its want of strength.

It is important not to confound stability with force, or the greatness of a thing with its duration. In democratic republics, the power which directs society is not stable; for it often changes hands, and assumes a new direction. But, whichever way it turns, its force is almost irresistible. The governments of the American republics appear to me to be as much centralized as those of the absolute monarchies of Europe, and more energetic than they are. I do not, therefore, imagine that they will perish from weakness.

If ever the free institutions of America are destroyed, that event may be attributed to the omnipotence of the majority, which may at some future time urge the minorities to desperation, and oblige them to have recourse to physical force. Anarchy will then be the result, but it will have been brought about by despotism.

Mr. Madison expresses the same opinion in the Federalist, No. 51. "It is of great importance in a republic, not only to guard the society against the oppression of its rulers, but to guard one part of the society against the injustice of the other part. Justice is the end of government. It is the end of civil society. It ever has been, and ever will be, pursued until it be obtained, or until liberty be lost in the pursuit. In a society, under the forms of which the stronger faction can readily unite and oppress the weaker, anarchy may as truly be said to reign as in a state of nature, where the weaker individual is not secured against the violence of the stronger: and as, in the latter state, even the stronger individuals are prompted by the uncertainty of their condition to submit to a government which may protect the weak as well as themselves, so, in the former state, will the more powerful factions be gradually induced by a like motive to wish for a government which will protect all parties, the weaker as well as the more powerful. It can be little doubted, that, if the State of Rhode Island was separated from the Confederacy and left to itself, the insecurity of right under the popular form of government within such narrow limits would be displayed by such reiterated oppressions of the factious majorities, that some power altogether independent of the people would soon be called for by the voice of the very factions whose misrule had proved the necessity of it."

Jefferson also said: "The executive power in our government is not the only, perhaps not even the principal, object of my solicitude. The tyranny of the legislature is really the danger most to be feared, and will continue to be so for many years to come. The tyranny of the executive power will come in its turn, but at a more distant period."

I am glad to cite the opinion of Jefferson upon this subject rather than that of any other, because I consider him the most powerful advocate democracy has ever had.

13. Causes Which Mitigate the Tyranny of the Majority in the United States.

Absence of Centralized Administration.

I HAVE already pointed out the distinction between a centralized government and a centralized administration. The former exists in America, but the latter is nearly unknown there. If the directing power of the American communities had both these instruments of government at its disposal, and united the habit of executing its commands to the right of commanding; if, after having established the general principles of government, it descended to the details of their application; and if, having regulated the great interests of the country, it could descend to the circle of individual interests, freedom would soon be banished from the New World.

But in the United States, the majority, which so frequently displays the tastes and the propensities of a despot, is still destitute of the most perfect instruments of tyranny. In the American republics, the central government has never as yet busied itself but with a small number of objects, sufficiently prominent to attract its attention. The secondary affairs of so-

ciety have never been regulated by its authority; and nothing
has hitherto betrayed its desire of even interfering in them. The
majority is become more and more absolute, but has not
increased the prerogatives of the central government; those
great prerogatives have been confined to a certain sphere; and,
although the despotism of the majority may be galling upon
one point, it cannot be said to extend to all. However the predominant party in the nation may be carried away by its passions, however ardent it may be in the pursuit of its projects,
it cannot oblige all the citizens to comply with its desires in
the same manner, and at the same time, throughout the country. When the central government which represents that majority has issued a decree, it must intrust the execution of its
will to agents, over whom it frequently has no control, and
whom it cannot perpetually direct. The townships, municipal
bodies, and counties form so many concealed breakwaters,
which check or part the tide of popular determination. If an
oppressive law were passed, liberty would still be protected
by the mode of executing that law; the majority cannot descend
to the details and what may be called the puerilities of administrative tyranny. It does not even imagine that it can do so,
for it has not a full consciousness of its authority. It knows only
the extent of its natural powers, but is unacquainted with the
art of increasing them.

This point deserves attention; for if a democratic republic,
similar to that of the United States, were ever founded in a
country where the power of one man had previously established a centralized administration, and had sunk it deep into
the habits and the laws of the people, I do not hesitate to assert,
that, in such a republic, a more insufferable despotism would
prevail than in any of the absolute monarchies of Europe; or,
indeed, than any which could be found on this side of Asia.

The Profession of the Law Serves to Counterpoise the Democracy.

In visiting the Americans and studying their laws, we perceive that the authority they have intrusted to members of the
legal profession, and the influence which these individuals exercise in the government, is the most powerful existing security
against the excesses of democracy. . . . Men who have made
a special study of the laws derive from this occupation certain
habits of order, a taste for formalities, and a kind of instinctive
regard for the regular connection of ideas, which naturally
render them very hostile to the revolutionary spirit and the
unreflecting passions of the multitude.

The special information which lawyers derive from their studies insures them a separate rank in society, and they constitute a sort of privileged body in the scale of intellect. This notion of their superiority perpetually recurs to them in the practice of their profession: they are the masters of a science which is necessary, but which is not very generally known: they serve as arbiters between the citizens; and the habit of directing to their purpose the blind passions of parties in litigation, inspires them with a certain contempt for the judgment of the multitude. Add to this, that they naturally constitute *a body;* not by any previous understanding, or by an agreement which directs them to a common end; but the analogy of their studies and the uniformity of their methods connect their minds together, as a common interest might unite their endeavors. Some of the tastes and the habits of the aristocracy may consequently be discovered in the characters of lawyers. They participate in the same instinctive love of order and formalities; and they entertain the same repugnance to the actions of the multitude, and the same secret contempt of the government of the people. . . .

I do not, then, assert that *all* the members of the legal profession are, at *all* times, the friends of order and the opponents of innovation, but merely that most of them are usually so. In a community in which lawyers are allowed to occupy without opposition that high station which naturally belongs to them, their general spirit will be eminently conservative and anti-democratic. When an aristocracy excludes the leaders of that profession from its ranks, it excites enemies who are the more formidable as they are independent of the nobility by their labors, and feel themselves to be their equals in intelligence, though inferior in opulence and power. But whenever an aristocracy consents to impart some of its privileges to these same individuals, the two classes coalesce very readily, and assume, as it were, family interests. . . .

Lawyers are attached to public order beyond every other consideration, and the best security of public order is authority. It must not be forgotten, also, that, if they prize freedom much, they generally value legality still more: they are less afraid of tyranny than of arbitrary power; and, provided the legislature undertakes of itself to deprive men of their independence, they are not dissatisfied. . . .

The government of democracy is favorable to the political power of lawyers; for when the wealthy, the noble, and the prince are excluded from the government, the lawyers take possession of it, in their own right, as it were, since they are the only men of information and sagacity, beyond the sphere

of the people, who can be the object of the popular choice.
If, then, they are led by their tastes towards the aristocracy
and the prince, they are brought in contact with the people by
their interests. They like the government of democracy, without participating in its propensities and without imitating its
weaknesses; whence they derive a twofold authority from it
and over it. The people in democratic states do not mistrust
the members of the legal profession, because it is known that
they are interested to serve the popular cause; and the people
listen to them without irritation, because they do not attribute to them any sinister designs. The lawyers do not, indeed,
wish to overthrow the institutions of democracy, but they constantly endeavor to turn it away from its real direction by
means which are foreign to its nature. Lawyers belong to the
people by birth and interest, and to the aristocracy by habit
and taste; they may be looked upon as the connecting link of
the two great classes of society. . . .

In America, there are no nobles or literary men, and the
people are apt to mistrust the wealthy; lawyers consequently
form the highest political class, and the most cultivated portion of society. They have therefore nothing to gain by innovation, which adds a conservative interest to their natural taste
for public order. If I were asked where I place the American
aristocracy, I should reply, without hesitation, that it is not
among the rich, who are united by no common tie, but that
it occupies the judicial bench and the bar.

The more we reflect upon all that occurs in the United
States, the more shall we be persuaded that the lawyers, as a
body, form the most powerful, if not the only, counterpoise
to the democratic element. In that country, we easily perceive
how the legal profession is qualified by its attributes, and even
by its faults, to neutralize the vices inherent in popular government. When the American people are intoxicated by passion, or carried away by the impetuosity of their ideas, they
are checked and stopped by the almost invisible influence of
their legal counsellors. These secretly oppose their aristocratic propensities to the nation's democratic instincts, their superstitious attachment to what is old to its love of novelty, their
narrow views to its immense designs, and their habitual pro-
crastination to its ardent impatience.

The courts of justice are the visible organs by which the legal
profession is enabled to control the democracy. The judge is
a lawyer, who, independently of the taste for regularity and
order which he has contracted in the study of law, derives an
additional love of stability from the inalienability of his own
functions. His legal attainments have already raised him to

a distinguished rank amongst his fellows; his political power
completes the distinction of his station, and gives him the instincts of the privileged classes. Armed with the power of
declaring the laws to be unconstitutional, the American magistrate perpetually interferes in political affairs. He cannot force
the people to make laws, but at least he can oblige them not
to disobey their own enactments, and not to be inconsistent
with themselves. . . .

It must not, moreover, be supposed that the legal spirit is
confined, in the United States, to the courts of justice; it extends far beyond them. As the lawyers form the only enlightened class whom the people do not mistrust, they are
naturally called upon to occupy most of the public stations.
They fill the legislative assemblies, and are at the head of the
administration; they consequently exercise a powerful influence upon the formation of the law, and upon its execution.
The lawyers are, however, obliged to yield to the current of
public opinion, which is too strong for them to resist; but it
is easy to find indications of what they would do, if they were
free to act. The Americans, who have made so many innovations in their political laws, have introduced very sparing
alterations in their civil laws, and that with great difficulty,
although many of these laws are repugnant to their social condition. The reason of this is, that, in matters of civil law, the
majority are obliged to defer to the authority of the legal profession, and the American lawyers are disinclined to innovate
when they are left to their own choice. . . .

The influence of legal habits extends beyond the precise
limits I have pointed out. Scarcely any political question arises
in the United States which is not resolved, sooner or later, into
a judicial question. Hence all parties are obliged to borrow,
in their daily controversies, the ideas, and even the language,
peculiar to judicial proceedings. As most public men are, or
have been, legal practitioners, they introduce the customs and
technicalities of their profession into the management of public
affairs. The jury extends this habitude to all classes. The language of the law thus becomes, in some measure, a vulgar
tongue; the spirit of the law, which is produced in the schools
and courts of justice, gradually penetrates beyond their walls
into the bosom of society, where it descends to the lowest
classes, so that at last the whole people contract the habits and
the tastes of the judicial magistrate. The lawyers of the United
States form a party which is but little feared and scarcely perceived, which has no badge peculiar to itself, which adapts
itself with great flexibility to the exigencies of the time, and
accommodates itself without resistance to all the movements

of the social body. But this party extends over the whole community, and penetrates into all the classes which compose it; it acts upon the country imperceptibly, but finally fashions it to suit its own purposes.

Trial by Jury.

Since my subject has led me to speak of the administration of justice in the United States, I will not pass over it without adverting to the institution of the jury. Trial by jury may be considered in two separate points of view; as a judicial, and as a political institution. . . .

My present purpose is to consider the jury as a political institution. . . . It would be a very narrow view to look upon the jury as a mere judicial institution; for, however great its influence may be upon the decisions of the courts, it is still greater on the destinies of society at large. The jury is, above all, a political institution, and it must be regarded in this light in order to be duly appreciated. By the jury, I mean a certain number of citizens chosen by lot, and invested with a temporary right of judging. Trial by jury, as applied to the repression of crime, appears to me an eminently republican element in the government, for the following reasons.

The institution of the jury may be aristocratic or democratic, according to the class from which the jurors are taken; but it always preserves its republican character, in that it places the real direction of society in the hands of the governed, or of a portion of the governed, and not in that of the government. Force is never more than a transient element of success, and after force, comes the notion of right. A government which should be able to reach its enemies only upon a field of battle would soon be destroyed. The true sanction of political laws is to be found in penal legislation; and if that sanction be wanting, the law will sooner or later lose its cogency. He who punishes the criminal is therefore the real master of society. Now, the institution of the jury raises the people itself, or at least a class of citizens, to the bench of judges. The institution of the jury consequently invests the people, or that class of citizens, with the direction of society. . . . The jury cannot fail to exercise a powerful influence upon the national character. . . . The jury . . . serves to communicate the spirit of the judges to the minds of all the citizens; and this spirit, with the habits which attend it, is the soundest preparation for free institutions. It imbues all classes with a respect for the thing judged, and with the notion of right. If these two elements be removed, the love of independence becomes a mere destructive passion.

It teaches men to practise equity; every man learns to judge his neighbor as he would himself be judged. And this is especially true of the jury in civil causes; for, whilst the number of persons who have reason to apprehend a criminal prosecution is small, every one is liable to have a lawsuit. The jury teaches every man not to recoil before the responsibility of his own actions, and impresses him with that manly confidence without which no political virtue can exist. It invests each citizen with a kind of magistracy; it makes them all feel the duties which they are bound to discharge towards society, and the part which they take in its government. By obliging men to turn their attention to other affairs than their own, it rubs off that private selfishness which is the rust of society.

The jury contributes powerfully to form the judgment and to increase the natural intelligence of a people; and this, in my opinion, is its greatest advantage. It may be regarded as a gratuitous public school, ever open, in which every juror learns his rights, enters into daily communication with the most learned and enlightened members of the upper classes, and becomes practically acquainted with the laws, which are brought within the reach of his capacity by the efforts of the bar, the advice of the judge, and even by the passions of the parties. I think that the practical intelligence and political good sense of the Americans are mainly attributable to the long use which they have made of the jury in civil causes. . . .

The jury, then, which seems to restrict the rights of the judiciary, does in reality consolidate its power; and in no country are the judges so powerful as where the people share their privileges. It is especially by means of the jury in civil causes, that the American magistrates imbue even the lower classes of society with the spirit of their profession. Thus the jury, which is the most energetic means of making the people rule, is also the most efficacious means of teaching it how to rule well.

14. Causes Which Tend to Maintain Democracy.

Accidental or Providential Causes.

. . . A THOUSAND circumstances, independent of the will of man, facilitate the maintenance of a democratic republic in the United States. . . .

The Americans have no neighbors, and consequently they have no great wars, or financial crises, or inroads, or conquest, to dread; they require neither great taxes, nor large armies, nor great generals; and they have nothing to fear from a scourge which is more formidable to republics than all these evils combined, namely, military glory. It is impossible to deny the inconceivable influence which military glory exercises upon the spirit of a nation. . . .

America has no great capital city, whose direct or indirect influence is felt over the whole extent of the country; this I hold to be one of the first causes of the maintenance of republican institutions in the United States. In cities, men cannot be prevented from concerting together, and awakening a mutual excitement which prompts sudden and passionate resolutions. Cities may be looked upon as large assemblies, of which all the inhabitants are members; their populace exercise a prodigious influence upon the magistrates, and frequently execute their own wishes without the intervention of public officers.

To subject the provinces to the metropolis is, therefore, to place the destiny of the empire in the hands, not only of a portion of the community, which is unjust, but in the hands of a populace carrying out its own impulses, which is very dangerous. The preponderance of capital cities is therefore a serious injury to the representative system; and it exposes modern republics to the same defect as the republics of antiquity, which all perished from not having known this system. . . .

The Americans had the chances of birth in their favor; and their forefathers imported that equality of condition and of intellect into the country whence the democratic republic has very naturally taken its rise. Nor was this all; for besides this republican condition of society, the early settlers bequeathed to their descendants the customs, manners, and opinions which contribute most to the success of a republic. When I reflect upon the consequences of this primary fact, methinks I see the destiny of America embodied in the first Puritan who landed on those shores, just as the whole human race was represented by the first man.

The chief circumstance which has favored the establishment and the maintenance of a democratic republic in the United States, is the nature of the territory which the Americans inhabit. Their ancestors gave them the love of equality and of freedom; but God himself gave them the means of remaining equal and free, by placing them upon a boundless continent. General prosperity is favorable to the stability of all governments, but more particularly of a democratic one, which depends upon the will of the majority, and especially upon the will of that portion of the community which is most exposed to want. When the people rule, they must be rendered happy, or they will overturn the state: and misery stimulates them to those excesses to which ambition rouses kings. The physical causes, independent of the laws, which promote general prosperity, are more numerous in America than they ever have been in any other country in the world, at any other period of history. In the United States, not only is legislation democratic, but Nature herself favors the cause of the people. . . .

That continent still presents, as it did in the primeval time, rivers which rise from never-failing sources, green and moist solitudes, and limitless fields which the plough-share of the husbandman has never turned. In this state, it is offered to man, not barbarous, ignorant, and isolated, as he was in the early ages, but already in possession of the most important secrets of nature, united to his fellowmen, and instructed by the experience of fifty centuries. At this very time, . . . millions of civilized Europeans are peaceably spreading over those fertile plains, with whose resources and extent they are not yet themselves accurately acquainted. Three or four thousand soldiers drive before them the wandering races of the aborigines; these are followed by the pioneers, who pierce the woods, scare off the beasts of prey, explore the courses of the inland streams, and make ready the triumphal march of civilization across the desert. . . .

An erroneous notion is generally entertained, that the deserts of America are peopled by European emigrants, who annually disembark upon the coasts of the New World, whilst the American population increase and multiply upon the soil which their forefathers tilled. The European settler usually arrives in the United States without friends, and often without resources. In order to subsist, he is obliged to work for hire, and he rarely proceeds beyond that belt of industrious population which adjoins the ocean. The desert cannot be explored without capital or credit; and the body must be accustomed to the rigors of a new climate, before it can be exposed in the midst of the forest. It is the Americans themselves who daily quit the spots which gave them birth, to acquire extensive domains in a remote region. Thus the European leaves his cottage for the Transatlantic shores, and the American, who is born on that very coast, plunges in his turn into the wilds of central America. This double emigration is incessant; it begins in the middle of Europe, it crosses the Atlantic Ocean, and it advances over the solitudes of the New World. Millions of men are marching at once towards the same horizon: their language, their religion, their manners differ; their object is the same. Fortune has been promised to them somewhere in the West, and to the West they go to find it. . . .

Sometimes the progress of man is so rapid that the desert reappears behind him. The woods stoop to give him a passage, and spring up again when he is past. It is not uncommon, in crossing the new States of the West, to meet with deserted dwellings in the midst of the wilds; the traveller frequently discovers the vestiges of a log-house in the most solitary retreat, which bear witness to the power, and no less to the inconstancy, of man. In these abandoned fields, and over these ruins of a day, the primeval forest soon scatters a fresh vegetation; the beasts resume the haunts which were once their own; and Nature comes smiling to cover the traces of man with green branches and flowers, which obliterate his ephemeral track.

I remember, that, in crossing one of the woodland districts which still cover the State of New York, I reached the shores of a lake which was embosomed in forests coeval with the world. A small island, covered with woods whose thick foliage concealed its banks, rose from the centre of the waters. Upon the shores of the lake, no object attested the presence of man, except a column of smoke, which might be seen on the horizon rising from the tops of the trees to the clouds, and seeming to hang from heaven rather than to be mounting to it. An Indian canoe was hauled up on the sand, which tempted me to visit the islet that had first attracted my attention, and in a few minutes I set foot upon its banks. The whole island formed one of those delicious solitudes of the New World, which almost lead civilized man to regret the haunts of the savage. A luxuriant vegetation bore witness to the incomparable fruitfulness of the soil. The deep silence, which is common to the wilds of North America, was only broken by the monotonous cooing of the wood-pigeons, and the tapping of the woodpecker upon the bark of trees. I was far from supposing that this spot had ever been inhabited, so completely did Nature seem to be left to herself; but when I reached the centre of the isle, I thought that I discovered some traces of man. I then proceeded to examine the surrounding objects with care, and I soon perceived that a European had undoubtedly been led to seek a refuge in this place. Yet what changes had taken place in the scene of his labors! The logs which he had hastily hewn to build himself a shed had sprouted afresh; the very props were intertwined with living verdure, and his cabin was transformed into a bower. In the midst of these shrubs, a few stones were to be seen, blackened with fire and sprinkled with thin ashes; here the hearth had no doubt been, and the chimney in falling had covered it with rubbish. I stood for some time in silent admiration of the resources of Nature and the littleness of

man; and when I was obliged to leave that enchanting solitude,
I exclaimed with sadness, "Are ruins, then, already here?"

In Europe, we are wont to look upon a restless disposition,
an unbounded desire of riches, and an excessive love of independence, as propensities very dangerous to society. Yet these
are the very elements which insure a long and peaceful future
to the republics of America. Without these unquiet passions,
the population would collect in certain spots, and would soon
experience wants like those of the Old World, which it is difficult to satisfy; for such is the present good fortune of the New
World, that the vices of its inhabitants are scarcely less favorable to society than their virtues. These circumstances exercise a great influence on the estimation in which human actions
are held in the two hemispheres. What we should call cupidity, the Americans frequently term a laudable industry; and
they blame as faint-heartedness what we consider to be the
virtue of moderate desires. . . .

*The Laws Contribute More to the Maintenance of the
Democratic Republic in the United States Than the
Physical Circumstances of the Country, and the Man-
ners More Than the Laws.*

. . . The maintenance of democratic institutions in the
United States is attributable to the circumstances, the laws,
and the manners of that country. Most Europeans are acquainted with only the first of these three causes, and they are
apt to give it a preponderant importance which it does not
really possess.

It is true that the Anglo-Americans settled in the New World
in a state of social equality; the low-born and the noble were
not to be found amongst them; and professional prejudices
were always as unknown as the prejudices of birth. Thus, as
the condition of society was democratic, the rule of democracy
was established without difficulty. But this circumstance is not
peculiar to the United States; almost all the American colonies
were founded by men equal amongst themselves, or who became so by inhabiting them. In no one part of the New World
have Europeans been able to create an aristocracy. Nevertheless, democratic institutions prosper nowhere but in the United
States.

The American Union has no enemies to contend with; it
stands in the wilds like an island in the ocean. But the
Spaniards of South America were no less isolated by nature;
yet their position has not relieved them from the charge of
standing armies. They make war upon each other when they

have no foreign enemies to oppose; and the Anglo-American democracy is the only one which has hitherto been able to maintain itself in peace.

The territory of the Union presents a boundless field to human activity, and inexhaustible materials for labor. The passion for wealth takes the place of ambition, and the heat of faction is mitigated by a consciousness of prosperity. But in what portion of the globe shall we find more fertile plains, mightier rivers, or more unexplored and inexhaustible riches, than in South America? Yet South America has been unable to maintain democratic institutions. If the welfare of nations depended on their being placed in a remote position, with an unbounded space of habitable territory before them, the Spaniards of South America would have no reason to complain of their fate. And although they might enjoy less prosperity than the inhabitants of the United States, their lot might still be such as to excite the envy of some nations in Europe. There are, however, no nations upon the face of the earth more miserable than those of South America.

Thus, not only are physical causes inadequate to produce results analogous to those which occur in North America, but they cannot raise the population of South America above the level of European states, where they act in a contrary direction. Physical causes do not therefore affect the destiny of nations so much as has been supposed. . . .

The Americans, then, have not relied upon the nature of their country to counterpoise those dangers which originate in their Constitution and their political laws. To evils which are common to all democratic nations, they have applied remedies which none but themselves had ever thought of; and, although they were the first to make the experiment, they have succeeded in it. The manners and laws of the Americans are not the only ones which may suit a democratic people; but the Americans have shown that it would be wrong to despair of regulating democracy by the aid of manners and laws. If other nations should borrow this general and pregnant idea from the Americans, without, however, intending to imitate them in the peculiar application which they have made of it; if they should attempt to fit themselves for that social condition which it seems to be the will of Providence to impose upon the generations of this age, and so to escape from the despotism or the anarchy which threatens them,—what reason is there to suppose that their efforts would not be crowned with success? The organization and the establishment of democracy in Christendom is the great political problem of our times. The Americans, unquestionably, have not resolved this problem, but they furnish useful data to those who undertake to resolve it.

Importance of What Precedes with Respect to the State of Europe.

. . . The question here discussed is interesting not only to the United States, but to the whole world; it concerns, not a nation only, but all mankind. If those nations whose social condition is democratic could remain free only while they inhabit uncultivated regions, we must despair of the future destiny of the human race; for democracy is rapidly acquiring a more extended sway, and the wilds are gradually peopled with men. If it were true that laws and manners are insufficient to maintain democratic institutions, what refuge would remain open to the nations, except the despotism of one man? I am aware that there are many worthy persons at the present time who are not alarmed at this alternative, and who are so tired of liberty as to be glad of repose far from its storms. But these persons are ill acquainted with the haven towards which they are bound. Preoccupied by their remembrances, they judge of absolute power by what it has been, and not by what it might become in our times.

If absolute power were re-established amongst the democratic nations of Europe, I am persuaded that it would assume a new form, and appear under features unknown to our fathers. There was a time in Europe when the laws and the consent of the people had invested princes with almost unlimited authority, but they scarcely ever availed themselves of it. I do not speak of the prerogatives of the nobility, of the authority of high courts of justice, of corporations and their chartered rights, or of provincial privileges, which served to break the blows of sovereign authority, and to keep up a spirit of resistance in the nation. Independently of these political institutions, —which, however opposed they might be to personal liberty, served to keep alive the love of freedom in the mind, and which may be esteemed useful in this respect,—the manners and opinions of the nation confined the royal authority within barriers which were not less powerful because less conspicuous. Religion, the affections of the people, the benevolence of the prince, the sense of honor, family pride, provincial prejudices, custom, and public opinion limited the power of kings, and restrained their authority within an invisible circle. The constitution of nations was despotic at that time, but their manners were free. Princes had the right, but they had neither the means nor the desire, of doing whatever they pleased.

But what now remains of those barriers which formerly arrested tyranny? Since religion has lost its empire over the souls of men, the most prominent boundary which divided good from evil is overthrown; everything seems doubtful and indeterminate in the moral world; kings and nations are guided by chance, and none can say where are the natural limits of despotism and the bounds of license. Long revolutions have forever destroyed the respect which surrounded the rulers of the state; and, since they have been relieved from the burden of public esteem, princes may henceforward surrender themselves without fear to the intoxication of arbitrary power.

When kings find that the hearts of their subjects are turned towards them, they are clement, because they are conscious of their strength; and they are chary of the affection of their people, because the affection of their people is the bulwark of the throne. A mutual interchange of good-will then takes place between the prince and the people, which resembles the gracious intercourse of domestic life. The subjects may murmur at the sovereign's decree, but they are grieved to displease him; and the sovereign chastises his subjects with the light hand of parental affection.

But when once the spell of royalty is broken in the tumult of revolution,—when successive monarchs have crossed the throne, so as alternately to display to the people the weakness of their right, and the harshness of their power,—the sovereign is no longer regarded by any as the father of the state, and he is feared by all as its master. If he is weak, he is despised; if he is strong, he is detested. He is himself full of animosity and alarm; he finds that he is a stranger in his own country, and he treats his subjects like conquered enemies.

When the provinces and the towns formed so many different nations in the midst of their common country, each of them had a will of its own, which was opposed to the general spirit of subjection; but, now that all the parts of the same empire, after having lost their immunities, their customs, their prejudices, their traditions, and even their names, have become accustomed to obey the same laws, it is not more difficult to oppress them all together than it was formerly to oppress one of them separately.

Whilst the nobles enjoyed their power, and indeed long after that power was lost, the honor of aristocracy conferred an extraordinary degree of force upon their personal opposition. Men could then be found who, notwithstanding their weakness, still entertained a high opinion of their personal value, and dared to cope single-handed with the public authority. But at the present day, when all ranks are more and more confounded,—when the individual disappears in the throng, and is easily lost in the midst of a common obscurity, when the honor of monarchy has almost lost its power, without being succeeded by virtue, and when nothing can enable man to rise above himself,—who shall say at what point the exigencies of power and the servility of weakness will stop?

As long as family feeling was kept alive, the antagonist of oppression was never alone; he looked about him, and found his clients, his hereditary friends, and his kinsfolk. If this support was wanting, he felt himself sustained by his ancestors, and animated by his posterity. But when patrimonial estates are divided, and when a few years suffice to confound the distinctions of race, where can family feeling be found? What force can there be in the customs of a country which has changed, and is still perpetually changing, its aspect,—in which every act of tyranny already has a precedent, and every crime an example,—in which there is nothing so old that its antiquity can save it from destruction, and nothing so unparalleled that its novelty can prevent it from being done? What resistance can be offered by manners of so pliant a make that they have already often yielded? What strength can even public opinion have retained, when no twenty persons are connected by a common tie,—when not a man, nor a family, nor chartered corporation, nor class, nor free institution, has the power of representing or exerting that opinion,—and when every citizen, being equally weak, equally poor, and equally isolated, has only his personal impotence to oppose to the organized force of the government?

The annals of France furnish nothing analogous to the condition in which that country might then be thrown. But it may more aptly be assimilated to the times of old, and to those hideous eras of Roman oppression, when the manners of the people were corrupted, their traditions obliterated, their habits destroyed, their opinions shaken, and freedom, expelled from the laws, could find no refuge in the land; when nothing protected the citizens, and the citizens no longer protected themselves; when human nature was the sport of man, and princes wearied out the clemency of Heaven before they exhausted the patience of their subjects. Those who hope to revive the monarchy of Henry IV. or of Louis XIV. appear to me to be afflicted with mental blindness; and when I consider the present condition of several European nations,—a condition to which all the others tend,—I am led to believe that they will soon be left with no other alternative than democratic liberty or the tyranny of the Cæsars.

Is not this deserving of consideration? If men must really

come to this point, that they are to be entirely emancipated or entirely enslaved,—all their rights to be made equal, or all to be taken away from them; if the rules of society were compelled either gradually to raise the crowd to their own level, or to allow all the citizens to fall below that of humanity,—would not the doubts of many be resolved, the consciences of many be confirmed, and the community prepared to make great sacrifices with little difficulty? In that case, the gradual growth of democratic manners and institutions should be regarded, not as the best, but as the only means of preserving freedom; and, without liking the government of democracy, it might be adopted as the most applicable, and the fairest remedy for the present ills of society.

It is difficult to make the people participate in the government; but it is still more difficult to supply them with experience, and to inspire them with the feelings which they need in order to govern well. I grant that the wishes of the democracy are capricious, its instruments rude, its laws imperfect. But, if it were true that soon no just medium would exist between the rule of democracy and the dominion of a single man, should we not rather incline towards the former, than submit voluntarily to the latter? And if complete equality be our fate, is it not better to be levelled by free institutions than by a despot?

Those who, after having read this book, should imagine that my intention in writing it was to propose the laws and manners of the Anglo-Americans for the imitation of all democratic communities, would make a great mistake; they must have paid more attention to the form than to the substance of my thought. My aim has been to show, by the example of America, that laws, and especially manners, may allow a democratic people to remain free. But I am very far from thinking that we ought to follow the example of the American democracy, and copy the means which it has employed to attain this end; for I am well aware of the influence which the nature of a country and its political antecedents exercise upon its political constitution; and I should regard it as a great misfortune for mankind if liberty were to exist all over the world under the same features.

But I am of opinion that, if we do not succeed in gradually introducing democratic institutions into France; if we despair of imparting to all the citizens those ideas and sentiments which first prepare them for freedom, and afterwards allow them to enjoy it,—there will be no independence at all, either for the middling classes or the nobility, for the poor or for the rich, but an equal tyranny over all; and I foresee that, if the peaceable dominion of the majority be not founded amongst

us in time, we shall sooner or later fall under the unlimited
authority of a single man.

15. Future Prospects of the United States.

. . . I am approaching the close of my inquiry: hitherto, in
speaking of the future destiny of the United States, I have
endeavored to divide my subject into distinct portions, in order
to study each of them with more attention. My present object
is to embrace the whole from one point of view; the remarks
I shall make will be less detailed, but they will be more sure.
I shall perceive each object less distinctly, but I shall descry
the principal facts with more certainty. A traveller, who has
just left a vast city, climbs the neighboring hill; as he goes farther off, he loses sight of the men whom he has just quitted;
their dwellings are confused in a dense mass; he can no longer
distinguish the public squares, and can scarcely trace out the
great thoroughfares; but his eye has less difficulty in following the boundaries of the city, and for the first time he sees the
shape of the whole. Such is the future destiny of the British
race in North America to my eye; the details of the immense
picture are lost in the shade, but I conceive a clear idea of the
entire subject.

The territory now occupied or possessed by the United
States of America forms about one twentieth part of the
habitable earth. But extensive as these bounds are, it must not
be supposed that the Anglo-American race will always remain
within them; indeed, it has already gone far beyond them.

There was a time when we also might have created a great
French nation in the American wilds, to counterbalance the
influence of the English upon the destinies of the New World.
France formerly possessed a territory in North America scarcely less extensive than the whole of Europe. The three greatest
rivers of that continent then flowed within her dominions. The
Indian tribes which dwelt between the mouth of the St.
Lawrence and the delta of the Mississippi were unaccustomed
to any other tongue than ours; and all the European settlements
scattered over that immense region recalled the traditions of
our country. Louisburg, Montmorency, Duquesne, Saint-Louis,
Vincennes, New Orleans, (for such were the names they bore,)
are words dear to France and familiar to our ears.

But a course of circumstances, which it would be tedious
to enumerate, have deprived us of this magnificent inheritance.
Wherever the French settlers were numerically weak and par-

tially established, they have disappeared: those who remain are collected on a small extent of country, and are now subject to other laws. The 400,000 French inhabitants of Lower Canada constitute at the present time the remnant of an old nation lost in the midst of a new people. A foreign population is increasing around them unceasingly and on all sides, who already penetrate amongst the former masters of the country, predominate in their cities, and corrupt their language. This population is identical with that of the United States; it is therefore with truth that I asserted that the British race is not confined within the frontiers of the Union, since it already extends to the northeast.

To the northwest, nothing is to be met with but a few insignificant Russian settlements; but to the southwest, Mexico presents a barrier to the Anglo-Americans. Thus, the Spaniards and the Anglo-Americans are, properly speaking, the two races which divide the possession of the New World. The limits of separation between them have been settled by treaty; but although the conditions of that treaty are favorable to the Anglo-Americans, I do not doubt that they will shortly infringe it. Vast provinces, extending beyond the frontiers of the Union towards Mexico, are still destitute of inhabitants. The natives of the United States will people these solitary regions before their rightful occupants. They will take possession of the soil, and establish social institutions, so that, when the legal owner at length arrives, he will find the wilderness under cultivation, and strangers quietly settled in the midst of his inheritance.

The lands of the New World belong to the first occupant; they are the natural reward of the swiftest pioneer. Even the countries which are already peopled will have some difficulty in securing themselves from this invasion. I have already alluded to what is taking place in the province of Texas. The inhabitants of the United States are perpetually migrating to Texas, where they purchase land; and although they conform to the laws of the country, they are gradually founding the empire of their own language and their own manners. The province of Texas is still part of the Mexican dominions, but it will soon contain no Mexicans; the same thing has occurred wherever the Anglo-Americans have come in contact with a people of a different origin.

It cannot be denied that the British race has acquired an amazing preponderance over all other European races in the New World; and it is very superior to them in civilization, industry, and power. As long as it is surrounded only by desert or thinly-peopled countries, as long as it encounters no dense population upon its route, through which it cannot work its

way, it will assuredly continue to spread. The lines marked
out by treaties will not stop it; but it will everywhere overleap
these imaginary barriers.

The geographical position of the British race in the New
World is peculiarly favorable to its rapid increase. Above its
northern frontiers the icy regions of the Pole extend; and a
few degrees below its southern confines lies the burning climate
of the Equator. The Anglo-Americans are therefore placed in
the most temperate and habitable zone of the continent.

It is generally supposed that the prodigious increase of population in the United States is posterior to their Declaration
of Independence. But this is an error: the population increased
as rapidly under the colonial system as at the present day; that
is to say, it doubled in about twenty-two years. But this proportion, which is now applied to millions, was then applied to
thousands, of inhabitants; and the same fact, which was scarcely noticeable a century ago, is now evident to every observer.

The English in Canada, who are dependent on a king,
augment and spread almost as rapidly as the British settlers of
the United States, who live under a republican government.
During the war of Independence, which lasted eight years, the
population continued to increase without intermission in the
same ratio. Although powerful Indian nations allied with the
English existed, at that time, upon the western frontiers, the
emigration westward was never checked. Whilst the enemy
laid waste the shores of the Atlantic, Kentucky, the western
parts of Pennsylvania, and the States of Vermont and of
Maine, were filling with inhabitants. Nor did the unsettled
state of things which succeeded the war prevent the increase
of the population, or stop its progress across the wilds. Thus,
the difference of laws, the various conditions of peace and war,
of order or anarchy, have exercised no perceptible influence
upon the continued development of the Anglo-Americans.
This may be readily understood, for no causes are sufficiently
general to exercise a simultaneous influence over the whole of
so extensive a territory. One portion of the country always
offers a sure retreat from the calamities which afflict another
part; and however great may be the evil, the remedy which is
at hand is greater still.

It must not, then, be imagined that the impulse of the British race in the New World can be arrested. The dismember-
ment of the Union, and the hostilities which might ensue, the
abolition of republican institutions, and the tyrannical government which might succeed, may retard this impulse, but they
cannot prevent the people from ultimately fulfilling their destinies. No power upon earth can shut out the emigrants from

that fertile wilderness which offers resources to all industry, and a refuge from all want. Future events, whatever they may be, will not deprive the Americans of their climate or their inland seas, their great rivers or their exuberant soil. Nor will bad laws, revolutions, and anarchy be able to obliterate that love of prosperity and spirit of enterprise which seem to be the distinctive characteristics of their race, or extinguish altogether the knowledge which guides them on their way.

Thus, in the midst of the uncertain future, one event at least is sure. At a period which may be said to be near,—for we are speaking of the life of a nation,—the Anglo-Americans alone will cover the immense space contained between the polar regions and the tropics, extending from the coasts of the Atlantic to those of the Pacific Ocean. The territory which will probably be occupied by the Anglo-Americans may perhaps equal three quarters of Europe in extent. The climate of the Union is, upon the whole, preferable to that of Europe, and its natural advantages are as great; it is therefore evident that its population will at some future time be proportionate to our own. Europe, divided as it is between so many nations, and torn as it has been by incessant wars growing out of the barbarous manners of the Middle Ages, has yet attained a population of 410 inhabitants to the square league. What cause can prevent the United States from having as numerous a population in time?

Many ages must elapse before the different offsets of the British race in America will cease to present the same physiognomy; and the time cannot be foreseen at which a permanent inequality of condition can be established in the New World. Whatever differences may arise, from peace or war, freedom or oppression, prosperity or want, between the destinies of the different descendants of the great Anglo-American family, they will all preserve at least a similar social condition, and will hold in common the customs and opinions to which that social condition has given birth.

In the Middle Ages, the tie of religion was sufficiently powerful to unite all the different populations of Europe in the same civilization. The British of the New World have a thousand other reciprocal ties; and they live at a time when the tendency to equality is general amongst mankind. The Middle Ages were a period when everything was broken up,—when each people, each province, each city, and each family tended strongly to maintain its distinct individuality. At the present time, an opposite tendency seems to prevail, and the nations seem to be advancing to unity. Our means of intellectual intercourse unite the remotest parts of the earth; and men cannot remain strangers to each other, or be ignorant of what is taking place in any corner of the globe. The consequence is, that there is less difference at the present day between the Europeans and their descendants in the New World, in spite of the ocean which divides them, than there was between certain towns in the thirteenth century, which were separated only by a river. If this tendency to assimilation brings foreign nations closer to each other, it must *a fortiori* prevent the descendants of the same people from becoming aliens to each other.

The time will therefore come, when one hundred and fifty millions of men will be living in North America, equal in condition, all belonging to one family, owing their origin to the same cause, and preserving the same civilization, the same language, the same religion, the same habits, the same manners, and imbued with the same opinions, propagated under the same forms. The rest is uncertain, but this is certain; and it is a fact new to the world,—a fact which the imagination strives in vain to grasp.

There are at the present time two great nations in the world, which started from different points, but seem to tend towards the same end. I allude to the Russians and the Americans. Both of them have grown up unnoticed; and whilst the attention of mankind was directed elsewhere, they have suddenly placed themselves in the front rank among the nations, and the world learned their existence and their greatness at almost the same time.

All other nations seem to have nearly reached their natural limits, and they have only to maintain their power; but these are still in the act of growth. All the others have stopped, or continue to advance with extreme difficulty; these alone are proceeding with ease and celerity along a path to which no limit can be perceived. The American struggles against the obstacles which nature opposes to him; the adversaries of the Russian are men. The former combats the wilderness and savage life; the latter, civilization with all its arms. The conquests of the American are therefore gained by the ploughshare; those of the Russian by the sword. The Anglo-American relies upon personal interest to accomplish his ends, and gives free scope to the unguided strength and common sense of the people; the Russian centres all the authority of society in a single arm. The principal instrument of the former is freedom; of the latter, servitude. Their starting-point is different, and their courses are not the same; yet each of them seems marked out by the will of Heaven to sway the destinies of half the globe.

PART TWO: *BOOK I*

☆

INFLUENCE OF DEMOCRACY UPON THE ACTION OF INTELLECT IN THE UNITED STATES

16. *Philosophical Method of the Americans.*

I THINK that in no country in the civilized world is less attention paid to philosophy than in the United States. The Americans have no philosophical school of their own; and they care but little for all the schools into which Europe is divided, the very names of which are scarcely known to them. Yet it is easy to perceive that almost all the inhabitants of the United States conduct their understanding in the same manner, and govern it by the same rules; that is to say, without ever having taken the trouble to define the rules, they have a philosophical method common to the whole people. To evade the bondage of system and habit, of family-maxims, class-opinions, and, in some degree, of national prejudices; to accept tradition only as a means of information, and existing facts only as a lesson to be used in doing otherwise and doing better; to seek the reason of things for one's self, and in one's self alone; to tend to results without being bound to means, and to aim at the substance through the form;—such are the principal characteristics of what I shall call the philosophical method of the Americans. But if I go further, and seek amongst these characteristics the principal one which includes almost all the rest, I discover that, in most of the operations of mind, each American appeals only to the individual effort of his own understanding.

America is therefore one of the countries where the precepts of Descartes are least studied, and are best applied. Nor is this surprising. The Americans do not read the works of Descartes, because their social condition deters them from speculative studies; but they follow his maxims, because this same social condition naturally disposes their minds to adopt them. In the midst of the continual movement which agitates a democrat-

ic community, the tie which unites one generation to another
is relaxed or broken; every man there readily loses all trace
of the ideas of his forefathers, or takes no care about them.
Men living in this state of society cannot derive their belief
from the opinions of the class to which they belong; for, so to
speak, there are no longer any classes, or those which still exist
are composed of such mobile elements, that the body can never
exercise any real control over its members. As to the influence
which the intellect of one man may have on that of another,
it must necessarily be very limited in a country where the citizens, placed on an equal footing, are all closely seen by each
other; and where, as no signs of incontestable greatness or
superiority are perceived in any one of them, they are constantly brought back to their own reason as the most obvious and
proximate source of truth. It is not only confidence in this or
that man which is destroyed, but the disposition for trusting
the authority of any man whatsoever. Every one shuts himself up in his own breast, and affects from that point to judge
the world.

The practice which obtains amongst the Americans, of fixing
the standard of their judgment in themselves alone, leads them
to other habits of mind. As they perceive that they succeed in
resolving without assistance all the little difficulties which
their practical life presents, they readily conclude that everything in the world may be explained, and that nothing in it
transcends the limits of the understanding. Thus they fall to
denying what they cannot comprehend; which leaves them
but little faith for whatever is extraordinary, and an almost
insurmountable distaste for whatever is supernatural. As it is
on their own testimony that they are accustomed to rely, they
like to discern the object which engages their attention with
extreme clearness; they therefore strip off as much as possible
all that covers it, they rid themselves of whatever separates
them from it, they remove whatever conceals it from sight, in
order to view it more closely and in the broad light of day.
This disposition of mind soon leads them to contemn forms,
which they regard as useless and inconvenient veils placed
between them and the truth. The Americans, then, have not
required to extract their philosophical method from books;
they have found it in themselves. The same thing may be
remarked in what has taken place in Europe. This same
method has only been established and made popular in Europe
in proportion as the condition of society has become more
equal, and men have grown more like each other. . . . .

It must never be forgotten that religion gave birth to Anglo-
American society. In the United States, religion is therefore

mingled with all the habits of the nation and all the feelings of patriotism, whence it derives a peculiar force. To this reason another of no less power may be added: in America, religion has, as it were, laid down its own limits. Religious institutions have remained wholly distinct from political institutions, so that former laws have been easily changed whilst former belief has remained unshaken. Christianity has therefore retained a strong hold on the public mind in America; and I would more particularly remark, that its sway is not only that of a philosophical doctrine which has been adopted upon inquiry, but of a religion which is believed without discussion. In the United States, Christian sects are infinitely diversified and perpetually modified; but Christianity itself is an established and irresistible fact, which no one undertakes either to attack or to defend. The Americans, having admitted the principal doctrines of the Christian religion without inquiry, are obliged to accept in like manner a great number of moral truths originating in it and connected with it. Hence the activity of individual analysis is restrained within narrow limits, and many of the most important of human opinions are removed from its influence.

The second circumstance to which I have alluded is, that the social condition and the constitution of the Americans are democratic, but they have not had a democratic revolution. They arrived upon the soil they occupy in nearly the condition in which we see them at the present day; and this is of considerable importance.

There are no revolutions which do not shake existing belief, enervate authority, and throw doubts over commonly received ideas. The effect of all revolutions is, therefore, more or less, to surrender men to their own guidance, and to open to the mind of every man a void and almost unlimited range of speculation. When equality of conditions succeeds a protracted conflict between the different classes of which the elder society was composed, envy, hatred, and uncharitableness, pride and exaggerated self-confidence, seize upon the human heart, and plant their sway in it for a time. This, independently of equality itself, tends powerfully to divide men,—to lead them to mistrust the judgment of each other, and to seek the light of truth nowhere but in themselves. Every one then attempts to be his own sufficient guide, and makes it his boast to form his own opinions on all subjects. Men are no longer bound together by ideas, but by interests; and it would seem as if human opinions were reduced to a sort of intellectual dust, scattered on every side, unable to collect, unable to cohere.

Thus, that independence of mind which equality supposes to exist is never so great, never appears so excessive, as at the time when equality is beginning to establish itself, and in the course of that painful labor by which it is established. That sort of intellectual freedom which equality may give ought, therefore, to be very carefully distinguished from the anarchy which revolution brings. Each of these two things must be separately considered, in order not to conceive exaggerated hopes or fears of the future.

I believe that the men who will live under the new forms of society will make frequent use of their private judgment, but I am far from thinking that they will often abuse it. This is attributable to a cause of more general application to all democratic countries, and which, in the long run, must needs restrain in them the independence of individual speculation within fixed, and sometimes narrow, limits. . . . At different periods, dogmatical belief is more or less common. It arises in different ways, and it may change its object and its form; but under no circumstances will dogmatical belief cease to exist, or, in other words, men will never cease to entertain some opinions on trust, and without discussion. If every one undertook to form all his own opinions, and to seek for truth by isolated paths struck out by himself alone, it would follow that no considerable number of men would ever unite in any common belief. But obviously without such common belief no society can prosper,—say, rather, no society can exist; for without ideas held in common, there is no common action, and without common action there may still be men, but there is no social body. In order that society should exist, and, *a fortiori*, that a society should prosper, it is required that all the minds of the citizens should be rallied and held together by certain predominant ideas; and this cannot be the case unless each of them sometimes draws his opinions from the common source, and consents to accept certain matters of belief already formed.

If I now consider man in his isolated capacity, I find that dogmatical belief is not less indispensable to him in order to live alone, than it is to enable him to co-operate with his fellows. If man were forced to demonstrate for himself all the truths of which he makes daily use, his task would never end. He would exhaust his strength in preparatory demonstrations, without ever advancing beyond them. As, from the shortness of his life, he has not the time, nor, from the limits of his intelligence, the capacity, to accomplish this, he is reduced to take upon trust a number of facts and opinions which he has not had either the time or the power to verify for himself, but which men of greater ability have sought out, or which the world adopts. On this groundwork he raises for himself the structure of his own thoughts; he is not led to proceed in this manner by choice, but is constrained by the inflexible law of his condition. There is no philosopher of so great parts in the world, but that he believes a million of things on the faith of other people, and supposes a great many more truths than he demonstrates.

This is not only necessary, but desirable. A man who should undertake to inquire into everything for himself, could devote to each thing but little time and attention. His task would keep his mind in perpetual unrest, which would prevent him from penetrating to the depth of any truth, or of grappling his mind firmly to any conviction. His intellect would be at once independent and powerless. He must therefore make his choice from amongst the various objects of human belief, and adopt many opinions without discussion, in order to search the better into that smaller number which he sets apart for investigation. It is true, that whoever receives an opinion on the word of another, does so far enslave his mind; but it is a salutary servitude which allows him to make a good use of freedom.

A principle of authority must then always occur, under all circumstances, in some part or other of the moral and intellectual world. Its place is variable, but a place it necessarily has. The independence of individual minds may be greater, or it may be less: unbounded it cannot be. Thus the question is, not to know whether any intellectual authority exists in the ages of democracy, but simply where it resides and by what standard it is to be measured.

I have shown in the preceding chapter how the equality of conditions leads men to entertain a sort of instinctive incredulity of the supernatural, and a very lofty and often exaggerated opinion of the human understanding. The men who live at a period of social equality are not therefore easily led to place that intellectual authority to which they bow either beyond or above humanity. They commonly seek for the sources of truth in themselves, or in those who are like themselves. This would be enough to prove that, at such periods, no new religion could be established, and that all schemes for such a purpose would be not only impious, but absurd and irrational. It may be foreseen that a democratic people will not easily give credence to divine missions; that they will laugh at modern prophets; and that they will seek to discover the chief arbiter of their belief within, and not beyond, the limits of their kind.

When the ranks of society are unequal, and men unlike each other in condition, there are some individuals wielding the power of superior intelligence, learning, and enlightenment, whilst the multitude are sunk in ignorance and prejudice. Men living at these aristocratic periods are therefore naturally induced to shape their opinions by the standard of a superior person, or superior class of persons, whilst they are averse to recognize the infallibility of the mass of the people. The contrary takes place in ages of equality. The nearer the people are drawn to the common level of an equal and similar condition, the less prone does each man become to place implicit faith in a certain man or a certain class of men. But his readiness to believe the multitude increases, and opinion is more than ever mistress of the world. Not only is common opinion the only guide which private judgment retains amongst a democratic people, but amongst such a people it possesses a power infinitely beyond what it has elsewhere. At periods of equality, men have no faith in one another, by reason of their common resemblance; but this very resemblance gives them almost unbounded confidence in the judgment of the public; for it would not seem probable, as they are all endowed with equal means of judging, but that the greater truth should go with the greater number.

When the inhabitant of a democratic country compares himself individually with all those about him, he feels with pride that he is the equal of any one of them; but when he comes to survey the totality of his fellows, and to place himself in contrast with so huge a body, he is instantly overwhelmed by the sense of his own insignificance and weakness. The same equality which renders him independent of each of his fellow-citizens, taken severally, exposes him alone and unprotected to the influence of the greater number. The public has therefore, among a democratic people, a singular power, which aristocratic nations cannot conceive of; for it does not persuade to certain opinions, but it enforces them, and infuses them into the intellect by a sort of enormous pressure of the minds of all upon the reason of each.

In the United States, the majority undertakes to supply a multitude of ready-made opinions for the use of individuals, who are thus relieved from the necessity of forming opinions of their own. Everybody there adopts great numbers of theories, on philosophy, morals, and politics, without inquiry, upon public trust; and if we look to it very narrowly, it will be perceived that religion herself holds sway there much less as a doctrine of revelation than as a commonly received opinion.

The fact that the political laws of the Americans are such that the majority rules the community with sovereign sway, materially increases the power which that majority naturally exercises over the mind. For nothing is more customary in man than to recognize superior wisdom in the person of his oppressor. This political omnipotence of the majority in the United States doubtless augments the influence which public opinion would obtain without it over the minds of each member of the community; but the foundations of that influence do not rest upon it. They must be sought for in the principle of equality itself, not in the more or less popular institutions which men living under that condition may give themselves. The intellectual dominion of the greater number would probably be less absolute amongst a democratic people governed by a king, than in the sphere of a pure democracy, but it will always be extremely absolute; and by whatever political laws men are governed in the ages of equality, it may be foreseen that faith in public opinion will become a species of religion there, and the majority its ministering prophet.

Thus intellectual authority will be different, but it will not be diminished; and far from thinking that it will disappear, I augur that it may readily acquire too much preponderance, and confine the action of private judgment within narrower limits than are suited either to the greatness or the happiness of the human race. In the principle of equality I very clearly discern two tendencies; the one leading the mind of every man to untried thoughts, the other which would prohibit him from thinking at all. And I perceive how, under the dominion of certain laws, democracy would extinguish that liberty of the mind to which a democratic social condition is favorable; so that, after having broken all the bondage once imposed on it by ranks or by men, the human mind would be closely fettered to the general will of the greatest number.

If the absolute power of a majority were to be substituted, by democratic nations, for all the different powers which checked or retarded overmuch the energy of individual minds, the evil would only have changed character. Men would not have found the means of independent life; they would simply have discovered (no easy task) a new physiognomy of servitude. There is,—and I cannot repeat it too often,—there is here matter for profound reflection to those who look on freedom of thought as a holy thing, and who hate not only the despot, but despotism. For myself, when I feel the hand of power lie heavy on my brow, I care but little to know who oppresses me; and I am not the more disposed to pass beneath the yoke because it is held out to me by the arms of a million of men.

17. Influence of Democracy on Religion.

. . . Men cannot do without dogmatical belief; and it is much to be desired that such belief should exist amongst them. . . . Of all the kinds of dogmatical belief, the most desirable appears to me to be dogmatical belief in matters of religion; and this is a clear inference, even from no higher consideration than the interests of this world. There is hardly any human action, however particular it may be, which does not originate in some very general idea men have conceived of the Deity, of his relation to mankind, of the nature of their souls, and of their duties to their fellow-creatures. Nor can anything prevent these ideas from being the common spring whence all the rest emanates. Men are therefore immeasurably interested in acquiring fixed ideas of God, of the soul, and of their general duties to their Creator and their fellow-men; for doubt on these first principles would abandon all their actions to chance, and would condemn them in some way to disorder and impotence.

This is, then, the subject on which it is most important for each of us to have fixed ideas; and unhappily it is also the subject on which it is most difficult for each of us, left to himself, to settle his opinions by the sole force of his reason. None but minds singularly free from the ordinary cares of life—minds at once penetrating, subtle, and trained by thinking—can, even with much time and care, sound the depths of these so necessary truths. And, indeed, we see that philosophers are themselves almost always surrounded with uncertainties; that at every step the natural light which illuminates their path grows dimmer and less secure; and that, in spite of all their efforts, they have as yet only discovered a few conflicting notions, on which the mind of man has been tossed about for thousands of years, without ever firmly grasping the truth, or finding novelty even in its errors. Studies of this nature are far above the average capacity of men; and, even if the majority of mankind were capable of such pursuits, it is evident that leisure to cultivate them would still be wanting.

Fixed ideas about God and human nature are indispensable to the daily practice of men's lives; but the practice of their lives prevents them from acquiring such ideas. The difficulty appears to be without a parallel. Amongst the sciences, there

150

are some which are useful to the mass of mankind, and are within its reach; others can be approached only by the few, and are not cultivated by the many, who require nothing beyond their more remote applications: but the daily practice of the science I speak of is indispensable to all, although the study of it is inaccessible to the greater number. General ideas respecting God and human nature are therefore the ideas above all others which it is most suitable to withdraw from the habitual action of private judgment, and in which there is most to gain and least to lose by recognizing a principle of authority.

The first object, and one of the principal advantages, of religion is to furnish to each of these fundamental questions a solution which is at once clear, precise, intelligible to the mass of mankind, and lasting. There are religions which are false and very absurd; but it may be affirmed that any religion which remains within the circle I have just traced, without pretending to go beyond it, (as many religions have attempted to do, for the purpose of restraining on every side the free movement of the human mind,) imposes a salutary restraint on the intellect; and it must be admitted that, if it does not save men in another world, it is at least very conducive to their happiness and their greatness in this. This is more especially true of men living in free countries. When the religion of a people is destroyed, doubt gets hold of the higher powers of the intellect, and half paralyzes all the others. Every man accustoms himself to have only confused and changing notions on the subjects most interesting to his fellow-creatures and himself. His opinions are ill-defended and easily abandoned; and, in despair of ever resolving by himself the hard problems respecting the destiny of man, he ignobly submits to think no more about them. Such a condition cannot but enervate the soul, relax the springs of the will, and prepare a people for servitude. Not only does it happen, in such a case, that they allow their freedom to be taken from them; they frequently themselves surrender it. When there is no longer any principle of authority in religion, any more than in politics, men are speedily frightened at the aspect of this unbounded independence. The constant agitation of all surrounding things alarms and exhausts them. As everything is at sea in the sphere of the mind, they determine at least that the mechanism of society shall be firm and fixed; and, as they cannot resume their ancient belief, they assume a master.

For my own part, I doubt whether man can ever support at the same time complete religious independence and entire political freedom. And I am inclined to think that, if faith be wanting in him, he must be subject; and if he be free, he must believe.

Perhaps, however, this great utility of religions is still more obvious amongst nations where equality of conditions prevails, than amongst others. It must be acknowledged that equality, which brings great benefits into the world, nevertheless suggests to men (as will be shown hereafter) some very dangerous propensities. It tends to isolate them from each other, to concentrate every man's attention upon himself; and it lays open the soul to an inordinate love of material gratification. The greatest advantage of religion is to inspire diametrically contrary principles. There is no religion which does not place the object of man's desires above and beyond the treasures of earth, and which does not naturally raise his soul to regions far above those of the senses. Nor is there any which does not impose on man some duties toward his kind, and thus draw him at times from the contemplation of himself. This occurs in religions the most false and dangerous.

Religious nations are therefore naturally strong on the very point on which democratic nations are weak, which shows of what importance it is for men to preserve their religion as their conditions become more equal.

I have neither the right nor the intention of examining the supernatural means which God employs to infuse religious belief into the heart of man. I am at this moment considering religions in a purely human point of view; my object is to inquire by what means they may most easily retain their sway in the democratic ages upon which we are entering. It has been shown that, at times of general cultivation and equality, the human mind consents only with reluctance to adopt dogmatical opinions, and feels their necessity acutely only in spiritual matters. This proves, in the first place, that, at such times, religions ought, more cautiously than at any other, to confine themselves within their own precincts; for in seeking to extend their power beyond religious matters, they incur a risk of not being believed at all. The circle within which they seek to restrict the human intellect ought therefore to be carefully traced, and, beyond its verge, the mind should be left entirely free to its own guidance. . . .

In speaking of philosophical method among the Americans, I have shown that nothing is more repugnant to the human mind, in an age of equality, than the idea of subjection to forms. Men living at such times are impatient of figures; to their eyes, symbols appear to be puerile artifices used to conceal or to set off truths which should more naturally be bared

to the light of day: they are unmoved by ceremonial observances, and are disposed to attach only a secondary importance
to the details of public worship.

Those who have to regulate the external forms of religion
in a democratic age should pay a close attention to these
natural propensities of the human mind, in order not to run
counter to them unnecessarily.

I firmly believe in the necessity of forms, which fix the
human mind in the contemplation of abstract truths, and
aid it in embracing them warmly and holding them with firmness. Nor do I suppose that it is possible to maintain a religion without external observances; but, on the other hand, I
am persuaded that, in the ages upon which we are entering,
it would be peculiarly dangerous to multiply them beyond
measure; and that they ought rather to be limited to as much
as is absolutely necessary to perpetuate the doctrine itself,
which is the substance of religion, of which the ritual is only
the form. A religion which should become more minute, more
peremptory, and more charged with small observances, at a
time when men are becoming more equal, would soon find
itself reduced to a band of fanatical zealots in the midst of an
infidel people.

I anticipate the objection that, as all religions have general and eternal truths for their object, they cannot thus shape
themselves to the shifting inclinations of every age, without
forfeiting their claim to certainty in the eyes of mankind. To
this I reply again, that the principal opinions which constitute
a creed, and which theologians call articles of faith, must
be very carefully distinguished from the accessories connected
with them. Religions are obliged to hold fast to the former,
whatever be the peculiar spirit of the age; but they should
take good care not to bind themselves in the same manner to
the latter, at a time when everything is in transition, and when
the mind, accustomed to the moving pageant of human affairs,
reluctantly allows itself to be fixed on any point. The fixity
of eternal and secondary things can afford a chance of duration only when civil society is itself fixed; under any other
circumstances, I hold it to be perilous.

We shall see that, of all the passions which originate in
or are fostered by equality, there is one which it renders
peculiarly intense, and which it also infuses into the heart
of every man,—I mean the love of well-being. The taste
for well-being is the prominent and indelible feature of
democratic times.

It may be believed that a religion which should undertake
to destroy so deep-seated a passion, would in the end be de-

stroyed by it; and if it attempted to wean men entirely from
the contemplation of the good things of this world, in order
to devote their faculties exclusively to the thought of another,
it may be foreseen that the minds of men would at length
escape its grasp, to plunge into the exclusive enjoyment of
present and material pleasures. The chief concern of religion
is to purify, to regulate, and to restrain the excessive and
exclusive taste for well-being which men feel at periods of
equality; but it would be an error to attempt to overcome it
completely, or to eradicate it. Men cannot be cured of the
love of riches; but they may be persuaded to enrich themselves by none but honest means.

This brings me to a final consideration, which comprises,
as it were, all the others. The more the conditions of men
are equalized and assimilated to each other, the more important is it for religion; whilst it carefully abstains from
the daily turmoil of secular affairs, not needlessly to run
counter to the ideas which generally prevail, or to the permanent interests which exist in the mass of the people. For,
as public opinion grows to be more and more the first and
most irresistible of existing powers, the religious principle
has no external support strong enough to enable it to resist
its attacks. This is not less true of a democratic people
ruled by a despot, than of a republic. In ages of equality
kings may often command obedience, but the majority always
commands belief: to the majority, therefore, deference is to
be paid in whatsoever is not contrary to the faith.

I showed in my former volume how the American clergy
stand aloof from secular affairs. This is the most obvious,
but not the only, example of their self-restraint. In America,
religion is a distinct sphere, in which the priest is sovereign,
but out of which he takes care never to go. Within its limits,
he is master of the mind; beyond them, he leaves men to themselves, and surrenders them to the independence and instability
which belong to their nature and their age. I have seen no
country in which Christianity is clothed with fewer forms, figures, and observances than in the United States; or where
it presents more distinct, simple, and general notions to the
mind. Although the Christians of America are divided into a
multitude of sects, they all look upon their religion in the
same light. This applies to Roman Catholicism as well as to
the other forms of belief. There are no Romish priests who
show less taste for the minute individual observances, for
extraordinary or peculiar means of salvation, or who cling
more to the spirit, and less to the letter, of the law, than the
Roman Catholic priests of the United States. Nowhere is that

doctrine of the Church which prohibits the worship reserved to God alone from being offered to the saints, more clearly inculcated or more generally followed. Yet the Roman Catholics of America are very submissive and very sincere.

Another remark is applicable to the clergy of every communion. The American ministers of the Gospel do not attempt to draw or to fix all the thoughts of man upon the life to come; they are willing to surrender a portion of his heart to the cares of the present; seeming to consider the goods of this world as important, though secondary, objects. If they take no part themselves in productive labor, they are at least interested in its progress, and they applaud its results; and whilst they never cease to point to the other world as the great object of the hopes and fears of the believer, they do not forbid him honestly to court prosperity in this. Far from attempting to show that these things are distinct and contrary to one another, they study rather to find out on what point they are most nearly and closely connected.

All the American clergy know and respect the intellectual supremacy exercised by the majority: they never sustain any but necessary conflicts with it. They take no share in the altercations of parties, but they readily adopt the general opinions of their country and their age: and they allow themselves to be borne away without opposition in the current of feeling and opinion by which everything around them is carried along. They endeavor to amend their contemporaries, but they do not quit fellowship with them. Public opinion is therefore never hostile to them: it rather supports and protects them; and their belief owes its authority at the same time to the strength which is its own, and to that which it borrows from the opinions of the majority.

Thus it is, that, by respecting all democratic tendencies not absolutely contrary to herself, and by making use of several of them for her own purposes, Religion sustains a successful struggle with that spirit of individual independence which is her most dangerous opponent.

America is the most democratic country in the world, and it is at the same time (according to reports worthy of belief) the country in which the Roman Catholic religion makes most progress. At first sight, this is surprising.

Two things must here be accurately distinguished: equality inclines men to wish to form their own opinions; but, on the other hand, it imbues them with the taste and the idea of unity, simplicity, and impartiality in the power which governs society. Men living in democratic times are therefore very prone to shake off all religious authority; but if they consent to subject themselves to any authority of this kind, they choose at least that it should be single and uniform. Religious powers not radiating from a common centre are naturally repugnant to their minds; and they almost as readily conceive that there should be no religion, as that there should be several.

At the present time, more than in any preceding age, Roman Catholics are seen to lapse into infidelity, and Protestants to be converted to Roman Catholicism. If the Roman Catholic faith be considered within the pale of the Church, it would seem to be losing ground; without that pale, to be gaining it. Nor is this difficult of explanation. The men of our days are naturally little disposed to believe; but, as soon as they have any religion, they immediately find in themselves a latent instinct which urges them unconsciously towards Catholicism. Many of the doctrines and practices of the Romish Church astonish them; but they feel a secret admiration for its discipline, and its great unity attracts them. If Catholicism could at length withdraw itself from the political animosities to which it has given rise, I have hardly any doubt but that the same spirit of the age which appears to be so opposed to it would become so favorable as to admit of its great and sudden advancement.

One of the most ordinary weaknesses of the human intellect is to seek to reconcile contrary principles, and to purchase peace at the expense of logic. Thus there have ever been, and will ever be, men who, after having submitted some portion of their religious belief to the principle of authority, will seek to exempt several other parts of their faith from it, and to keep their minds floating at random between liberty and obedience. But I am inclined to believe that the number of these thinkers will be less in democratic than in other ages; and that our posterity will tend more and more to a division into only two parts,—some relinquishing Christianity entirely, and others returning to the Church of Rome.

18. Equality Suggests to the Americans the Idea of the Indefinite Perfectibility of Man.

EQUALITY suggests to the human mind several ideas which would not have originated from any other source, and it modifies almost all those previously entertained. I take as an example the idea of human perfectibility, because it is one of the principal notions that the intellect can conceive, and because it constitutes of itself a great philosophical theory, which is everywhere to be traced by its consequences in the conduct of human affairs.

Although man has many points of resemblance with the brutes, one trait is peculiar to himself,—he improves: they are incapable of improvement. Mankind could not fail to discover this difference from the beginning. The idea of perfectibility is therefore as old as the world; equality did not give birth to it, but has imparted to it a new character.

When the citizens of a community are classed according to rank, profession, or birth, and when all men are constrained to follow the career which chance has opened before them, every one thinks that the utmost limits of human power are to be discerned in proximity to himself, and no one seeks any longer to resist the inevitable law of his destiny. Not, indeed, that an aristocratic people absolutely deny man's faculty of self-improvement, but they do not hold it to be indefinite; they can conceive amelioration, but not change: they imagine that the future condition of society may be better, but not essentially different; and, whilst they admit that humanity has made progress, and may still have some to make, they assign to it beforehand certain impassable limits.

Thus, they do not presume that they have arrived at the supreme good or at absolute truth, (what people or what man was ever wild enough to imagine it?) but they cherish a persuasion that they have pretty nearly reached that degree of greatness and knowledge which our imperfect nature admits of; and, as nothing moves about them, they are willing to fancy that everything is in its fit place. Then it is that the legislator affects to lay down eternal laws; that kings and nations will raise none but imperishable monuments; and that the present generation undertakes to spare generations to come the care of regulating their destinies.

In proportion as castes disappear and the classes of society approximate,—as manners, customs, and laws vary, from the tumultuous intercourse of men,—as new facts arise,—as new truths are brought to light,—as ancient opinions are dissipated, and others take their place,—the image of an ideal but always fugitive perfection presents itself to the human mind. Continual changes are then every instant occurring under the observation of every man: the position of some is rendered worse; and he learns but too well that no people and no individual, how enlightened soever they may be, can lay claim to infallibility: the condition of others is improved; whence he infers that man is endowed with an indefinite faculty of improvement. His reverses teach him that none have discovered absolute good,—his success stimulates him to the never-ending pursuit of it. Thus, forever seeking, forever falling to rise again,—often disappointed, but not discouraged,—he tends unceasingly towards that unmeasured greatness so indistinctly visible at the end of the long track which humanity has yet to tread.

It can hardly be believed how many facts naturally flow from the philosophical theory of the indefinite perfectibility of man, or how strong an influence it exercises even on those who, living entirely for the purposes of action and not of thought, seem to conform their actions to it, without knowing anything about it.

I accost an American sailor, and inquire why the ships of his country are built so as to last but for a short time; he answers without hesitation, that the art of navigation is every day making such rapid progress, that the finest vessel would become almost useless if it lasted beyond a few years. In these words, which fell accidentally, and on a particular subject, from an uninstructed man, I recognize the general and systematic idea upon which a great people direct all their concerns.

Aristocratic nations are naturally too apt to narrow the scope of human perfectibility; democratic nations, to expand it beyond reason.

19. The Example of the Americans Does Not Prove That a Democratic People Can Have No Aptitude and No Taste for Science, Literature, or Art.

It must be acknowledged that in few of the civilized nations of our time have the higher sciences made less progress than in the United States; and in few have great artists, distinguished poets, or celebrated writers, been more rare. Many Europeans, struck by this fact, have looked upon it as a natural and inevitable result of equality; and they have thought that, if a democratic state of society and democratic institutions were ever to prevail over the whole earth, the human mind would gradually find its beacon-lights grow dim, and men would relapse into a period of darkness.

To reason thus is, I think, to confound several ideas which it is important to divide and examine separately: it is to mingle, unintentionally, what is democratic with what is only

American. The religion professed by the first emigrants, and
bequeathed by them to their descendants,—simple in its forms,
austere and almost harsh in its principles, and hostile to external symbols and to ceremonial pomp,—is naturally unfavorable to the fine arts, and only yields reluctantly to the
pleasures of literature. The Americans are a very old and a
very enlightened people, who have fallen upon a new and
unbounded country, where they may extend themselves at
pleasure, and which they may fertilize without difficulty.
This state of things is without a parallel in the history of the
world. In America, every one finds facilities unknown elsewhere for making or increasing his fortune. The spirit of gain
is always on the stretch, and the human mind, constantly
diverted from the pleasures of imagination and the labors of
the intellect, is there swayed by no impulse but the pursuit of
wealth. Not only are manufacturing and commercial classes
to be found in the United States, as they are in all other countries; but, what never occurred elsewhere, the whole community are simultaneously engaged in productive industry and commerce. But I am convinced that, if the Americans had been
alone in the world, with the freedom and the knowledge acquired by their forefathers, and the passions which are their
own, they would not have been slow to discover that progress
cannot long be made in the application of the sciences without
cultivating the theory of them; that all the arts are perfected
by one another: and, however absorbed they might have been
by the pursuit of the principal object of their desires, they
would speedily have admitted that it is necessary to turn aside
from it occasionally, in order the better to attain it in the
end.

The taste for the pleasures of mind is moreover so natural to the heart of civilized man, that amongst the polite
nations, which are least disposed to give themselves up to
these pursuits, a certain number of persons are always to be
found who take part in them. This intellectual craving, once
felt, would very soon have been satisfied. But at the very time
when the Americans were naturally inclined to require nothing of science but its special applications to the useful arts
and the means of rendering life comfortable, learned and
literary Europe was engaged in exploring the common sources
of truth, and in improving at the same time all that can minister to the pleasures or satisfy the wants of man.

At the head of the enlightened nations of the Old World
the inhabitants of the United States more particularly distinguished one, to which they were closely united by a common
origin and by kindred habits. Amongst this people they found

distinguished men of science, able artists, writers of eminence, and they were enabled to enjoy the treasures of the intellect without laboring to amass them. In spite of the ocean which intervenes, I cannot consent to separate America from Europe. I consider the people of the United States as that portion of the English people who are commissioned to explore the forests of the New World; whilst the rest of the nation, enjoying more leisure and less harassed by the drudgery of life, may devote their energies to thought, and enlarge in all directions the empire of mind.

The position of the Americans is therefore quite exceptional, and it may be believed that no democratic people will ever be placed in a similar one. Their strictly Puritanical origin,—their exclusively commercial habits,—even the country they inhabit, which seems to divert their minds from the pursuit of science, literature, and the arts,—the proximity of Europe, which allows them to neglect these pursuits without relapsing into barbarism,—a thousand special causes, of which I have only been able to point out the most important, —have singularly concurred to fix the mind of the American upon purely practical objects. His passions, his wants, his education, and everything about him, seem to unite in drawing the native of the United States earthward: his religion alone bids him turn, from time to time, a transient and distracted glance to heaven. Let us cease, then, to view all democratic nations under the example of the American people, and attempt to survey them at length with their own features.

It is possible to conceive a people not subdivided into any castes or scale of ranks; among whom the law, recognizing no privileges, should divide inherited property into equal shares; but which, at the same time, should be without knowledge and without freedom. Nor is this an empty hypothesis: a despot may find that it is his interest to render his subjects equal and to leave them ignorant, in order more easily to keep them slaves. Not only would a democratic people of this kind show neither aptitude nor taste for science, literature, or art, but it would probably never arrive at the possession of them. The law of descent would of itself provide for the destruction of large fortunes at each succeeding generation; and no new fortunes would be acquired. The poor man, without either knowledge or freedom, would not so much as conceive the idea of raising himself to wealth; and the rich man would allow himself to be degraded to poverty, without a notion of self-defence. Between these two members of the community complete and invincible equality would soon be established. No one would then have time or taste to devote himself to the pursuits or pleasures of the intellect; but all men would remain paralyzed in a state of common ignorance and equal servitude.

When I conceive a democratic society of this kind, I fancy myself in one of those low, close, and gloomy abodes, where the light which breaks in from without soon faints and fades away. A sudden heaviness overpowers me, and I grope through the surrounding darkness, to find an opening which will restore me to the air and the light of day. But all this is not applicable to men already enlightened who retain their freedom, after having abolished those peculiar and hereditary rights which perpetuated the tenure of property in the hands of certain individuals or certain classes.

When men living in a democratic state of society are enlightened, they readily discover that they are not confined and fixed by any limits which constrain them to take up with their present fortune. They all, therefore, conceive the idea of increasing it,—if they are free, they all attempt it; but all do not succeed in the same manner. The legislature, it is true, no longer grants privileges, but nature grants them. As natural inequality is very great, fortunes become unequal as soon as every man exerts all his faculties to get rich.

The law of descent prevents the establishment of wealthy families, but it does not prevent the existence of wealthy individuals. It constantly brings back the members of the community to a common level, from which they as constantly escape; and the inequality of fortunes augments in proportion as their knowledge is diffused and their liberty increased.

A sect which arose in our time, and was celebrated for its talents and its extravagance, proposed to concentrate all property in the hands of a central power, whose function it should afterwards be to parcel it out to individuals, according to their merits. This would have been a method of escaping from that complete and eternal equality which seems to threaten democratic society. But it would be a simpler and less dangerous remedy to grant no privilege to any, giving to all equal cultivation and equal independence, and leaving every one to determine his own position. Natural inequality will soon make way for itself, and wealth will spontaneously pass into the hands of the most capable.

Free and democratic communities, then, will always contain a multitude of people enjoying opulence or a competency. The wealthy will not be so closely linked to each other as the members of the former aristocratic class of society; their inclinations will be different, and they will scarcely ever enjoy leisure as secure or complete; but they will be far more numerous than those who belonged to that class of society could ever be. These persons will not be strictly confined to the cares of practical life; and they will still be able, though in different degrees, to indulge in the pursuits and pleasures of the intellect. In those pleasures they will indulge; for, if it be true that the human mind leans on one side to the limited, the material, and the useful, it naturally rises on the other to the infinite, the spiritual, and the beautiful. Physical wants confine it to the earth; but, as soon as the tie is loosened, it will rise of itself.

Not only will the number of those who can take an interest in the productions of mind be greater, but the taste for intellectual enjoyment will descend, step by step, even to those who, in aristocratic societies, seem to have neither time nor ability to indulge in them. When hereditary wealth, the privileges of rank, and the prerogatives of birth have ceased to be, and when every man derives his strength from himself alone, it becomes evident that the chief cause of disparity between the fortunes of men is the mind. Whatever tends to invigorate, to extend, or to adorn the mind, instantly rises to a high value. The utility of knowledge becomes singularly conspicuous even to the eyes of the multitude: those who have no taste for its charms set store upon its results, and make some efforts to acquire it.

In free and enlightened democratic times there is nothing to separate men from each other, or to retain them in their place: they rise or sink with extreme rapidity. All classes live in continual intercourse, from their great proximity to each other. They communicate and intermingle every day; they imitate and emulate one another: this suggests to the people many ideas, notions, and desires which they would never have entertained if the distinctions of rank had been fixed, and society at rest. In such nations, the servant never considers himself as an entire stranger to the pleasures and toils of his master, nor the poor man to those of the rich; the rural population assimilates itself to that of the towns, and the provinces to the capital. No one easily allows himself to be reduced to the mere material cares of life; and the humblest artisan casts at times an eager and a furtive glance into the higher regions of the intellect. People do not read with the same notions or in the same manner as they do in aristocratic communities; but the circle of readers is unceasingly expanded, till it includes all the people.

As soon as the multitude begin to take an interest in the labors of the mind, it finds out that to excel in some of them is a powerful means of acquiring fame, power, or wealth.

The restless ambition which equality begets instantly takes this direction, as it does all others. The number of those who cultivate science, letters, and the arts, becomes immense. The intellectual world starts into prodigious activity: every one endeavors to open for himself a path there, and to draw the eyes of the public after him. Something analogous occurs to what happens in society in the United States politically considered. What is done is often imperfect, but the attempts are innumerable; and, although the results of individual effort are commonly very small, the total amount is always very large. It is therefore not true to assert, that men living in democratic times are naturally indifferent to science, literature, and the arts: only it must be acknowledged that they cultivate them after their own fashion, and bring to the task their own peculiar qualifications and deficiencies.

20. Why the Americans Are More Addicted to Practical Than to Theoretical Science.

IF A democratic state of society and democratic institutions do not retard the onward course of the human mind, they incontestably guide it in one direction in preference to another. Their efforts, thus circumscribed, are still exceedingly great; and I may be pardoned if I pause for a moment to contemplate them.

We had occasion, in speaking of the philosophical method of the American people, to make several remarks, which must here be turned to account. Equality begets in man the desire of judging of everything for himself: it gives him, in all things, a taste for the tangible and the real, a contempt for tradition and for forms. These general tendencies are principally discernible in the peculiar subject of this chapter.

Those who cultivate the sciences amongst a democratic people are always afraid of losing their way in visionary speculation. They mistrust systems; they adhere closely to facts, and study facts with their own senses. As they do not easily defer to the mere name of any fellow-man, they are never inclined to rest upon any man's authority; but, on the contrary, they are unremitting in their efforts to find out the weaker points of their neighbors' doctrine. Scientific precedents have little weight with them; they are never long detained by the subtilty of the schools, nor ready to accept big words for sterling coin; they penetrate, as far as they can,

into the principal parts of the subject which occupies them,
and they like to expound them in the vulgar tongue. Scientific
pursuits then follow a freer and safer course, but a less lofty
one.

The mind may, as it appears to me, divide science into
three parts. The first comprises the most theoretical principles,
and those more abstract notions, whose application is either
unknown or very remote. The second is composed of those
general truths which still belong to pure theory, but lead
nevertheless by a straight and short road to practical results.
Methods of application and means of execution make up the
third. Each of these different portions of science may be separately cultivated, although reason and experience prove that
neither of them can prosper long, if it be absolutely cut off
from the two others.

In America, the purely practical part of science is admirably understood, and careful attention is paid to the theoretical portion, which is immediately requisite to application.
On this head, the Americans always display a clear, free,
original, and inventive power of mind. But hardly any one in
the United States devotes himself to the essentially theoretical
and abstract portion of human knowledge. In this respect, the
Americans carry to excess a tendency which is, I think, discernible, though in a less degree, amongst all democratic
nations.

Nothing is more necessary to the culture of the higher sciences, or of the more elevated departments of science, than
meditation; and nothing is less suited to meditation than the
structure of democratic society. We do not find there, as
amongst an aristocratic people, one class which keeps in repose because it is well off; and another, which does not venture to stir because it despairs of improving its condition.
Every one is in motion: some in quest of power, others of
gain. In the midst of this universal tumult,—this incessant
conflict of jarring interests,—this continual striving of men
after fortune,—where is that calm to be found which is necessary for the deeper combinations of the intellect? How can
the mind dwell upon any single point, when everything whirls
around it, and man himself is swept and beaten onwards by
the heady current which rolls all things in its course?

But the permanent agitation which subsists in the bosom of
a peaceable and established democracy must be distinguished
from the tumultuous and revolutionary movements which almost always attend the birth and growth of democratic society.
When a violent revolution occurs amongst a highly-civilized
people, it cannot fail to give a sudden impulse to their feelings

and ideas. This is more particularly true of democratic revolutions, which stir up at once all the classes of which a people is composed, and beget at the same time inordinate ambition in the breast of every member of the community. The French made surprising advances in the exact sciences at the very time at which they were finishing the destruction of the remains of their former feudal society; yet this sudden fecundity is not to be attributed to democracy, but to the unexampled revolution which attended its growth. What happened at that period was a special incident, and it would be unwise to regard it as the test of a general principle.

Great revolutions are not more common amongst democratic than amongst other nations: I am even inclined to believe that they are less so. But there prevails amongst those populations a small, distressing motion, a sort of incessant jostling of men, which annoys and disturbs the mind without exciting or elevating it.

Men who live in democratic communities not only seldom indulge in meditation, but they naturally entertain very little esteem for it. A democratic state of society and democratic institutions keep the greater part of men in constant activity; and the habits of mind which are suited to an active life are not always suited to a contemplative one. The man of action is frequently obliged to content himself with the best he can get, because he would never accomplish his purpose if he chose to carry every detail to perfection. He has perpetually occasion to rely on ideas which he has not had leisure to search to the bottom; for he is much more frequently aided by the seasonableness of an idea than by its strict accuracy; and, in the long run, he risks less in making use of some false principles, than in spending his time in establishing all his principles, on the basis of truth. The world is not led by long or learned demonstrations: a rapid glance at particular incidents, the daily study of the fleeting passions of the multitude, the accidents of the moment and the art of turning them to account, decide all its affairs.

In the ages in which active life is the condition of almost every one, men are therefore generally led to attach an excessive value to the rapid bursts and superficial conceptions of the intellect; and, on the other hand, to depreciate unduly its slower and deeper labors. This opinion of the public influences the judgment of the men who cultivate the sciences; they are persuaded that they may succeed in those pursuits without meditation, or are deterred from such pursuits as demand it.

There are several methods of studying the sciences.

Amongst a multitude of men you will find a selfish, mercantile, and trading taste for the discoveries of the mind, which must not be confounded with that disinterested passion which is kindled in the heart of a few. A desire to utilize knowledge is one thing; the pure desire to know is another. I do not doubt that in a few minds, and at long intervals, an ardent, inexhaustible love of truth springs up, self-supported, and living in ceaseless fruition, without ever attaining full satisfaction. This ardent love it is—this proud, disinterested love of what is true—which raises men to the abstract sources of truth, to draw their mother knowledge thence.

If Pascal had had nothing in view but some large gain, or even if he had been stimulated by the love of fame alone, I cannot conceive that he would ever have been able to rally all the powers of his mind, as he did, for the better discovery of the most hidden things of the Creator. When I see him, as it were, tear his soul from all the cares of life to devote it wholly to these researches, and, prematurely snapping the links which bind the frame to life, die of old age before forty, I stand amazed, and perceive that no ordinary cause is at work to produce efforts so extraordinary.

The future will prove whether these passions, at once so rare and so productive, come into being and into growth as easily in the midst of democratic as in aristocratic communities. For myself, I confess that I am slow to believe it.

In aristocratic societies, the class which gives the tone to opinion, and has the guidance of affairs, being permanently and hereditarily placed above the multitude, naturally conceives a lofty idea of itself and of man. It loves to invent for him noble pleasures, to carve out splendid objects for his ambition. Aristocracies often commit very tyrannical and inhuman actions, but they rarely entertain grovelling thoughts; and they show a kind of haughty contempt of little pleasures, even whilst they indulge in them. The effect is greatly to raise the general pitch of society. In aristocratic ages, vast ideas are commonly entertained of the dignity, the power, and the greatness of man. These opinions exert their influence on those who cultivate the sciences, as well as on the rest of the community. They facilitate the natural impulse of the mind to the highest regions of thought; and they naturally prepare it to conceive a sublime, almost a divine, love of truth.

Men of science at such periods are consequently carried away towards theory; and it even happens that they frequently conceive an inconsiderate contempt for practice. "Archimedes," says Plutarch, "was of so lofty a spirit, that he never condescended to write any treatise on the manner of constructing all these engines of war. And as he held this science of inventing and putting together engines, and all arts generally speaking which tended to any useful end in practice, to be vile, low, and mercenary, he spent his talents and his studious hours in writing of those things only whose beauty and subtilty had in them no admixture of necessity." Such is the aristocratic aim of science: it cannot be the same in democratic nations.

The greater part of the men who constitute these nations are extremely eager in the pursuit of actual and physical gratification. As they are always dissatisfied with the position which they occupy, and are always free to leave it, they think of nothing but the means of changing their fortune, or increasing it. To minds thus predisposed, every new method which leads by a shorter road to wealth, every machine which spares labor, every instrument which diminishes the cost of production, every discovery which facilitates pleasures or augments them, seems to be the grandest effort of the human intellect. It is chiefly from these motives that a democratic people addicts itself to scientific pursuits,—that it understands and respects them. In aristocratic ages, science is more particularly called upon to furnish gratification to the mind; in democracies, to the body.

You may be sure that the more a nation is democratic, enlightened, and free, the greater will be the number of these interested promoters of scientific genius, and the more will discoveries immediately applicable to productive industry confer gain, fame, and even power, on their authors. For in democracies, the working class take a part in public affairs; and public honors, as well as pecuniary remuneration, may be awarded to those who deserve them.

In a community thus organized, it may easily be conceived that the human mind may be led insensibly to the neglect of theory; and that it is urged, on the contrary, with unparalleled energy, to the applications of science, or at least to that portion of theoretical science which is necessary to those who make such applications. In vain will some instinctive inclination raise the mind towards the loftier spheres of the intellect; interest draws it down to the middle zone. There it may develop all its energy and restless activity, and bring forth wonders. These very Americans, who have not discovered one of the general laws of mechanics, have introduced into navigation an engine which changes the aspect of the world.

Assuredly I do not contend that the democratic nations of our time are destined to witness the extinction of the great luminaries of man's intelligence, or even that they will

never bring new lights into existence. At the age at which
the world has now arrived, and amongst so many cultivated
nations perpetually excited by the fever of productive industry, the bonds which connect the different parts of science
cannot fail to strike the observer; and the taste for practical
science itself, if it be enlightened, ought to lead men not to
neglect theory. In the midst of so many attempted applications of so many experiments, repeated every day, it is almost impossible that general laws should not frequently be
brought to light; so that great discoveries would be frequent,
though great inventors may be few.

I believe, moreover, in high scientific vocations. If the
democratic principle does not, on the one hand, induce men
to cultivate science for its own sake, on the other, it enormous-
ly increases the number of those who do cultivate it. Nor is it
credible that, amid so great a multitude, a speculative genius
should not from time to time arise inflamed by the love of
truth alone. Such an one, we may be sure, would dive into
the deepest mysteries of nature, whatever be the spirit of his
country and his age. He requires no assistance in his course,—
it is enough that he is not checked in it. All that I mean to
say is this: permanent inequality of conditions leads men to
confine themselves to the arrogant and sterile research of
abstract truths, whilst the social condition and the institutions of democracy prepare them to seek the immediate and
useful practical results of the sciences. This tendency is natural
and inevitable: it is curious to be acquainted with it, and it
may be necessary to point it out.

If those who are called upon to guide the nations of our
time clearly discerned from afar off these new tendencies,
which will soon be irresistible, they would understand that,
possessing education and freedom, men living in democratic
ages cannot fail to improve the industrial part of science; and
that henceforward all the efforts of the constituted authorities
ought to be directed to support the highest branches of learning, and to foster the nobler passion for science itself. In the
present age, the human mind must be coerced into theoretical
studies; it runs of its own accord to practical applications; and,
instead of perpetually referring it to the minute examination
of secondary effects, it is well to divert it from them sometimes,
in order to raise it up to the contemplation of primary
causes. . . .

21. In What Spirit the Americans Cultivate the Arts.

IT WOULD be to waste the time of my readers and my own, if I strove to demonstrate how the general mediocrity of fortunes, the absence of superfluous wealth, the universal desire of comfort, and the constant efforts by which every one attempts to procure it, make the taste for the useful predominate over the love of the beautiful in the heart of man. Democratic nations, amongst whom all these things exist, will therefore cultivate the arts which serve to render life easy, in preference to those whose object is to adorn it. They will habitually prefer the useful to the beautiful, and they will require that the beautiful should be useful.

It commonly happens that, in the ages of privilege, the practice of almost all the arts becomes a privilege; and that every profession is a separate walk, upon which it is not allowable for every one to enter. Even when productive industry is free, the fixed character which belongs to aristocratic nations gradually segregates all the persons who practise the same art, till they form a distinct class, always composed of the same families, whose members are all known to each other, and amongst whom a public opinion of their own, and a species of corporate pride, soon spring up. In a class or guild of this kind, each artisan has not only his fortune to make, but his reputation to preserve. He is not exclusively swayed by his own interest, or even by that of his customer, but by that of the body to which he belongs; and the interest of that body is, that each artisan should produce the best possible workmanship. In aristocratic ages, the object of the arts is therefore to manufacture as well as possible,—not with the greatest despatch, or at the lowest rate.

When, on the contrary, every profession is open to all,—when a multitude of persons are constantly embracing and abandoning it,—and when its several members are strangers, indifferent to, and from their numbers hardly seen by, each other,—the social tie is destroyed, and each workman, standing alone, endeavors simply to gain the most money at the least cost. The will of the customer is then his only limit. But at the same time, a corresponding change takes place in the customer also. In countries in which riches, as well as power, are concentrated and retained in the hands of a few, the use of the greater part of this world's goods belongs to a small number of individuals, who are always the same. Necessity, public opinion, or moderate desires, exclude all others from the enjoyment of them. As this aristocratic class remains fixed at the pinnacle of greatness on which it stands, without diminution or increase, it is always acted upon by the same wants, and affected by them in the same manner. The men of whom it is composed naturally derive from their superior and hereditary position a taste for what is extremely well made and lasting. This affects the general way of thinking of the nation in relation to the arts. It often occurs, among such a people, that even the peasant will rather go without the objects he covets, than procure them in a state of imperfection. In aristocracies, then, the handicraftsmen work for only a limited number of fastidious customers: the profit they hope to make depends principally on the perfection of their workmanship.

Such is no longer the case when, all privileges being abolished, ranks are intermingled, and men are forever rising or sinking upon the social scale. Amongst a democratic people, a number of citizens always exist whose patrimony is divided and decreasing. They have contracted, under more prosperous circumstances, certain wants, which remain after the means of satisfying such wants are gone; and they are anxiously looking out for some surreptitious method of providing for them. On the other hand, there are always in democracies a large number of men whose fortune is upon the increase, but whose desires grow much faster than their fortunes: and who gloat upon the gifts of wealth in anticipation, long before they have means to command them. Such men are eager to find some short cut to these gratifications, already almost within their reach. From the combination of these two causes the result is, that in democracies there is always a multitude of persons whose wants are above their means, and who are very willing to take up with imperfect satisfaction, rather than abandon the object of their desires altogether.

The artisan readily understands these passions, for he himself partakes in them: in an aristocracy, he would seek to sell his workmanship at a high price to the few; he now conceives that the more expeditious way of getting rich is to sell them at a low price to all. But there are only two ways of lowering the price of commodities. The first is to discover some better, shorter, and more ingenious method of producing them: the second is to manufacture a larger quantity of goods, nearly similar, but of less value. Amongst a democratic population, all the intellectual faculties of the workman are directed to these two objects: he strives to invent methods which may enable him not only to work better, but quicker and cheaper; or, if he cannot succeed in that, to diminish the intrinsic quality of the thing he makes, without rendering it wholly unfit for the use for which it is intended. When none but the wealthy had watches, they were almost all very good ones: few are now made which are worth much, but everybody has one in his pocket. Thus the democratic principle not only tends to direct the human mind to the useful arts, but it induces the artisan to produce with great rapidity many imperfect commodities, and the consumer to content himself with these commodities.

Not that, in democracies, the arts are incapable, in case of need, of producing wonders. This may occasionally be the case, if customers appear who are ready to pay for time and trouble. In this rivalry of every kind of industry, in the midst of this immense competition and these countless experiments, some excellent workmen are found, who reach the utmost limits of their craft. But they have rarely an opportunity of showing what they can do; they are scrupulously sparing of their powers; they remain in a state of accomplished mediocrity, which judges itself, and, though well able to shoot beyond the mark before it, aims only at what it hits. In aristocracies, on the contrary, workmen always do all they can; and when they stop, it is because they have reached the limit of their art.

When I arrive in a country where I find some of the finest productions of the arts, I learn from this fact nothing of the social condition or of the political constitution of the country. But if I perceive that the productions of the arts are generally of an inferior quality, very abundant and very cheap, I am convinced that, amongst the people where this occurs, privilege is on the decline, and that ranks are beginning to intermingle, and will soon be confounded together.

The handicraftsmen of democratic ages endeavor not only to bring their useful productions within the reach of the whole community, but they strive to give to all their commodities attractive qualities which they do not in reality possess. In the confusion of all ranks, every one hopes to appear what he is not, and makes great exertions to succeed in this object. This sentiment, indeed, which is but too natural to the heart of man, does not originate in the democratic principle; but that principle applies it to material objects. The hypocrisy of virtue is of every age, but the hypocrisy of luxury belongs more particularly to the ages of democracy.

To satisfy these new cravings of human vanity, the arts have recourse to every species of imposture; and these devices sometimes go so far as to defeat their own purpose. Imitation diamonds are now made which may be easily mistaken for real ones; as soon as the art of fabricating false diamonds shall become so perfect that they cannot be distinguished from real ones, it is probable that both will be abandoned, and become mere pebbles again.

This leads me to speak of those arts which are called, by way of distinction, the fine arts. I do not believe that it is a necessary effect of a democratic social condition and of democratic institutions to diminish the number of those who cultivate the fine arts; but these causes exert a powerful influence on the manner in which these arts are cultivated. Many of those who had already contracted a taste for the fine arts are impoverished: on the other hand, many of those who are not yet rich begin to conceive that taste, at least by imitation; the number of consumers increases, but opulent and fastidious consumers become more scarce. Something analogous to what I have already pointed out in the useful arts then takes place in the fine arts; the productions of artists are more numerous, but the merit of each production is diminished. No longer able to soar to what is great, they cultivate what is pretty and elegant; and appearance is more attended to than reality.

In aristocracies, a few great pictures are produced; in democratic countries, a vast number of insignificant ones. In the former, statues are raised of bronze; in the latter, they are modelled in plaster.

When I arrived for the first time at New York, by that part of the Atlantic Ocean which is called the East River, I was surprised to perceive along the shore, at some distance from the city, a number of little palaces of white marble, several of which were of ancient architecture. When I went the next day to inspect more closely one which had particularly attracted my notice, I found that its walls were of whitewashed brick, and its columns of painted wood. All the edifices which I had admired the night before were of the same kind.

The social condition and the institutions of democracy impart, moreover, certain peculiar tendencies to all the imitative arts, which it is easy to point out. They frequently withdraw them from the delineation of the soul, to fix them exclusively on that of the body; and they substitute the representation of motion and sensation for that of sentiment and thought: in a word, they put the Real in the place of the Ideal.

I doubt whether Raphael studied the minute intricacies of the mechanism of the human body as thoroughly as the draughtsmen of our own time. He did not attach the same importance as they do to rigorous accuracy on his point, because he aspired to surpass nature. He sought to make of man something which should be superior to man, and to embellish beauty itself. David and his scholars were, on the contrary, as good anatomists as they were painters. They wonderfully depicted the models which they had before their eyes, but they rarely imagined anything beyond them: they followed nature with fidelity, whilst Raphael sought for something better than nature. They have left us an exact portraiture of man; but he discloses in his works a glimpse of the Divinity.

This remark as to the manner of treating a subject is no less applicable to the choice of it. The painters of the Renaissance generally sought far above themselves, and away from their own time, for mighty subjects, which left to their imagination an unbounded range. Our painters often employ their talents in the exact imitation of the details of private life, which they have always before their eyes; and they are forever copying trivial objects, the originals of which are only too abundant in nature.

22. *Literary Characteristics of Democratic Times.*

WHEN a traveller goes into a bookseller's shop in the United States, and examines the American books upon the shelves, the number of works appears very great; whilst that of known authors seems, on the contrary, extremely small. He will first find a multitude of elementary treatises, destined to teach the rudiments of human knowledge. Most of these books are written in Europe; the Americans reprint them, adapting them to their own use. Next comes an enormous quantity of religious works, Bibles, sermons, edifying anecdotes, controversial divinity, and reports of charitable societies; lastly appears the long catalogue of political pamphlets. In America, parties do not write books to combat each other's opinions, but pamphlets, which are circulated for a day with incredible rapidity, and then expire.

In the midst of all these obscure productions of the human brain appear the more remarkable works of a small number of authors, whose names are, or ought to be, known to Europeans.

Although America is perhaps in our days the civilized country in which literature is least attended to, still a large number of persons there take an interest in the productions of mind, and make them, if not the study of their lives, at least the charm of their leisure hours. But England supplies these readers with most of the books which they require. Almost all important English books are republished in the United States. The literary genius of Great Britain still darts its rays into the recesses of the forests of the New World. There is hardly a pioneer's hut which does not contain a few odd volumes of Shakespeare. I remember that I read the feudal drama of Henry V. for the first time in a log-house.

Not only do the Americans constantly draw upon the treasures of English literature, but it may be said with truth that they find the literature of England growing on their own soil. The larger part of that small number of men in the United States who are engaged in the composition of literary works are English in substance, and still more so in form. Thus they transport into the midst of democracy the ideas and literary fashions which are current amongst the aristocratic nation they have taken for their model. They paint with colors borrowed from foreign manners; and as they hardly ever represent the country they were born in as it really is, they are seldom popular there.

The citizens of the United States are themselves so convinced that it is not for them that books are published, that, before they can make up their minds upon the merit of one of their authors, they generally wait till his fame has been ratified in England; just as, in pictures, the author of an original is held entitled to judge of the merit of a copy.

The inhabitants of the United States have then, at present, properly speaking, no literature. The only authors whom I acknowledge as American are the journalists. They indeed are not great writers, but they speak the language of their country, and make themselves heard. Other authors are aliens; they are to the Americans what the imitators of the Greeks and Romans were to us at the revival of learning,—an object of curiosity, not of general sympathy. They amuse the mind, but they do not act upon the manners of the people.

I have already said that this state of things is far from originating in democracy alone, and that the causes of it must be sought for in several peculiar circumstances independent of the democratic principle. If the Americans, retaining the same laws and social condition, had had a different origin, and had been transported into another country, I do not question that they would have had a literature. Even as they are, I am convinced that they will ultimately have one; but its character will be different from that which marks the American literary productions of our time, and that character will be peculiarly its own. Nor is it impossible to trace this character beforehand.

I suppose an aristocratic people amongst whom letters are cultivated; the labors of the mind, as well as the affairs of state, are conducted there by a ruling class in society. The literary as well as the political career is almost entirely confined to this class, or to those nearest to it in rank. These premises suffice for a key to all the rest.

When a small number of the same men are engaged at the same time upon the same objects, they easily concert with one another, and agree upon certain leading rules which are to govern them each and all. If the object which attracts the attention of these men is literature, the productions of the mind will soon be subjected by them to precise canons, from which it will no longer be allowable to depart. If these men occupy an hereditary position in the country, they will be naturally inclined, not only to adopt a certain number of fixed rules for themselves, but to follow those which their forefathers laid down for their own guidance; their code will be at once strict and traditional. As they are not necessarily engrossed by the cares of daily life,—as they have never been so, any more than their fathers were before them,—they have learned to take an interest, for several generations back, in the labors of mind. They have learned to understand literature as an art, to love it in the end for its own sake, and to feel a scholar-like satisfaction in seeing men conform to its rules. Nor is this all: the men of whom I speak began and will end their lives in easy or affluent circumstances; hence they have naturally conceived a taste for choice gratifications, and a love of refined and delicate pleasures. Nay, more: a kind of softness of mind and heart, which they frequently contract in the midst of this long and peaceful enjoyment of so much welfare, leads them to put aside, even from their pleasures, whatever might be too startling or too acute. They had rather be amused than intensely excited; they wish to be interested, but not to be carried away.

Now let us fancy a great number of literary performances executed by the men, or for the men, whom I have just described, and we shall readily conceive a style of literature in which everything will be regular and prearranged. The slightest work will be carefully touched in its least details; art and labor will be conspicuous in everything; each kind of writing will have rules of its own, from which it will not be allowed to swerve, and which distinguish it from all others. Style will be thought of almost as much importance as thought, and the form will be no less considered than the matter; the diction will be polished, measured, and uniform. The tone of the mind will be always dignified, seldom very animated; and writers will care more to perfect what they produce, than to multiply their productions. It will sometimes happen that the members of the literary class, always living amongst themselves, and writing for themselves alone, will entirely lose sight of the rest of the world, which will infect them with a false and labored style; they will lay down minute literary rules for their exclusive use, which will insensibly lead them to deviate from common sense, and finally to transgress the bounds of nature. By dint of striving after a mode of parlance different from the vulgar, they will arrive at a sort of aristocratic jargon, which is hardly less remote from pure language than is the coarse dialect of the people. Such are the natural perils of literature amongst aristocracies. Every aristocracy which keeps itself entirely aloof from the people becomes impotent,—a fact which is as true in literature as it is in politics.

Let us now turn the picture, and consider the other side of it: let us transport ourselves into the midst of a democracy not unprepared by ancient traditions and present culture to partake in the pleasures of mind. Ranks are there intermingled and confounded; knowledge and power are both infinitely subdivided, and, if I may use the expression, scattered on every side. Here, then, is a motley multitude whose intellectual wants are to be supplied. These new votaries of the pleasures of mind have not all received the same education; they do not resemble their fathers,—nay, they perpetually differ from themselves, for they live in a state of incessant change of place, feelings, and fortunes. The mind of each is therefore unattached to that of his fellows by tradition or common habits; and they have never had the power, the inclination, or the time to concert together. It is, however, from the bosom of this heterogeneous and agitated mass that authors spring; and from the same source their profits and their fame are distributed.

I can without difficulty understand that, under these circumstances, I must expect to meet in the literature of such a people with but few of those strict conventional rules which are admitted by readers and writers in aristocratic times. If it should happen that the men of some one period were agreed upon any such rules, that would prove nothing for the following period; for, amongst democratic nations, each new generation is a new people. Amongst such nations, then, literature will not easily be subjected to strict rules, and it is impossible that any such rules should ever be permanent.

In democracies, it is by no means the case that all who cultivate literature have received a literary education; and most of those who have some tinge of belles-lettres are either engaged in politics or in a profession which only allows them to taste occasionally and by stealth the pleasures of mind. These pleasures, therefore, do not constitute the principal charm of their lives; but they are considered as a transient and necessary recreation amidst the serious labors of life. Such men can never acquire a sufficiently intimate knowledge of the art of literature to appreciate its more delicate beauties; and the minor shades of expression must escape them. As the time they can devote to letters is very short, they seek to make the best use of the whole of it. They prefer books which may be easily procured, quickly read, and which require no learned researches to be understood. They ask for beauties self-proffered, and easily enjoyed; above all, they must have what is unexpected and new. Accustomed to the struggle, the crosses, and the monotony of practical life, they require strong and rapid emotions, startling passages,—truths or errors brilliant enough to rouse them up, and to plunge them at once, as if by violence, into the midst of the subject.

Why should I say more? or who does not understand what is about to follow, before I have expressed it? Taken as a whole, literature in democratic ages can never present, as it does in the periods of aristocracy, an aspect of order, regularity, science, and art; its form will, on the contrary, ordinarily be slighted, sometimes despised. Style will frequently be fantastic, incorrect, overburdened, and loose,—almost always vehement and bold. Authors will aim at rapidity of execution, more than at perfection of detail. Small productions will be more common than bulky books: there will be more wit than erudition, more imagination than profundity; and literary performances will bear marks of an untutored and rude vigor of thought,—frequently of great variety and singular fecundity. The object of authors will be to astonish rather than to please, and to stir the passions more than to charm the taste.

Here and there, indeed, writers will doubtless occur who will choose a different track, and who will, if they are gifted with superior abilities, succeed in finding readers, in spite of their defects or their better qualities; but these exceptions will be rare; and even the authors who shall so depart from the received practice in the main subject of their works, will always relapse into it in some lesser details.

I have just depicted two extreme conditions: the transition by which a nation passes from the former to the latter is not sudden, but gradual, and marked with shades of very various intensity. In the passage which conducts a lettered people from the one to the other, there is almost always a moment at which

the literary genius of democratic nations has its confluence
with that of aristocracies, and both seek to establish their joint
sway over the human mind. Such epochs are transient, but very
brilliant: they are fertile without exuberance, and animated
without confusion. The French literature of the eighteenth
century may serve as an example.

I should say more than I mean, if I were to assert that the
literature of a nation is always subordinate to its social state
and its political constitution. I am aware that, independently
of these causes, there are several others which confer certain
characteristics on literary productions; but these appear to me
to be the chief. The relations which exist between the social
and political condition of a people and the genius of its authors
are always numerous: whoever knows the one, is never completely ignorant of the other.

23. Of Some Sources of Poetry Amongst Democratic Nations.

MANY different significations have been given to the word
Poetry. It would weary my readers if I were to lead them to
discuss which of these definitions ought to be selected: I prefer
telling them at once that which I have chosen. In my opinion,
Poetry is the search after, and the delineation of, the Ideal.

The Poet is he who, by suppressing a part of what exists, by
adding some imaginary touches to the picture, and by combining certain real circumstances which do not in fact happen
together, completes and extends the work of nature. Thus, the
object of poetry is not to represent what is true, but to adorn it,
and to present to the mind some loftier image. Verse, regarded
as the ideal beauty of language, may be eminently poetical;
but verse does not of itself constitute poetry.

I now proceed to inquire whether, amongst the actions, the
sentiments, and the opinions of democratic nations, there are
any which lead to a conception of the ideal, and which may
for this reason be considered as natural sources of poetry.

It must, in the first place, be acknowledged that the taste
for ideal beauty, and the pleasure derived from the expression
of it, are never so intense or so diffused amongst a democratic
as amongst an aristocratic people. In aristocratic nations, it
sometimes happens that the body acts as it were spontaneously,
whilst the higher faculties are bound and burdened by repose.
Amongst these nations, the people will often display poetic

tastes, and their fancy sometimes ranges beyond and above what surrounds them.

But in democracies, the love of physical gratification, the notion of bettering one's condition, the excitement of competition, the charm of anticipated success, are so many spurs to urge men onward in the active professions they have embraced, without allowing them to deviate for an instant from the track. The main stress of the faculties is to this point. The imagination is not extinct; but its chief function is to devise what may be useful, and to represent what is real. The principle of equality not only diverts men from the description of ideal beauty; it also diminishes the number of objects to be described.

Aristocracy, by maintaining society in a fixed position, is favorable to the solidity and duration of positive religions, as well as to the stability of political institutions. It not only keeps the human mind within a certain sphere of belief, but it predisposes the mind to adopt one faith rather than another. An aristocratic people will always be prone to place intermediate powers between God and man. In this respect, it may be said that the aristocratic element is favorable to poetry. When the universe is peopled with supernatural beings, not palpable to sense, but discovered by the mind, the imagination ranges freely; and poets, finding a thousand subjects to delineate, also find a countless audience to take an interest in their productions.

In democratic ages, it sometimes happens, on the contrary, that men are as much afloat in matters of faith as they are in their laws. Scepticism then draws the imagination of poets back to earth, and confines them to the real and visible world. Even when the principle of equality does not disturb religious conviction, it tends to simplify it, and to divert attention from secondary agents, to fix it principally on the Supreme Power.

Aristocracy naturally leads the human mind to the contemplation of the past, and fixes it there. Democracy, on the contrary, gives men a sort of instinctive distaste for what is ancient. In this respect, aristocracy is far more favorable to poetry; for things commonly grow larger and more obscure as they are more remote; and, for this two-fold reason, they are better suited to the delineation of the ideal.

After having deprived poetry of the past, the principle of equality robs it in part of the present. Amongst aristocratic nations, there are a certain number of privileged personages, whose situation is, as it were, without and above the condition of man: to these, power, wealth, fame, wit, refinement, and distinction in all things appear peculiarly to belong. The crowd never sees them very closely, or does not watch them in minute details; and little is needed to make the description of such men poetical. On the other hand, amongst the same people, you will meet with classes so ignorant, low, and enslaved, that they are no less fit objects for poetry, from the excess of their rudeness and wretchedness, than the former are from their greatness and refinement. Besides, as the different classes of which an aristocratic community is composed are widely separated, and imperfectly acquainted with each other, the imagination may always represent them with some addition to, or some subtraction from, what they really are.

In democratic communities, where men are all insignificant and very much alike, each man instantly sees all his fellows when he surveys himself. The poets of democratic ages can never, therefore, take any man in particular as the subject of a piece; for an object of slender importance, which is distinctly seen on all sides, will never lend itself to an ideal conception.

Thus the principle of equality, in proportion as it has established itself in the world, has dried up most of the old springs of poetry. Let us now attempt to show what new ones it may disclose.

When scepticism had depopulated heaven, and the progress of equality had reduced each individual to smaller and better-known proportions, the poets, not yet aware of what they could substitute for the great themes which were departing together with the aristocracy, turned their eyes to inanimate nature. As they lost sight of gods and heroes, they set themselves to describe streams and mountains. Thence originated, in the last century, that kind of poetry which has been called, by way of distinction, *descriptive*. Some have thought that this embellished delineation of all the physical and inanimate objects which cover the earth was the kind of poetry peculiar to democratic ages; but I believe this to be an error, and that it belongs only to a period of transition.

I am persuaded that, in the end, democracy diverts the imagination from all that is external to man, and fixes it on man alone. Democratic nations may amuse themselves for a while with considering the productions of nature; but they are excited in reality only by a survey of themselves. Here, and here alone, the true sources of poetry amongst such nations are to be found; and it may be believed that the poets who shall neglect to draw their inspirations hence, will lose all sway over the minds which they would enchant, and will be left in the end with none but unimpassioned spectators of their transports.

I have shown how the ideas of progression and of the

indefinite perfectibility of the human race belong to democratic ages. Democratic nations care but little for what has been, but they are haunted by visions of what will be; in this direction, their unbounded imagination grows and dilates beyond all measure. Here, then, is the widest range open to the genius of poets, which allows them to remove their performances to a sufficient distance from the eye. Democracy, which shuts the past against the poet, opens the future before him.

As all the citizens who compose a democratic community are nearly equal and alike, the poet cannot dwell upon any one of them; but the nation itself invites the exercise of his powers. The general similitude of individuals, which renders any one of them taken separately an improper subject of poetry, allows poets to include them all in the same imagery, and to take a general survey of the people itself. Democratic nations have a clearer perception than any others of their own aspect; and an aspect so imposing is admirably fitted to the delineation of the ideal.

I readily admit that the Americans have no poets; I cannot allow that they have no poetic ideas. In Europe, people talk a great deal of the wilds of America, but the Americans themselves never think about them: they are insensible to the wonders of inanimate nature, and they may be said not to perceive the mighty forests which surround them till they fall beneath the hatchet. Their eyes are fixed upon another sight: the American people views its own march across these wilds, —drying swamps, turning the course of rivers, peopling solitudes, and subduing nature. This magnificent image of themselves does not meet the gaze of the Americans at intervals only; it may be said to haunt every one of them in his least as well as in his most important actions, and to be always flitting before his mind.

Nothing conceivable is so petty, so insipid, so crowded with paltry interests, in one word, so anti-poetic, as the life of a man in the United States. But amongst the thoughts which it suggests, there is always one which is full of poetry, and this is the hidden nerve which gives vigor to the whole frame.

In aristocratic ages, each people, as well as each individual, is prone to stand separate and aloof from all others. In democratic ages, the extreme fluctuations of men, and the impatience of their desires, keep them perpetually on the move; so that the inhabitants of different countries intermingle, see, listen to, and borrow from each other. It is not only, then, the members of the same community who grow more alike; communities themselves are assimilated to one another, and the whole assemblage presents to the eye of the spectator one vast democracy, each citizen of which is a nation. This displays the aspect of mankind for the first time in the broadest light. All that belongs to the existence of the human race taken as a whole, to its vicissitudes and its future, becomes an abundant mine of poetry.

The poets who lived in aristocratic ages have been eminently successful in their delineations of certain incidents in the life of a people or a man; but none of them ever ventured to include within his performances the destinies of mankind,—a task which poets writing in democratic ages may attempt.

At that same time at which every man, raising his eyes above his country, begins at length to discern mankind at large, the Deity is more and more manifest to the human mind in full and entire majesty. If, in democratic ages, faith in positive religion be often shaken, and the belief in intermediate agents, by whatever name they are called, be overcast; on the other hand, men are disposed to conceive a far broader idea of Providence itself, and its interference in human affairs assumes a new and more imposing appearance to their eyes. Looking at the human race as one great whole, they easily conceive that its destinies are regulated by the same design; and in the actions of every individual they are led to acknowledge a trace of that universal and eternal plan on which God rules our race. This consideration may be taken as another prolific source of poetry which is opened in democratic times.

Democratic poets will always appear trivial and frigid if they seek to invest gods, demons, or angels with corporeal forms, and if they attempt to draw them down from heaven to dispute the supremacy of earth. But if they strive to connect the great events they commemorate with the general providential designs which govern the universe, and, without showing the finger of the Supreme Governor, reveal the thoughts of the Supreme Mind, their works will be admired and understood, for the imagination of their contemporaries takes this direction of its own accord.

It may be foreseen in like manner, that poets living in democratic times will prefer the delineation of passions and ideas to that of persons and achievements. The language, the dress, and the daily actions of men in democracies are repugnant to conceptions of the ideal. These things are not poetical in themselves; and if it were otherwise, they would cease to be so, because they are too familiar to all those to whom the poet would speak of them. This forces the poet constantly to search below the external surface which is palpable to the senses, in order to read the inner soul; and nothing lends itself more to the delineation of the ideal, than the scrutiny of the hidden depths in the immaterial nature of man. I need not traverse earth and sky to discover a wondrous object woven of contrasts, of infinite greatness and littleness, of intense gloom and amazing brightness,—capable at once of exciting pity, admiration, terror, contempt. I have only to look at myself. Man springs out of nothing, crosses time, and disappears forever in the bosom of God; he is seen but for a moment, wandering on the verge of the two abysses, and there he is lost.

If man were wholly ignorant of himself, he would have no poetry in him; for it is impossible to describe what the mind does not conceive. If man clearly discerned his own nature, his imagination would remain idle, and would have nothing to add to the picture. But the nature of man is sufficiently disclosed for him to apprehend something of himself, and sufficiently obscure for all the rest to be plunged in thick darkness, in which he gropes forever,—and forever in vain, —to lay hold on some completer notion of his being.

Amongst a democratic people, poetry will not be fed with legends or the memorials of old traditions. The poet will not attempt to people the universe with supernatural beings, in whom his readers and his own fancy have ceased to believe; nor will he coldly personify virtues and vices, which are better received under their own features. All these resources fail him; but Man remains, and the poet needs no more. The destinies of mankind—man himself, taken aloof from his country and his age, and standing in the presence of Nature and of God, with his passions, his doubts, his rare prosperities and inconceivable wretchedness—will become the chief, if not the sole, theme of poetry amongst these nations.

Experience may confirm this assertion, if we consider the productions of the greatest poets who have appeared since the world has been turned to democracy. The authors of our age who have so admirably delineated the features of Faust, Childe Harold, Réné, and Jocelyn, did not seek to record the actions of an individual, but to enlarge and to throw light on some of the obscurer recesses of the human heart.

Such are the poems of democracy. The principle of equality does not then destroy all the subjects of poetry: it renders them less numerous, but more vast.

24. Why American Writers and Orators Often Use an Inflated Style.

I HAVE frequently remarked that the Americans, who generally treat of business in clear, plain language, devoid of all ornament, and so extremely simple as to be often coarse, are apt to become inflated as soon as they attempt a more poetical diction. They then vent their pomposity from one end of a harangue to the other; and to hear them lavish imagery on every occasion, one might fancy that they never spoke of anything with simplicity.

The English less frequently commit a similar fault. The cause of this may be pointed out without much difficulty. In democratic communities, each citizen is habitually engaged in the contemplation of a very puny object, namely, himself. If he ever raises his looks higher, he perceives only the immense form of society at large, or the still more imposing aspect of mankind. His ideas are all either extremely minute and clear, or extremely general and vague: what lies between is a void. When he has been drawn out of his own sphere, therefore, he always expects that some amazing object will be offered to his attention; and it is on these terms alone that he consents to tear himself for a moment from the petty, complicated cares which form the charm and the excitement of his life.

This appears to me sufficiently to explain why men in democracies, whose concerns are in general so paltry, call upon their poets for conceptions so vast and descriptions so unlimited.

The authors, on their part, do not fail to obey a propensity of which they themselves partake; they perpetually inflate their imaginations, and, expanding them beyond all bounds, they not unfrequently abandon the great in order to reach the gigantic. By these means, they hope to attract the observation of the multitude, and to fix it easily upon themselves: nor are their hopes disappointed; for, as the multitude seeks for nothing in poetry but objects of vast dimensions, it has neither the time to measure with accuracy the proportions of all the objects set before it, nor a taste sufficiently correct to perceive at once in what respect they are out of proportion. The author and the public at once vitiate one another.

We have also seen, that, amongst democratic nations, the sources of poetry are grand, but not abundant. They are soon exhausted: and poets, not finding the elements of the ideal in what is real and true, abandon them entirely and create monsters. I do not fear that the poetry of democratic nations will prove insipid, or that it will fly too near the ground; I rather apprehend that it will be forever losing itself in the clouds, and that it will range at last to purely imaginary regions. I fear that the productions of democratic poets may often be surcharged with immense and incoherent imagery, with exaggerated descriptions and strange creations; and that the fantastic beings of their brain may sometimes make us regret the world of reality.

25. *Some Characteristics of Historians in Democratic Times.*

HISTORIANS who write in aristocratic ages are wont to refer all occurrences to the particular will and character of certain individuals; and they are apt to attribute the most important revolutions to slight accidents. They trace out the smallest causes with sagacity, and frequently leave the greatest unperceived.

Historians who live in democratic ages exhibit precisely opposite characteristics. Most of them attribute hardly any influence to the individual over the destiny of the race, or to citizens over the fate of a people; but, on the other hand, they assign great general causes to all petty incidents. These contrary tendencies explain each other.

When the historian of aristocratic ages surveys the theatre of the world, he at once perceives a very small number of prominent actors, who manage the whole piece. These great personages, who occupy the front of the stage, arrest attention, and fix it on themselves; and whilst the historian is bent on penetrating the secret motives which make these persons speak and act, the others escape his memory. The importance of the things which some men are seen to do, gives him an exaggerated estimate of the influence which one man may possess; and naturally leads him to think, that, in order to explain the impulses of the multitude, it is necessary to refer them to the particular influence of some one individual.

When, on the contrary, all the citizens are independent of one another, and each of them is individually weak, no one is seen to exert a great, or still less a lasting, power over the community. At first sight, individuals appear to be absolutely devoid of any influence over it; and society would seem to advance alone by the free and voluntary action of all the men who compose it. This naturally prompts the mind to search for that general reason which operates upon so many men's faculties at once, and turns them simultaneously in the same direction.

I am very well convinced that, even amongst democratic nations, the genius, the vices, or the virtues of certain individuals retard or accelerate the natural current of a people's history; but causes of this secondary and fortuitous nature are infinitely more various, more concealed, more complex, less powerful, and consequently less easy to trace, in periods of equality than in ages of aristocracy, when the task of the historian is simply to detach from the mass of general events the particular influence of one man or of a few men. In the former case, the historian is soon wearied by the toil; his mind loses itself in this labyrinth; and, in his inability clearly to discern or conspicuously to point out the influence of individuals, he denies that they have any. He prefers talking about the characteristics of race, the physical conformation of the country, or the genius of civilization,—which abridges his own labors, and satisfies his reader better at less cost.

M. de Lafayette says somewhere in his Memoirs, that the exaggerated system of general causes affords surprising consolations to second-rate statesmen. I will add, that its effects are not less consolatory to second-rate historians; it can always furnish a few mighty reasons to extricate them from the most difficult part of their work, and it indulges the indolence or incapacity of their minds, whilst it confers upon them the honors of deep thinking.

For myself, I am of opinion that, at all times, one great portion of the events of this world is attributable to very general facts, and another to special influences. These two kinds of cause are always in operation; their proportion only varies. General facts serve to explain more things in democratic than in aristocratic ages, and fewer things are then assignable to individual influences. During periods of aristocracy, the reverse takes place: special influences are stronger, general causes weaker; unless, indeed, we consider as a general cause the fact itself of the inequality of condition, which allows some individuals to baffle the natural tendencies of all the rest.

The historians who seek to describe what occurs in democratic societies are right, therefore, in assigning much to general causes, and in devoting their chief attention to discover them; but they are wrong in wholly denying the special influence of individuals, because they cannot easily trace or follow it.

The historians who live in democratic ages are not only prone to assign a great cause to every incident, but they are also given to connect incidents together so as to deduce a system from them. In aristocratic ages, as the attention of historians is constantly drawn to individuals, the connection of events escapes them; or, rather, they do not believe in any such connection. To them, the clew of history seems every instant crossed and broken by the step of man. In democratic ages, on the contrary, as the historian sees much more of actions than of actors, he may easily establish some kind of sequence and methodical order amongst the former.

Ancient literature, which is so rich in fine historical compositions, does not contain a single great historical system, whilst the poorest of modern literatures abound with them. It would appear that the ancient historians did not make sufficient use of those general theories which our historical writers are ever ready to carry to excess.

Those who write in democratic ages have another more dangerous tendency. When the traces of individual action upon nations are lost, it often happens that the world goes on to move, though the moving agent is no longer discoverable. As it becomes extremely difficult to discern and analyze the reasons which, acting separately on the will of each member of the community, concur in the end to produce movement in the whole mass, men are led to believe that this movement is involuntary, and that societies unconsciously obey some superior force ruling over them. But even when the general fact which governs the private volition of all individuals is supposed to be discovered upon the earth, the principle of human free-will is not secured. A cause sufficiently extensive to affect millions of men at once, and sufficiently strong to bend them all together in the same direction, may well seem irresistible: having seen that mankind do yield to it, the mind is close upon the inference that mankind cannot resist it.

Historians who live in democratic ages, then, not only deny that the few have any power of acting upon the destiny of a people, but they deprive the people themselves of the power of modifying their own condition, and they subject them either to an inflexible Providence or to some blind necessity. According to them, each nation is indissolubly bound by its position, its origin, its antecedents, and its character, to a certain lot which no efforts can ever change. They involve generation in generation, and thus, going back from age to age, and from necessity to necessity, up to the origin of the world, they forge a close and enormous chain, which girds and binds the human race. To their minds it is not enough to show what events have occurred: they would fain show that events could not have occurred otherwise. They take a nation arrived at a certain stage of its history, and they affirm that it could not but follow the track which brought it thither. It is easier to make such an assertion than to show how the nation might have adopted a better course.

In reading the historians of aristocratic ages, and especially those of antiquity, it would seem that, to be master of his lot and to govern his fellow-creatures, man requires only to be master of himself. In perusing the historical volumes which our age has produced, it would seem that man is utterly powerless over himself and over all around him. The historians of antiquity taught how to command: those of our time teach only how to obey; in their writings the author often appears great, but humanity is always diminutive.

If this doctrine of necessity, which is so attractive to those who write history in democratic ages, passes from authors to their readers, till it infects the whole mass of the community and gets possession of the public mind, it will soon paralyze the activity of modern society, and reduce Christians to the level of the Turks.

I would moreover observe, that such doctrines are peculiarly dangerous at the period at which we are arrived. Our contemporaries are but too prone to doubt of human free-will, because each of them feels himself confined on every side by his own weakness; but they are still willing to acknowledge the strength and independence of men united in society. Let not this principle be lost sight of; for the great object in our time is to raise the faculties of men, not to complete their prostration.

BOOK II

☆

INFLUENCE OF DEMOCRACY ON THE FEELINGS
OF THE AMERICANS

26. Why Democratic Nations Show a More Ardent and Enduring Love of Equality Than of Liberty.

THE first and most intense passion which is produced by equality of condition is, I need hardly say, the love of that equality. My readers will therefore not be surprised that I speak of this feeling before all others.

Everybody has remarked that, in our time, and especially in France, this passion for equality is every day gaining ground in the human heart. It has been said a hundred times, that our contemporaries are far more ardently and tenaciously attached to equality than to freedom; but, as I do not find that the causes of the fact have been sufficiently analyzed, I shall endeavor to point them out.

It is possible to imagine an extreme point at which freedom and equality would meet and be confounded together. Let us suppose that all the people take a part in the government, and that each one of them has an equal right to take a part in it. As no one is different from his fellows, none can exercise a tyrannical power; men will be perfectly free, because they are all entirely equal; and they will all be perfectly equal, because they are entirely free. To this ideal state democratic nations tend. This is the only complete form that equality can assume upon earth; but there are a thousand others which, without being equally perfect, are not less cherished by those nations.

The principle of equality may be established in civil society, without prevailing in the political world. Equal rights may exist of indulging in the same pleasures, of entering the same professions, of frequenting the same places; in a word, of living in the same manner and seeking wealth by the same means,—although all men do not take an equal share in the government. A kind of equality may even be established in the political world, though there should be no political freedom there. A man may be the equal of all his countrymen save one, who is the master of all without distinction, and who selects equally from among them all the agents of his power. Several other combinations might be easily imagined, by which very great equality would be united to institutions more or less free, or even to institutions wholly without freedom.

Although men cannot become absolutely equal unless they are entirely free; and consequently equality, pushed to its furthest extent, may be confounded with freedom, yet there is good reason for distinguishing the one from the other. The taste which men have for liberty, and that which they feel for equality, are, in fact, two different things; and I am not afraid to add, that, amongst democratic nations, they are two unequal things.

Upon close inspection, it will be seen that there is in every age some peculiar and preponderating fact with which all others are connected; this fact almost always gives birth to some pregnant idea or some ruling passion, which attracts to itself and bears away in its course all the feelings and opinions of the time: it is like a great stream, towards which each of the neighboring rivulets seems to flow.

Freedom has appeared in the world at different times and under various forms; it has not been exclusively bound to any social condition, and it is not confined to democracies. Freedom cannot, therefore, form the distinguishing characteristic of democratic ages. The peculiar and preponderating fact which marks those ages as its own is the equality of condition; the ruling passion of men in those periods is the love of this equality. Ask not what singular charm the men of democratic ages find in being equal, or what special reasons they may have for clinging so tenaciously to equality rather than to the other advantages which society holds out to them: equality is the distinguishing characteristic of the age they live in; that, of itself, is enough to explain that they prefer it to all the rest.

But independently of this reason, there are several others, which will at all times habitually lead men to prefer equality to freedom.

If a people could ever succeed in destroying, or even in diminishing, the equality which prevails in its own body, they could do so only by long and laborious efforts. Their social condition must be modified, their laws abolished, their opinions superseded, their habits changed, their manners corrupted. But political liberty is more easily lost; to neglect to hold it fast, is to allow it to escape. Men therefore cling to equality

Democracy in America ☆ PART II / Book Two 191

not only because it is dear to them; they also adhere to it because they think it will last forever.

That political freedom may compromise in its excesses the tranquillity, the property, the lives of individuals, is obvious even to narrow and unthinking minds. On the contrary, none but attentive and clear-sighted men perceive the perils with which equality threatens us, and they commonly avoid pointing them out. They know that the calamities they apprehend are remote, and flatter themselves that they will only fall upon future generations, for which the present generation takes but little thought. The evils which freedom sometimes brings with it are immediate; they are apparent to all, and all are more or less affected by them. The evils which extreme equality may produce are slowly disclosed; they creep gradually into the social frame; they are seen only at intervals; and at the moment at which they become most violent, habit already causes them to be no longer felt.

The advantages which freedom brings are only shown by the lapse of time; and it is always easy to mistake the cause in which they originate. The advantages of equality are immediate, and they may always be traced from their source.

Political liberty bestows exalted pleasures, from time to time, upon a certain number of citizens. Equality every day confers a number of small enjoyments on every man. The charms of equality are every instant felt, and are within the reach of all; the noblest hearts are not insensible to them, and the most vulgar souls exult in them. The passion which equality creates must therefore be at once strong and general. Men cannot enjoy political liberty unpurchased by some sacrifices, and they never obtain it without great exertions. But the pleasures of equality are self-proffered: each of the petty incidents of life seems to occasion them; and in order to taste them, nothing is required but to live.

Democratic nations are at all times fond of equality, but there are certain epochs at which the passion they entertain for it swells to the height of fury. This occurs at the moment when the old social system, long menaced, is overthrown after a severe intestine struggle, and the barriers of rank are at length thrown down. At such times, men pounce upon equality as their booty, and they cling to it as to some precious treasure which they fear to lose. The passion for equality penetrates on every side into men's hearts, expands there, and fills them entirely. Tell them not that, by this blind surrender of themselves to an exclusive passion, they risk their dearest interests: they are deaf. Show them not freedom escaping from their grasp, whilst they are looking another way: they are blind, or, rather, they can discern but one object to be desired in the universe.

What I have said is applicable to all democratic nations; what I am about to say concerns the French alone. Amongst most modern nations, and especially amongst all those of the continent of Europe, the taste and the idea of freedom only began to exist and to be developed at the time when social conditions were tending to equality, and as a consequence of that very equality. Absolute kings were the most efficient levellers of ranks amongst their subjects. Amongst these nations, equality preceded freedom: equality was therefore a fact of some standing when freedom was still a novelty; the one had already created customs, opinions, and laws belonging to it, when the other, alone and for the first time, came into actual existence. Thus the latter was still only an affair of opinion and of taste, whilst the former had already crept into the habits of the people, possessed itself of their manners, and given a particular turn to the smallest actions in their lives. Can it be wondered at that the men of our own time prefer the one to the other?

I think that democratic communities have a natural taste for freedom: left to themselves, they will seek it, cherish it, and view any privation of it with regret. But for equality, their passion is ardent, insatiable, incessant, invincible: they call for equality in freedom; and if they cannot obtain that, they still call for equality in slavery. They will endure poverty, servitude, barbarism; but they will not endure aristocracy.

This is true at all times, and especially in our own day. All men and all powers seeking to cope with this irresistible passion will be overthrown and destroyed by it. In our age, freedom cannot be established without it, and despotism itself cannot reign without its support.

27. Of Individualism in Democratic Countries.

I HAVE shown how it is that, in ages of equality, every man seeks for his opinions within himself: I am now to show how it is that, in the same ages, all his feelings are turned towards himself alone. *Individualism* is a novel expression, to which a novel idea has given birth. Our fathers were only acquainted with *égoïsme* (selfishness). Selfishness is a passionate and exaggerated love of self, which leads a man to connect everything with himself, and to prefer himself to everything in the world. Individualism is a mature and calm feeling, which disposes each member of the community to sever himself from the mass of his fellows, and to draw apart with his family and his friends; so that, after he has thus formed a little circle of his own, he willingly leaves society at large to itself. Selfishness originates in blind instinct: individualism proceeds from erroneous judgment more than from depraved feelings; it originates as much in deficiencies of mind as in perversity of heart.

Selfishness blights the germ of all virtue: individualism, at first, only saps the virtues of public life; but, in the long run, it attacks and destroys all others, and is at length absorbed in downright selfishness. Selfishness is a vice as old as the world, which does not belong to one form of society more than to another: individualism is of democratic origin, and it threatens to spread in the same ratio as the equality of condition.

Amongst aristocratic nations, as families remain for centuries in the same condition, often on the same spot, all generations become, as it were, contemporaneous. A man almost always knows his forefathers, and respects them: he thinks he already sees his remote descendants, and he loves them. He willingly imposes duties on himself towards the former and the latter; and he will frequently sacrifice his personal gratifications to those who went before and to those who will come after him. Aristocratic institutions have, moreover, the effect of closely binding every man to several of his fellow-citizens. As the classes of an aristocratic people are strongly marked and permanent, each of them is regarded by its own members as a sort of lesser country, more tangible and more cherished than the country at large. As, in aristocratic communities, all the citizens occupy fixed positions, one above the other, the result is, that each of them always sees a man above himself whose patronage is necessary to him, and, below himself, another man whose co-operation he may claim. Men living in aristocratic ages are therefore almost always closely attached to something placed out of their own sphere, and they are often disposed to forget themselves. It is true that, in these ages, the notion of human fellowship is faint, and that men seldom think of sacrificing themselves for mankind; but they often sacrifice themselves for other men. In democratic times, on the contrary, when the duties of each individual to the race are much more clear, devoted service to any one man becomes more rare; the bond of human affection is extended, but it is relaxed.

Amongst democratic nations, new families are constantly

springing up, others are constantly falling away, and all that remain change their condition; the woof of time is every instant broken, and the track of generations effaced. Those who went before are soon forgotten; of those who will come after, no one has any idea: the interest of man is confined to those in close propinquity to himself. As each class approximates to other classes, and intermingles with them, its members become indifferent, and as strangers to one another. Aristocracy had made a chain of all the members of the community, from the peasant to the king: democracy breaks that chain, and severs every link of it.

As social conditions become more equal, the number of persons increases who, although they are neither rich nor powerful enough to exercise any great influence over their fellows, have nevertheless acquired or retained sufficient education and fortune to satisfy their own wants. They owe nothing to any man, they expect nothing from any man; they acquire the habit of always considering themselves as standing alone, and they are apt to imagine that their whole destiny is in their own hands.

Thus, not only does democracy make every man forget his ancestors, but it hides his descendants and separates his contemporaries from him; it throws him back forever upon himself alone, and threatens in the end to confine him entirely within the solitude of his own heart.

28. *That the Americans Combat the Effects of Individualism by Free Institutions.*

DESPOTISM, which is of a very timorous nature, is never more secure of continuance than when it can keep men asunder; and all its influence is commonly exerted for that purpose. No vice of the human heart is so acceptable to it as selfishness: a despot easily forgives his subjects for not loving him, provided they do not love each other. He does not ask them to assist him in governing the state; it is enough that they do not aspire to govern it themselves. He stigmatizes as turbulent and unruly spirits those who would combine their exertions to promote the prosperity of the community; and, perverting the natural meaning of words, he applauds as good citizens those who have no sympathy for any but themselves.

Thus the vices which despotism produces are precisely those which equality fosters. These two things mutually and perniciously complete and assist each other. Equality places men side by side, unconnected by any common tie; despotism raises barriers to keep them asunder: the former predisposes them not to consider their fellow-creatures, the latter makes general indifference a sort of public virtue.

Despotism, then, which is at all times dangerous, is more particularly to be feared in democratic ages. It is easy to see that in those same ages men stand most in need of freedom. When the members of a community are forced to attend to public affairs, they are necessarily drawn from the circle of their own interests, and snatched at times from self-observation. As soon as a man begins to treat of public affairs in public, he begins to perceive that he is not so independent of his fellow-men as he had at first imagined, and that, in order to obtain their support, he must often lend them his co-operation.

When the public govern, there is no man who does not feel the value of public good-will, or who does not endeavor to court it by drawing to himself the esteem and affection of those amongst whom he is to live. Many of the passions which congeal and keep asunder human hearts, are then obliged to retire and hide below the surface. Pride must be dissembled; disdain dares not break out; selfishness fears its own self. Under a free government, as most public offices are elective, the men whose elevated minds or aspiring hopes are too closely circumscribed in private life constantly feel that they cannot do without the people who surround them. Men learn at such times to think of their fellow-men from ambitious motives; and they frequently find it, in a manner, their interest to forget themselves.

I may here be met by an objection derived from electioneering intrigues, the meanness of candidates, and the calumnies of their opponents. These are occasions of enmity which occur the oftener, the more frequent elections become. Such evils are doubtless great, but they are transient; whereas the benefits which attend them remain. The desire of being elected may lead some men for a time to violent hostility; but this same desire leads all men in the long run mutually to support each other; and, if it happens that an election accidentally severs two friends, the electoral system brings a multitude of citizens permanently together, who would otherwise always have remained unknown to each other. Freedom produces private animosities, but despotism gives birth to general indifference.

The Americans have combated by free institutions the tendency of equality to keep men asunder, and they have subdued it. The legislators of America did not suppose that a general

representation of the whole nation would suffice to ward off
a disorder at once so natural to the frame of democratic
society, and so fatal: they also thought that it would be well
to infuse political life into each portion of the territory, in
order to multiply to an infinite extent opportunities of acting
in concert for all the members of the community, and to make
them constantly feel their mutual dependence on each other.
The plan was a wise one. The general affairs of a country only
engage the attention of leading politicians, who assemble from
time to time in the same places; and, as they often lose sight
of each other afterwards, no lasting ties are established between
them. But if the object be to have the local affairs of a district
conducted by the men who reside there, the same persons are
always in contact, and they are, in a manner, forced to be
acquainted, and to adapt themselves to one another.

It is difficult to draw a man out of his own circle to interest
him in the destiny of the state, because he does not clearly
understand what influence the destiny of the state can have
upon his own lot. But if it be proposed to make a road cross
the end of his estate, he will see at a glance that there is a
connection between this small public affair and his greatest
private affairs; and he will discover, without its being shown
to him, the close tie which unites private to general interest.
Thus, far more may be done by intrusting to the citizens the
administration of minor affairs than by surrendering to them
the control of important ones, towards interesting them in the
public welfare, and convincing them that they constantly
stand in need one of another in order to provide for it. A
brilliant achievement may win for you the favor of a people
at one stroke; but to earn the love and respect of the population
which surrounds you, a long succession of little services rendered and of obscure good deeds,—a constant habit of kindness, and an established reputation for disinterestedness,—
will be required. Local freedom, then, which leads a great
number of citizens to value the affection of their neighbors
and of their kindred, perpetually brings men together, and
forces them to help one another, in spite of the propensities
which sever them.

In the United States, the more opulent citizens take great
care not to stand aloof from the people; on the contrary, they
constantly keep on easy terms with the lower classes: they
listen to them, they speak to them every day. They know that
the rich in democracies always stand in need of the poor; and
that, in democratic times, you attach a poor man to you more
by your manner than by benefits conferred. The magnitude
of such benefits, which sets off the difference of condition,

causes a secret irritation to those who reap advantage from them; but the charm of simplicity of manners is almost irresistible: affability carries men away, and even want of polish is not always displeasing. This truth does not take root at once in the minds of the rich. They generally resist it as long as the democratic revolution lasts, and they do not acknowledge it immediately after that revolution is accomplished. They are very ready to do good to the people, but they still choose to keep them at arm's length; they think that is sufficient, but they are mistaken. They might spend fortunes thus without warming the hearts of the population around them;—that population does not ask them for the sacrifice of their money, but of their pride.

It would seem as if every imagination in the United States were upon the stretch to invent means of increasing the wealth and satisfying the wants of the public. The best-informed inhabitants of each district constantly use their information to discover new truths which may augment the general prosperity; and, if they have made any such discoveries, they eagerly surrender them to the mass of the people.

When the vices and weaknesses frequently exhibited by those who govern in America are closely examined, the prosperity of the people occasions, but improperly occasions, surprise. Elected magistrates do not make the American democracy flourish; it flourishes because the magistrates are elective.

It would be unjust to suppose that the patriotism and the zeal which every American displays for the welfare of his fellow-citizens are wholly insincere. Although private interest directs the greater part of human actions in the United States, as well as elsewhere, it does not regulate them all. I must say that I have often seen Americans make great and real sacrifices to the public welfare; and I have remarked a hundred instances in which they hardly ever failed to lend faithful support to each other. The free institutions which the inhabitants of the United States possess, and the political rights of which they make so much use, remind every citizen, and in a thousand ways, that he lives in society. They every instant impress upon his mind the notion that it is the duty, as well as the interest, of men to make themselves useful to their fellow-creatures; and as he sees no particular ground of animosity to them, since he is never either their master or their slave, his heart readily leans to the side of kindness. Men attend to the interests of the public, first by necessity, afterwards by choice: what was intentional becomes an instinct; and by dint of working for the good of one's fellow-citizens, the habit and the taste for serving them is at length acquired.

Many people in France consider equality of condition as
one evil, and political freedom as a second. When they are
obliged to yield to the former, they strive at least to escape
from the latter. But I contend that, in order to combat the
evils which equality may produce, there is only one effectual
remedy,—namely, political freedom.

29. Of the Use Which the Americans Make of Public Associations in Civil Life.

I DO not propose to speak of those political associations by the
aid of which men endeavor to defend themselves against the
despotic action of a majority, or against the aggressions of
regal power. That subject I have already treated. If each
citizen did not learn, in proportion as he individually becomes
more feeble, and consequently more incapable of preserving
his freedom single-handed, to combine with his fellow-citizens
for the purpose of defending it, it is clear that tyranny would
unavoidably increase together with equality.

Those associations only which are formed in civil life,
without reference to political objects, are here adverted to. The
political associations which exist in the United States are only
a single feature in the midst of the immense assemblage of
associations in that country. Americans of all ages, all conditions, and all dispositions, constantly form associations. They
have not only commercial and manufacturing companies, in
which all take part, but associations of a thousand other kinds,
—religious, moral, serious, futile, general or restricted, enormous or diminutive. The Americans make associations to give
entertainments, to found seminaries, to build inns, to construct
churches, to diffuse books, to send missionaries to the antipodes; they found in this manner hospitals, prisons, and schools.
If it be proposed to inculcate some truth, or to foster some
feeling by the encouragement of a great example, they form
a society. Wherever, at the head of some new undertaking, you
see the government in France, or a man of rank in England,
in the United States you will be sure to find an association.

I met with several kinds of associations in America of
which I confess I had no previous notion; and I have often
admired the extreme skill with which the inhabitants of the
United States succeed in proposing a common object to the
exertions of a great many men, and in inducing them voluntarily to pursue it.

I have since travelled over England, whence the Americans have taken some of their laws and many of their customs; and it seemed to me that the principle of association was by no means so constantly or adroitly used in that country. The English often perform great things singly, whereas the Americans form associations for the smallest undertakings. It is evident that the former people consider association as a powerful means of action, but the latter seem to regard it as the only means they have of acting.

Thus, the most democratic country on the face of the earth is that in which men have, in our time, carried to the highest perfection the art of pursuing in common the object of their common desires, and have applied this new science to the greatest number of purposes. Is this the result of accident? or is there in reality any necessary connection between the principle of association and that of equality?

Aristocratic communities always contain, amongst a multitude of persons who by themselves are powerless, a small number of powerful and wealthy citizens, each of whom can achieve great undertakings single-handed. In aristocratic societies, men do not need to combine in order to act, because they are strongly held together. Every wealthy and powerful citizen constitutes the head of a permanent and compulsory association, composed of all those who are dependent upon him, or whom he makes subservient to the execution of his designs.

Amongst democratic nations, on the contrary, all the citizens are independent and feeble; they can do hardly anything by themselves, and none of them can oblige his fellow-men to lend him their assistance. They all, therefore, become powerless, if they do not learn voluntarily to help each other. If men living in democratic countries had no right and no inclination to associate for political purposes, their independence would be in great jeopardy; but they might long preserve their wealth and their cultivation: whereas, if they never acquired the habit of forming associations in ordinary life, civilization itself would be endangered. A people amongst whom individuals should lose the power of achieving great things single-handed, without acquiring the means of producing them by united exertions, would soon relapse into barbarism.

Unhappily, the same social condition which renders associations so necessary to democratic nations, renders their formation more difficult amongst those nations than amongst all other. When several members of an aristocracy agree to combine, they easily succeed in doing so: as each of them brings great strength to the partnership, the number of its members may be very limited; and when the members of an association are limited in number, they may easily become mutually acquainted, understand each other, and establish fixed regulations. The same opportunities do not occur amongst democratic nations, where the associated members must always be very numerous for their association to have any power.

I am aware that many of my countrymen are not in the least embarrassed by this difficulty. They contend, that, the more enfeebled and incompetent the citizens become, the more able and active the government ought to be rendered, in order that society at large may execute what individuals can no longer accomplish. They believe this answers the whole difficulty, but I think they are mistaken.

A government might perform the part of some of the largest American companies; and several States, members of the Union, have already attempted it; but what political power could ever carry on the vast multitude of lesser undertakings which the American citizens perform every day, with the assistance of the principle of association? It is easy to foresee that the time is drawing near when man will be less and less able to produce, of himself alone, the commonest necessaries of life. The task of the governing power will therefore perpetually increase, and its very efforts will extend it every day. The more it stands in the place of associations, the more will individuals, losing the notion of combining together, require its assistance: these are causes and effects which unceasingly create each other. Will the administration of the country ultimately assume the management of all the manufactures which no single citizen is able to carry on? And if a time at length arrives when, in consequence of the extreme subdivision of landed property, the soil is split into an infinite number of parcels, so that it can only be cultivated by companies of husbandmen, will it be necessary that the head of the government should leave the helm of state to follow the plough? The morals and the intelligence of a democratic people would be as much endangered as its business and manufactures, if the government ever wholly usurped the place of private companies.

Feelings and opinions are recruited, the heart is enlarged, and the human mind is developed, only by the reciprocal influence of men upon each other. I have shown that these influences are almost null in democratic countries; they must therefore be artificially created, and this can only be accomplished by associations.

When the members of an aristocratic community adopt a new opinion, or conceive a new sentiment, they give it a station, as it were, beside themselves, upon the lofty platform where they stand; and opinions or sentiments so conspicuous to the eyes of the multitude are easily introduced into the minds or hearts of all around. In democratic countries, the governing power alone is naturally in a condition to act in this manner; but it is easy to see that its action is always inadequate, and often dangerous. A government can no more be competent to keep alive and to renew the circulation of opinions and feelings amongst a great people, than to manage all the speculations of productive industry. No sooner does a government attempt to go beyond its political sphere, and to enter upon this new track, than it exercises, even unintentionally, an insupportable tyranny; for a government can only dictate strict rules, the opinions which it favors are rigidly enforced, and it is never easy to discriminate between its advice and its commands. Worst still will be the case, if the government really believes itself interested in preventing all circulation of ideas; it will then stand motionless and oppressed by the heaviness of voluntary torpor. Governments, therefore, should not be the only active powers: associations ought, in democratic nations, to stand in lieu of those powerful private individuals whom the equality of conditions has swept away.

As soon as several of the inhabitants of the United States have taken up an opinion or a feeling which they wish to promote in the world, they look out for mutual assistance; and as soon as they have found each other out, they combine. From that moment they are no longer isolated men, but a power seen from afar, whose actions serve for an example, and whose language is listened to. The first time I heard in the United States that a hundred thousand men had bound themselves publicly to abstain from spirituous liquors, it appeared to me more like a joke than a serious engagement; and I did not at once perceive why these temperate citizens could not content themselves with drinking water by their own firesides. I at last understood that these hundred thousand Americans, alarmed by the progress of drunkenness around them, had made up their minds to patronize temperance. They acted just in the same way as a man of high rank who should dress very plainly, in order to inspire the humbler orders with a contempt of luxury. It is probable that, if these hundred thousand men had lived in France, each of them would singly have memorialized the government to watch the public houses all over the kingdom.

Nothing, in my opinion, is more deserving of our attention than the intellectual and moral associations of America. The political and industrial associations of that country strike us forcibly; but the others elude our observation, or, if we discover them, we understand them imperfectly, because we have hardly ever seen anything of the kind. It must, however, be acknowledged, that they are as necessary to the American people as the former, and perhaps more so. In democratic countries, the science of association is the mother of science; the progress of all the rest depends upon the progress it has made.

Amongst the laws which rule human societies, there is one which seems to be more precise and clear than all others. If men are to remain civilized, or to become so, the art of associating together must grow and improve in the same ratio in which the equality of conditions is increased.

30. Of the Relation Between Public Associations and the Newspapers.

WHEN men are no longer united amongst themselves by firm and lasting ties, it is impossible to obtain the co-operation of any great number of them, unless you can persuade every man whose help you require that his private interest obliges him voluntarily to unite his exertions to the exertions of all the others. This can be habitually and conveniently effected only by means of a newspaper: nothing but a newspaper can drop the same thought into a thousand minds at the same moment. A newspaper is an adviser who does not require to be sought, but who comes of his own accord, and talks to you briefly every day of the common weal, without distracting you from your private affairs.

Newspapers therefore become more necessary in proportion as men become more equal, and individualism more to be feared. To suppose that they only serve to protect freedom would be to diminish their importance: they maintain civilization. I shall not deny that, in democratic countries, newspapers frequently lead the citizens to launch together into very ill-digested schemes; but if there were no newspapers, there would be no common activity. The evil which they produce is therefore much less than that which they cure.

The effect of a newspaper is not only to suggest the same purpose to a great number of persons, but to furnish means for executing in common the designs which they may have singly conceived. The principal citizens who inhabit an aristocratic country discern each other from afar; and if they wish to unite their forces, they move towards each other, drawing a multitude of men after them. It frequently happens, on the contrary, in democratic countries, that a great number of men who wish or who want to combine cannot accomplish it, because, as they are very insignificant and lost amidst the crowd, they cannot see, and know not where to find, one another. A newspaper then takes up the notion or the feeling which had occurred simultaneously, but singly, to each of them. All are then immediately guided towards this beacon; and these wandering minds, which had long sought each other in darkness, at length meet and unite. The newspaper brought them together, and the newspaper is still necessary to keep them united.

In order that an association amongst a democratic people should have any power, it must be a numerous body. The persons of whom it is composed are therefore scattered over a wide extent, and each of them is detained in the place of his domicile by the narrowness of his income, or by the small unremitting exertions by which he earns it. Means must then be found to converse every day without seeing each other, and to take steps in common without having met. Thus, hardly any democratic association can do without newspapers.

There is, consequently, a necessary connection between public associations and newspapers: newspapers make associations, and associations make newspapers; and if it has been correctly advanced, that associations will increase in number as the conditions of men become more equal, it is not less certain that the number of newspapers increases in proportion to that of associations. Thus it is, in America, that we find at the same time the greatest number of associations and of newspapers.

This connection between the number of newspapers and that of associations leads us to the discovery of a further connection between the state of the periodical press and the form of the administration in a country, and shows that the number of newspapers must diminish or increase amongst a democratic people, in proportion as its administration is more or less centralized. For, amongst democratic nations, the exercise of local powers cannot be intrusted to the principal members of the community, as in aristocracies. Those powers must either be abolished, or placed in the hands of very large numbers of men, who then in fact constitute an association permanently established by law, for the purpose of administering the affairs of a certain extent of territory; and they require a journal, to bring to them every day, in the midst of their own minor concerns, some intelligence of the state of their public weal. The more numerous local powers are, the

greater is the number of men in whom they are vested by law;
and as this want is hourly felt, the more profusely do newspapers abound.

The extraordinary subdivision of administrative power has
much more to do with the enormous number of American
newspapers, than the great political freedom of the country
and the absolute liberty of the press. If all the inhabitants of
the Union had the suffrage,—but a suffrage which should
extend only to the choice of their legislators in Congress,—
they would require but few newspapers, because they would
have to act together only on very important, but very rare,
occasions. But within the great national association, lesser
associations have been established by law in every county,
every city, and indeed in every village, for the purposes of local
administration. The laws of the country thus compel every
American to co-operate every day of his life with some of his
fellow-citizens for a common purpose, and each one of them
requires a newspaper to inform him what all the others are
doing.

I am of opinion that a democratic people, without any
national representative assemblies, but with a great number
of small local powers, would have in the end more newspapers
than another people governed by a centralized administration
and an elective legislature. What best explains to me the
enormous circulation of the daily press in the United States
is, that, amongst the Americans, I find the utmost national
freedom combined with local freedom of every kind.

There is a prevailing opinion in France and England, that
the circulation of newspapers would be indefinitely increased
by removing the taxes which have been laid upon the press.
This is a very exaggerated estimate of the effects of such a
reform. Newspapers increase in numbers, not according to
their cheapness, but according to the more or less frequent
want which a great number of men may feel for intercommuni-
cation and combination.

In like manner, I should attribute the increasing influence
of the daily press to causes more general than those by which
it is commonly explained. A newspaper can only subsist on
the condition of publishing sentiments or principles common
to a large number of men. A newspaper, therefore, always
represents an association which is composed of its habitual
readers. This association may be more or less defined, more
or less restricted, more or less numerous; but the fact that the
newspaper keeps alive, is a proof that at least the germ of such
an association exists in the minds of its readers.

This leads me to a last reflection, with which I shall conclude this chapter. The more equal the conditions of men become, and the less strong men individually are the more easily do they give way to the current of the multitude, and the more difficult it is for them to adhere by themselves to an opinion which the multitude discard. A newspaper represents an association; it may be said to address each of its readers in the name of all the others, and to exert its influence over them in proportion to their individual weakness. The power of the newspaper press must therefore increase as the social conditions of men become more equal.

31. Relation of Civil to Political Associations.

THERE is only one country on the face of the earth where the citizens enjoy unlimited freedom of association for political purposes. This same country is the only one in the world where the continual exercise of the right of association has been introduced into civil life, and where all the advantages which civilization can confer are procured by means of it.

In all the countries where political associations are prohibited, civil associations are rare. It is hardly probable that this is the result of accident; but the inference should rather be, that there is a natural, and perhaps a necessary, connection between these two kinds of associations.

Certain men happen to have a common interest in some concern; either a commercial undertaking is to be managed, or some speculation in manufactures to be tried: they meet, they combine, and thus, by degrees, they become familiar with the principle of association. The greater the multiplicity of small affairs, the more do men, even without knowing it, acquire facility in prosecuting great undertakings in common.

Civil associations, therefore, facilitate political association; but, on the other hand, political association singularly strengthens and improves associations for civil purposes. In civil life, every man may, strictly speaking, fancy that he can provide for his own wants; in politics, he can fancy no such thing. When a people, then, have any knowledge of public life, the notion of association, and the wish to coalesce, present themselves every day to the minds of the whole community: whatever natural repugnance may restrain men from acting in concert, they will always be ready to combine for the sake of a party. Thus political life makes the love and practice of association more general; it imparts a desire of union, and teaches the means of combination to numbers of men who otherwise would have always lived apart.

Politics not only give birth to numerous associations, but to associations of great extent. In civil life, it seldom happens that any one interest draws a very large number of men to act in concert; much skill is required to bring such an interest into existence: but in politics, opportunities present themselves every day. Now it is solely in great associations that the general value of the principle of association is displayed. Citizens who are individually powerless do not very clearly anticipate the strength which they may acquire by uniting together; it must be shown to them in order to be understood. Hence it is often easier to collect a multitude for a public purpose than a few persons; a thousand citizens do not see what interest they have in combining together; ten thousand will be perfectly aware of it. In politics, men combine for great undertakings; and the use they make of the principle of association in important affairs practically teaches them that it is their interest to help each other in those of less moment. A political association draws a number of individuals at the same time out of their own circle; however they may be naturally kept asunder by age, mind, and fortune, it places them nearer together, and brings them into contact. Once met, they can always meet again.

Men can embark in few civil partnerships without risking a portion of their possessions; this is the case with all manufacturing and trading companies. When men are as yet but little versed in the art of association, and are unacquainted with its principal rules, they are afraid, when first they combine in this manner, of buying their experience dear. They therefore prefer depriving themselves of a powerful instrument of success, to running the risks which attend the use of it. They are, however, less reluctant to join political associations, which appear to them to be without danger, because they adventure no money in them. But they cannot belong to these associations for any length of time, without finding out how order is maintained amongst a large number of men, and by what contrivance they are made to advance, harmoniously and methodically, to the same object. Thus they learn to surrender their own will to that of all the rest, and to make their own exertions subordinate to the common impulse,—things which it is not less necessary to know in civil than in political associations. Political associations may therefore be considered as large free schools, where all the members of the community go to learn the general theory of association.

But even if political association did not directly contribute to the progress of civil association, to destroy the former would be to impair the latter. When citizens can only meet in public for certain purposes, they regard such meetings as a strange proceeding of rare occurrence, and they rarely think at all about it. When they are allowed to meet freely for all purposes, they ultimately look upon public association as the universal, or in a manner the sole, means which men can employ to accomplish the different purposes they may have in view. Every new want instantly revives the notion. The art of association then becomes, as I have said before, the mother of action, studied and applied by all.

When some kinds of associations are prohibited and others allowed, it is difficult to distinguish the former from the latter beforehand. In this state of doubt, men abstain from them altogether, and a sort of public opinion passes current, which tends to cause any association whatsoever to be regarded as a bold, and almost an illicit enterprise.

It is therefore chimerical to suppose that the spirit of association, when it is repressed on some one point, will nevertheless display the same vigor on all others; and that, if men be allowed to prosecute certain undertakings in common, that is quite enough for them eagerly to set about them. When the members of a community are allowed and accustomed to combine for all purposes, they will combine as readily for the lesser as for the more important ones; but if they are only allowed to combine for small affairs, they will be neither inclined nor able to effect it. It is in vain that you will leave them entirely free to prosecute their business on joint-stock account: they will hardly care to avail themselves of the rights you have granted to them; and, after having exhausted your strength in vain efforts to put down prohibited associations, you will be surprised that you cannot persuade men to form the associations you encourage.

I do not say that there can be no civil associations in a country where political association is prohibited; for men can never live in society without embarking in some common undertakings: but I maintain that, in such a country, civil associations will always be few in number, feebly planned, unskilfully managed, that they will never form any vast designs, or that they will fail in the execution of them.

This naturally leads me to think that freedom of association in political matters is not so dangerous to public tranquillity as is supposed; and that possibly, after having agitated society for some time, it may strengthen the state in the end. In democratic countries, political associations are, so to speak, the only powerful persons who aspire to rule the state. Accordingly, the governments of our time look upon associations of this kind just as sovereigns in the Middle Ages regarded the great vassals of the crown: they entertain a sort of instinctive abhorrence of them, and combat them on all occasions. They bear, on the contrary, a natural good-will to civil associations, because they readily discover that, instead of directing the minds of the community to public affairs, these institutions serve to divert them from such reflections; and that, by engaging them more and more in the pursuit of objects which cannot be attained without public tranquillity, they deter them from revolutions. But these governments do not attend to the fact, that political associations tend amazingly to multiply and facilitate those of a civil character, and that, in avoiding a dangerous evil, they deprive themselves of an efficacious remedy.

When you see the Americans freely and constantly forming associations for the purpose of promoting some political principle, of raising one man to the head of affairs, or of wresting power from another, you have some difficulty in understanding how men so independent do not constantly fall into the abuse of freedom. If, on the other hand, you survey the infinite number of trading companies which are in operation in the United States, and perceive that the Americans are on every side unceasingly engaged in the execution of important and difficult plans, which the slightest revolution would throw into confusion, you will readily comprehend why people so well employed are by no means tempted to perturb the state, nor to destroy that public tranquillity by which they all profit.

Is it enough to observe these things separately, or should we not discover the hidden tie which connects them? In their political associations, the Americans, of all conditions, minds, and ages, daily acquire a general taste for association, and grow accustomed to the use of it. There they meet together in large numbers,—they converse, they listen to each other, and they are mutually stimulated to all sorts of undertakings. They afterwards transfer to civil life the notions they have thus acquired, and make them subservient to a thousand purposes. Thus it is by the enjoyment of a dangerous freedom that the Americans learn the art of rendering the dangers of freedom less formidable.

If a certain moment in the existence of a nation be selected, it is easy to prove that political associations perturb the state and paralyze productive industry; but take the whole life of a people, and it may perhaps be easy to demonstrate, that freedom of association in political matters is favorable to the prosperity, and even to the tranquillity, of the community.

I said in the former part of this work: "The unrestrained liberty of political association cannot be entirely assimilated to the liberty of the press. The one is at the same time less necessary and more dangerous than the other. A nation may confine it within certain limits, without ceasing to be mistress of itself; and it may sometimes be obliged to do so, in order to maintain its own authority." And, further on, I added: "It cannot be denied that the unrestrained liberty of association for political purposes is the last degree of liberty which a people is fit for. If it does not throw them into anarchy, it perpetually brings them, as it were, to the verge of it." Thus, I do not think that a nation is always at liberty to invest its citizens with an absolute right of association for political purposes; and I doubt whether, in any country or in any age, it be wise to set no limits to freedom of association.

A certain nation, it is said, could not maintain tranquillity in the community, cause the laws to be respected, or establish a lasting government, if the right of association were not confined within narrow limits. These blessings are doubtless invaluable; and I can imagine that, to acquire or to preserve them, a nation may impose upon itself severe temporary restrictions: but still it is well that the nation should know at what price these blessings are purchased. I can understand that it may be advisable to cut off a man's arm in order to save his life; but it would be ridiculous to assert that he will be as dexterous as he was before he lost it.

32. Of the Taste for Physical Well-Being in America.

IN AMERICA, the passion for physical well-being is not always exclusive, but it is general; and if all do not feel it in the same manner, yet it is felt by all. Carefully to satisfy even the least wants of the body, and to provide the little conveniences of life, is uppermost in every mind. Something of an analogous character is more and more apparent in Europe. Amongst the causes which produce these similar consequences in both hemispheres, several are so connected with my subject as to deserve notice.

When riches are hereditarily fixed in families, a great number of men enjoy the comforts of life without feeling an exclusive taste for those comforts. The heart of man is not so much caught by the undisturbed possession of anything valuable, as by the desire, as yet imperfectly satisfied, of possessing it, and by the incessant dread of losing it. In aristocratic communities, the wealthy, never having experienced a condition different from their own, entertain no fear of changing it; the existence of such conditions hardly occurs to them. The comforts of life are not to them the end of life, but simply a way of living; they regard them as existence itself,—enjoyed, but scarcely thought of. As the natural and instinctive taste which all men feel for being well off is thus satisfied without trouble and without apprehension, their faculties are turned elsewhere, and applied to more arduous and lofty undertakings, which excite and engross their minds.

Hence it is that, in the very midst of physical gratifications, the members of an aristocracy often display a haughty contempt of these very enjoyments, and exhibit singular powers of endurance under the privation of them. All the revolutions which have ever shaken or destroyed aristocracies have shown how easily men accustomed to superfluous luxuries can do without the necessaries of life; whereas men who have toiled to acquire a competency can hardly live after they have lost it.

If I turn my observation from the upper to the lower classes, I find analogous effects produced by opposite causes. Amongst a nation where aristocracy predominates in society, and keeps it stationary, the people in the end get as much accustomed to poverty as the rich to their opulence. The latter bestow no anxiety on their physical comforts, because they enjoy them without an effort; the former do not think of things which they despair of obtaining, and which they hardly know enough of to desire them. In communities of this kind, the imagination of the poor is driven to seek another world; the miseries of real life enclose it around, but it escapes from their control, and flies to seek its pleasures far beyond.

When, on the contrary, the distinctions of ranks are confounded together and privileges are destroyed,—when hereditary property is subdivided, and education and freedom widely diffused, the desire of acquiring the comforts of the world haunts the imagination of the poor, and the dread of losing them that of the rich. Many scanty fortunes spring up; those who possess them have a sufficient share of physical gratifications to conceive a taste for these pleasures,—not enough to satisfy it. They never procure them without exertion, and they never indulge in them without apprehension. They are therefore always straining to pursue or to retain gratifications so delightful, so imperfect, so fugitive.

If I were to inquire what passion is most natural to men

who are stimulated and circumscribed by the obscurity of their birth or the mediocrity of their fortune, I could discover none more peculiarly appropriate to their condition than this love of physical prosperity. The passion for physical comforts is essentially a passion of the middle classes: with those classes it grows and spreads, with them it preponderates. From them it mounts into the higher orders of society, and descends into the mass of the people.

I never met in America with any citizen so poor as not to cast a glance of hope and envy on the enjoyments of the rich, or whose imagination did not possess itself by anticipation of those good things which fate still obstinately withheld from him.

On the other hand, I never perceived amongst the wealthier inhabitants of the United States that proud contempt of physical gratifications which is sometimes to be met with even in the most opulent and dissolute aristocracies. Most of these wealthy persons were once poor: they have felt the sting of want; they were long a prey to adverse fortunes; and now that the victory is won, the passions which accompanied the contest have survived it: their minds are, as it were, intoxicated by the small enjoyments which they have pursued for forty years.

Not but that in the United States, as elsewhere, there are a certain number of wealthy persons, who, having come into their property by inheritance, possess without exertion an opulence they have not earned. But even these men are not less devotedly attached to the pleasures of material life. The love of well-being is now become the predominant taste of the nation; the great current of human passions runs in that channel, and sweeps everything along in its course. It may be supposed, from what has just been said, that the love of physical gratification must constantly urge the Americans to irregularities in morals, disturb the peace of families, and threaten the security of society at large. But it is not so: the passion for physical gratifications produces in democracies effects very different from those which it occasions in aristocratic nations.

It sometimes happens that, wearied with public affairs and sated with opulence, amidst the ruin of religious belief and the decline of the state, the heart of an aristocracy may by degrees be seduced to the pursuit of sensual enjoyment alone. At other times, the power of the monarch or the weakness of the people, without stripping the nobility of their fortune, compels them to stand aloof from the administration of affairs, and, whilst the road to mighty enterprise is closed,

abandons them to the inquietude of their own desires; they
then fall back heavily upon themselves, and seek in the
pleasures of the body oblivion of their former greatness.

When the members of an aristocratic body are thus exclusively devoted to the pursuit of physical gratifications,
they commonly turn in that direction all the energy which
they derive from their long experience of power. Such men
are not satisfied with the pursuit of comfort; they require
sumptuous depravity and splendid corruption. The worship
they pay the senses is a gorgeous one; and they seem to vie
with each other in the art of degrading their own natures.
The stronger, the more famous, and the more free an aristocracy has been, the more depraved will it then become; and,
however brilliant may have been the lustre of its virtues, I
dare predict that they will always be surpassed by the splendor
of its vices.

The taste for physical gratifications leads a democratic
people into no such excesses. The love of well-being is there
displayed as a tenacious, exclusive, universal passion; but its
range is confined. To build enormous palaces, to conquer or
to mimic nature, to ransack the world in order to gratify the
passions of a man, is not thought of: but to add a few roods
of land to your field, to plant an orchard, to enlarge a dwelling,
to be always making life more comfortable and convenient,
to avoid trouble, and to satisfy the smallest wants without
effort and almost without cost. These are small objects, but
the soul clings to them; it dwells upon them closely and day
by day, till they at last shut out the rest of the world, and
sometimes intervene between itself and Heaven.

This, it may be said, can only be applicable to those members of the community who are in humble circumstances;
wealthier individuals will display taste akin to those which
belonged to them in aristocratic ages. I contest the proposition: in point of physical gratifications, the most opulent
members of a democracy will not display tastes very different
from those of the people; whether it be that, springing from
the people, they really share those tastes, or that they esteem
it a duty to submit to them. In democratic society, the
sensuality of the public has taken a moderate and tranquil
course, to which all are bound to conform: it is as difficult
to depart from the common rule by one's vices as by one's
virtues. Rich men who live amidst democratic nations are
therefore more intent on providing for their smallest wants,
than for their extraordinary enjoyments; they gratify a number of petty desires, without indulging in any great irregulari-

ties of passion: thus, they are more apt to become enervated than debauched.

The special taste which the men of democratic times entertain for physical enjoyments is not naturally opposed to the principles of public order; nay, it often stands in need of order, that it may be gratified. Nor is it adverse to regularity of morals, for good morals contribute to public tranquillity and are favorable to industry. It may even be frequently combined with a species of religious morality: men wish to be as well off as they can in this world, without foregoing their chance of another. Some physical gratifications cannot be indulged in without crime; from such they strictly abstain. The enjoyment of others is sanctioned by religion and morality; to these the heart, the imagination, and life itself, are unreservedly given up; till, in snatching at these lesser gifts, men lose sight of those more precious possessions which constitute the glory and the greatness of mankind.

The reproach I address to the principle of equality is not that it leads men away in the pursuit of forbidden enjoyments, but that it absorbs them wholly in quest of those which are allowed. By these means, a kind of virtuous materialism may ultimately be established in the world, which would not corrupt, but enervate, the soul, and noiselessly unbend its springs of action.

33. What Causes Almost All Americans to Follow Industrial Callings.

AGRICULTURE is, perhaps, of all the useful arts, that which improves most slowly amongst democratic nations. Frequently, indeed, it would seem to be stationary, because other arts are making rapid strides towards perfection. On the other hand, almost all the tastes and habits which the equality of condition produces naturally lead men to commercial and industrial occupations.

Suppose an active, enlightened, and free man, enjoying a competency, but full of desires: he is too poor to live in idleness; he is rich enough to feel himself protected from the immediate fear of want, and he thinks how he can better his condition. This man has conceived a taste for physical gratifications, which thousands of his fellow-men indulge in around him; he has himself begun to enjoy these pleasures, and he is eager to increase his means of satisfying these tastes more completely. But life is slipping away, time is urgent;— to what is he to turn? The cultivation of the ground promises an almost certain result to his exertions, but a slow one; men are not enriched by it without patience and toil. Agriculture is therefore only suited to those who have already large superfluous wealth, or to those whose penury bids them only seek a bare subsistence. The choice of such a man as we have supposed is soon made; he sells his plot of ground, leaves his dwelling, and embarks in some hazardous but lucrative calling.

Democratic communities abound in men of this kind; and, in proportion as the equality of conditions becomes greater, their multitude increases. Thus, democracy not only swells the number of working-men, but it leads men to prefer one kind of labor to another; and, whilst it diverts them from agriculture, it encourages their taste for commerce and manufactures.

This spirit may be observed even amongst the richest members of the community. In democratic countries, however opulent a man is supposed to be, he is almost always discontented with his fortune, because he finds that he is less rich than his father was, and he fears that his sons will be less rich than himself. Most rich men in democracies are therefore constantly haunted by the desire of obtaining wealth, and they naturally turn their attention to trade and manufactures, which appear to offer the readiest and most efficient means of success. In this respect, they share the instincts of the poor without feeling the same necessities, say, rather, they feel the most imperious of all necessities, that of not sinking in the world.

In aristocracies, the rich are at the same time the governing power. The attention which they unceasingly devote to important public affairs diverts them from the lesser cares which trade and manufactures demand. But if an individual happens to turn his attention to business, the will of the body to which he belongs will immediately prevent him from pursuing it; for, however men may declaim against the rule of numbers, they cannot wholly escape it; and even amongst those aristocratic bodies which most obstinately refuse to acknowledge the rights of the national majority, a private majority is formed which governs the rest.

In democratic countries, where money does not lead those who possess it to political power, but often removes them from it, the rich do not know how to spend their leisure. They are driven into active life by the inquietude and the greatness of their desires, by the extent of their resources, and by the taste for what is extraordinary, which is almost always felt by those who rise, by whatsoever means, above the crowd. Trade is the only road open to them. In democracies, nothing is more great or more brilliant than commerce: it attracts the attention of the public, and fills the imagination of the multitude; all energetic passions are directed towards it. Neither their own prejudices nor those of anybody else can prevent the rich from devoting themselves to it. The wealthy members of democracies never form a body which has manners and regulations of its own; the opinions peculiar to their class do not restrain them, and the common opinions of their country urge them on. Moreover, as all the large fortunes which are found in a democratic community are of commercial growth, many generations must succeed each other before their possessors can have entirely laid aside their habits of business.

Circumscribed within the narrow space which politics leave them, rich men in democracies eagerly embark in commercial enterprise: there they can extend and employ their natural advantages; and indeed, it is even by the boldness and the magnitude of their industrial speculations that we may measure the slight esteem in which productive industry would have been held by them, if they had been born amidst an aristocracy.

A similar observation is likewise applicable to all men living in democracies, whether they be poor or rich. Those who live in the midst of democratic fluctuations have always before their eyes the image of chance; and they end by liking all undertakings in which chance plays a part. They are therefore all led to engage in commerce, not only for the sake of the profit it holds out to them, but for the love of the constant excitement occasioned by that pursuit.

The United States of America have only been emancipated for half a century from the state of colonial dependence in which they stood to Great Britain: the number of large fortunes there is small, and capital is still scarce. Yet no people in the world have made such rapid progress in trade and manufactures as the Americans; they constitute at the present day the second maritime nation in the world; and although their manufactures have to struggle with almost insurmountable natural impediments, they are not prevented from making great and daily advances.

In the United States, the greatest undertakings and speculations are executed without difficulty, because the whole population are engaged in productive industry, and because the poorest as well as the most opulent members of the commonwealth are ready to combine their efforts for these purposes. The consequence is, that a stranger is constantly amazed by the immense public works executed by a nation which contains, so to speak, no rich men. The Americans arrived but as yesterday on the territory which they inhabit, and they have already changed the whole order of nature for their own advantage. They have joined the Hudson to the Mississippi, and made the Atlantic Ocean communicate with the Gulf of Mexico, across a continent of more than five hundred leagues in extent which separates the two seas. The longest railroads which have been constructed, up to the present time, are in America.

But what most astonishes me in the United States is not so much the marvellous grandeur of some undertakings, as the innumerable multitude of small ones. Almost all the farmers of the United States combine some trade with agriculture; most of them make agriculture itself a trade. It seldom happens that an American farmer settles for good upon the land which he occupies: especially in the districts of the Far West, he brings land into tillage in order to sell it again, and not to farm it: he builds a farm-house on the speculation, that, as the state of the country will soon be changed by the increase of population, a good price may be obtained for it.

Every year, a swarm of people from the North arrive in the Southern States, and settle in the parts where the cotton-plant and the sugar-cane grow. These men cultivate the soil in order to make it produce in a few years enough to enrich them; and they already look forward to the time when they may return home to enjoy the competency thus acquired. Thus the Americans carry their business-like qualities into agriculture; and their trading passions are displayed in that, as in their other pursuits.

The Americans make immense progress in productive industry, because they all devote themselves to it at once; and for this same reason, they are exposed to unexpected and formidable embarrassments. As they are all engaged in commerce, their commercial affairs are affected by such various and complex causes, that it is impossible to foresee what difficulties may arise. As they are all more or less engaged in productive industry, at the least shock given to business, all private fortunes are put in jeopardy at the same time, and the state is shaken. I believe that the return of these commercial panics is an endemic disease of the democratic nations of our age. It may be rendered less dangerous, but it cannot be cured; because it does not originate in accidental circumstances, but in the temperament of these nations.

34. How an Aristocracy May Be Created by Manufactures.

I HAVE shown how democracy favors the growth of manufactures, and increases without limit the numbers of the manufacturing classes: we shall now see by what side-road manufacturers may possibly, in their turn, bring men back to aristocracy.

It is acknowledged, that, when a workman is engaged every day upon the same details, the whole commodity is produced with greater ease, promptitude, and economy. It is likewise acknowledged, that the cost of production of manufactured goods is diminished by the extent of the establishment in which they are made, and by the amount of capital employed or of credit. These truths had long been imperfectly discerned, but in our time they have been demonstrated. They have been already applied to many very important kinds of manufactures, and the humblest will gradually be governed by them. I know of nothing in politics which deserves to fix the attention of the legislator more closely than these two new axioms of the science of manufactures.

When a workman is unceasingly and exclusively engaged in the fabrication of one thing, he ultimately does his work with singular dexterity; but, at the same time, he loses the general faculty of applying his mind to the direction of the work. He every day becomes more adroit and less industrious; so that it may be said of him, that, in proportion as the workman improves, the man is degraded. What can be expected of a man who has spent twenty years of his life in making heads for pins? and to what can that mighty human intelligence, which has so often stirred the world, be applied in him, except it be to investigate the best method of making pins' heads? When a workman has spent a considerable portion of his existence in this manner, his thoughts are forever set upon the object of his daily toil; his body has contracted certain fixed habits, which it can never shake off: in a word, he no longer belongs to himself, but to the calling which he has chosen. It is in vain that laws and manners have been at pains to level all the barriers round such a man, and to open to him on every side a thousand different paths to fortune; a theory of manufactures more powerful than manners and laws binds him to a craft, and frequently to a spot, which he cannot leave: it assigns to him a certain place in society, beyond which he cannot go: in the midst of universal movement, it has rendered him stationary.

In proportion as the principle of the division of labor is more extensively applied, the workman becomes more weak, more narrow-minded, and more dependent. The art advances, the artisan recedes. On the other hand, in proportion as it becomes more manifest that the productions of manufactures are by so much the cheaper and better as the manufacture is larger, and the amount of capital employed more considerable, wealthy and educated men come forward to embark in manufactures, which were heretofore abandoned to poor or ignorant handicraftsmen. The magnitude of the efforts required, and the importance of the results to be obtained, attract them. Thus, at the very time at which the science of manufactures lowers the class of workmen, it raises the class of masters.

While the workman concentrates his faculties more and more upon the study of a single detail, the master surveys an extensive whole, and the mind of the latter is enlarged in proportion as that of the former is narrowed. In a short time, the one will require nothing but physical strength without intelligence; the other stands in need of science, and almost of genius, to insure success. This man resembles more and more the administrator of a vast empire,—that man, a brute.

The master and the workman have then here no similarity, and their differences increase every day. They are only connected as the two rings at the extremities of a long chain. Each of them fills the station which is made for him, and which he does not leave: the one is continually, closely, and necessarily dependent upon the other, and seems as much born to obey, as that other is to command. What is this but aristocracy?

As the conditions of men constituting the nation become more and more equal, the demand for manufactured commodities becomes more general and extensive; and the cheapness which places these objects within the reach of slender fortunes becomes a great element of success. Hence, there are every day more men of great opulence and education who devote their wealth and knowledge to manufactures; and who seek, by opening large establishments, and by a strict division of labor, to meet the fresh demands which are made on all sides. Thus, in proportion as the mass of the nation turns to democracy, that particular class which is engaged in manufactures becomes more aristocratic. Men grow more alike in the one, more different in the other; and inequality increases in the less numerous class, in the same ratio in which it decreases in the community. Hence it would appear, on searching to the bottom, that aristocracy should naturally spring out of the bosom of democracy.

But this kind of aristocracy by no means resembles those kinds which preceded it. It will be observed at once, that, as it applies exclusively to manufactures and to some manufacturing callings, it is a monstrous exception in the general aspect of society. The small aristocratic societies which are formed by some manufacturers in the midst of the immense democracy of our age, contain, like the great aristocratic societies of former ages, some men who are very opulent, and a multitude who are wretchedly poor. The poor have few means of escaping from their condition and becoming rich; but the rich are constantly becoming poor, or they give up business when they have realized a fortune. Thus the elements of which the class of the poor is composed are fixed; but the elements of which the class of the rich is composed are not so. To say the truth, though there are rich men, the class of rich men does not exist; for these rich individuals have no feelings or purposes in common, no mutual traditions or mutual hopes; there are individuals, therefore, but no definite class.

Not only are the rich not compactly united amongst themselves, but there is no real bond between them and the poor. Their relative position is not a permanent one; they are constantly drawn together or separated by their interests. The workman is generally dependent on the master, but not on any particular master: these two men meet in the factory, but know not each other elsewhere; and whilst they come into contact on one point, they stand very wide apart on all others. The manufacturer asks nothing of the workman but his labor; the workman expects nothing from him but his wages. The one contracts no obligation to protect, nor the other to defend; and they are not permanently connected either by habit or duty. The aristocracy created by business rarely settles in the midst of the manufacturing population which it directs: the object is not to govern that population, but to use it. An aristocracy thus constituted can have no great hold upon those whom it employs; and, even if it succeed in retaining them at one moment, they escape the next: it knows not how to will, and it cannot act.

The territorial aristocracy of former ages was either bound by law, or thought itself bound by usage, to come to the relief of its serving-men, and to succor their distresses. But the manufacturing aristocracy of our age first impoverishes and debases the men who serve it, and then abandons them to be supported by the charity of the public. This is a natural consequence of what has been said before. Between the workman and the master there are frequent relations, but no real association.

I am of opinion, upon the whole, that the manufacturing aristocracy which is growing up under our eyes is one of the harshest which ever existed in the world; but, at the same time, it is one of the most confined and least dangerous. Nevertheless, the friends of democracy should keep their eyes anxiously fixed in this direction; for if ever a permanent inequality of conditions and aristocracy again penetrate into the world, it may be predicted that this is the gate by which they will enter.

BOOK III

☆

INFLUENCE OF DEMOCRACY ON MANNERS
PROPERLY SO CALLED

35. How Democracy Renders the Habitual Intercourse of the Americans Simple and Easy.

DEMOCRACY does not attach men strongly to each other; but it places their habitual intercourse upon an easier footing.

If two Englishmen chance to meet at the Antipodes, where they are surrounded by strangers whose language and manners are almost unknown to them, they will first stare at each other with much curiosity, and a kind of secret uneasiness; they will then turn away, or, if one accosts the other, they will take care only to converse with a constrained and absent air, upon very unimportant subjects. Yet there is no enmity between these men; they have never seen each other before, and each believes the other to be a respectable person. Why then should they stand so cautiously apart? We must go back to England to learn the reason.

When it is birth alone, independent of wealth, which classes men in society, every one knows exactly what his own position is upon the social scale; he does not seek to rise, he does not fear to sink. In a community thus organized, men of different castes communicate very little with each other; but if accident brings them together, they are ready to converse without hoping or fearing to lose their own position. Their intercourse is not upon a footing of equality, but it is not constrained.

When a moneyed aristocracy succeeds to an aristocracy of birth, the case is altered. The privileges of some are still extremely great, but the possibility of acquiring those privileges is open to all: whence it follows, that those who possess them are constantly haunted by the apprehension of losing them, or of other men's sharing them; those who do not yet enjoy them long to possess them at any cost, or, if they fail, to appear at least to possess them,—which is not impossible. As the social importance of men is no longer ostensibly and permanently fixed by blood, and is infinitely varied by wealth, ranks still exist, but it is not easy clearly to distinguish at a glance those who respectively belong to them. Secret hostilities then arise in the community; one set of men endeavor by innumerable artifices to penetrate, or to appear to penetrate, amongst those who are above them; another set are constantly in arms against these usurpers of their rights; or, rather, the same individual does both at once, and whilst he seeks to raise himself into a higher circle, he is always on the defensive against the intrusion of those below him.

Such is the condition of England at the present time; and I am of opinion that the peculiarity just adverted to must be attributed principally to this cause. As aristocratic pride is still extremely great amongst the English, and as the limits of aristocracy are ill-defined, everybody lives in constant dread lest advantage should be taken of his familiarity. Unable to judge at once of the social position of those he meets, an Englishman prudently avoids all contact with them. Men are afraid lest some slight service rendered should draw them into an unsuitable acquaintance; they dread civilities, and they avoid the obtrusive gratitude of a stranger quite as much as his hatred.

Many people attribute these singular anti-social propensities, and the reserved and taciturn bearing of the English, to purely physical causes. I may admit that there is something of it in their race, but much more of it is attributable to their social condition, as is proved by the contrast of the Americans.

In America, where the privileges of birth never existed, and where riches confer no peculiar rights on their possessors, men unacquainted with each other are very ready to frequent the same places, and find neither peril nor advantage in the free interchange of their thoughts. If they meet by accident, they neither seek nor avoid intercourse; their manner is therefore natural, frank, and open; it is easy to see that they hardly expect or apprehend anything from each other, and that they do not care to display, any more than to conceal, their position in the world. If their demeanor is often cold and serious, it is never haughty or constrained; and if they do not converse, it is because they are not in a humor to talk, not because they think it their interest to be silent.

In a foreign country two Americans are at once friends, simply because they are Americans. They are repulsed by no prejudice; they are attracted by their common country.

For two Englishmen, the same blood is not enough; they must be brought together by the same rank. The Americans remark this unsociable mood of the English as much as the French do, and are not less astonished by it. Yet the Americans are connected with England by their origin, their religion, their language, and partially by their manners: they only differ in their social condition. It may therefore be inferred, that the reserve of the English proceeds from the constitution of their country, much more than from that of its inhabitants.

36. Why the Americans Show So Little Sensitiveness in Their Own Country, and Are So Sensitive in Europe.

THE temper of the Americans is vindictive, like that of all serious and reflecting nations. They hardly ever forget an offence, but it is not easy to offend them; and their resentment is as slow to kindle as it is to abate.

In aristocratic communities, where a small number of persons manage everything, the outward intercourse of men is subject to settled conventional rules. Every one then thinks he knows exactly what marks of respect or of condescension he ought to display, and none are presumed to be ignorant of the science of etiquette. These usages of the first class in society afterwards serve as a model to all the others; besides which, each of the latter lays down a code of its own, to which all its members are bound to conform. Thus the rules of politeness form a complex system of legislation, which it is difficult to be perfectly master of, but from which it is dangerous for any one to deviate; so that men are constantly exposed involuntarily to inflict or to receive bitter affronts.

But as the distinctions of rank are obliterated, as men differing in education and in birth meet and mingle in the same places of resort, it is almost impossible to agree upon the rules of good breeding. As its laws are uncertain, to disobey them is not a crime, even in the eyes of those who know what they are: men attach more importance to intentions than to forms, and they grow less civil, but at the same time less quarrelsome.

There are many little attentions which an American does not care about; he thinks they are not due to him, or he presumes that they are not known to be due: he therefore either does not perceive a rudeness, or he forgives it; his manners become less courteous, and his character more plain and masculine.

The mutual indulgence which the Americans display, and the manly confidence with which they treat each other, also result from another deeper and more general cause, which I have already adverted to in the preceding chapter. In the United States, the distinctions of rank in civil society are slight, in political society they are null; an American, therefore, does not think himself bound to pay particular attentions to any of his fellow-citizens, nor does he require such attentions from them towards himself. As he does not see that it is his interest eagerly to seek the company of any of his countrymen, he is slow to fancy that his own company is declined: despising no one on account of his station, he does not imagine that any one can despise him for that cause; and until he has clearly perceived an insult, he does not suppose that an affront was intended. The social condition of the Americans naturally accustoms them not to take offence in small matters; and, on the other hand, the democratic freedom which they enjoy transfuses this same mildness of temper into the character of the nation.

The political institutions of the United States constantly bring citizens of all ranks into contact, and compel them to pursue great undertakings in concert. People thus engaged have scarcely time to attend to the details of etiquette, and they are besides too strongly interested in living harmoniously for them to stick at such things. They therefore soon acquire a habit of considering the feelings and opinions of those whom they meet more than their manners, and they do not allow themselves to be annoyed by trifles.

I have often remarked, in the United States, that it is not easy to make a man understand that his presence may be dispensed with; hints will not always suffice to shake him off. I contradict an American at every word he says, to show him that his conversation bores me; he instantly labors with fresh pertinacity to convince me: I preserve a dogged silence, and he thinks I am meditating deeply on the truths which he is uttering: at last, I rush from his company, and he supposes that some urgent business hurries me elsewhere. This man will never understand that he wearies me to death, unless I tell him so; and the only way to get rid of him is to make him my enemy for life.

It appears surprising, at first sight, that the same man, transported to Europe, suddenly becomes so sensitive and captious, that I often find it as difficult to avoid offending him here, as it was there to put him out of countenance. These two opposite effects proceed from the same cause. Democratic institutions generally give men a lofty notion of their country and of themselves. An American leaves his country with a heart swollen with pride: on arriving in Europe, he at once finds out that we are not so engrossed by the United States and the great people who inhabit them as he had supposed; and this begins to annoy him. He has been informed that the conditions of society are not equal in our part of the globe; and he observes that, among the nations of Europe, the traces of rank are not wholly obliterated,—that wealth and birth still retain some indeterminate privileges, which force themselves upon his notice whilst they elude definition. He is therefore profoundly ignorant of the place which he ought to occupy in this half-ruined scale of classes, which are sufficiently distinct to hate and despise each other, yet sufficiently alike for him to be always confounding them. He is afraid of ranging himself too high, still more is he afraid of being ranged too low: this twofold peril keeps his mind constantly on the stretch, and embarrasses all he says and does.

He learns from tradition that in Europe ceremonial observances were infinitely varied according to different ranks; this recollection of former times completes his perplexity, and he is the more afraid of not obtaining those marks of respect which are due to him, as he does not exactly know in what they consist. He is like a man surrounded by traps: society is not a recreation for him, but a serious toil: he weighs your least actions, interrogates your looks, and scrutinizes all you say, lest there should be some hidden allusion to affront him. I doubt whether there was ever a provincial man of quality so punctilious in breeding as he is: he endeavors to attend to the slightest rules of etiquette, and does not allow one of them to be waived towards himself: he is full of scruples, and at the same time of pretensions; he wishes to do enough, but fears to do too much; and as he does not very well know the limits of the one or of the other, he keeps up a haughty and embarrassed air of reserve.

But this is not all: here is yet another double of the human heart. An American is forever talking of the admirable equality which prevails in the United States: aloud, he makes it the boast of his country, but in secret, he deplores it for himself; and he aspires to show that, for his part, he is an exception to the general state of things which he vaunts. There is hardly an American to be met with who does not claim some remote kindred with the first founders of the Colonies;

and as for the scions of the noble families of England, America seemed to me to be covered with them. When an opulent American arrives in Europe, his first care is to surround himself with all the luxuries of wealth: he is so afraid of being taken for the plain citizen of a democracy, that he adopts a hundred distorted ways of bringing some new instance of his wealth before you every day. His house will be in the most fashionable part of the town: he will always be surrounded by a host of servants. I have heard an American complain that, in the best houses of Paris, the society was rather mixed; the taste which prevails there was not pure enough for him; and he ventured to hint that, in his opinion, there was a want of elegance of manner; he could not accustom himself to see wit concealed under such unpretending forms.

These contrasts ought not to surprise us. If the vestiges of former aristocratic distinctions were not so completely effaced in the United States, the Americans would be less simple and less tolerant in their own country; they would require less, and be less fond of borrowed manners, in ours.

37. Influence of Democracy on Wages.

. . . As the gradations of the social scale come to be less observed, whilst the great sink and the humble rise, and poverty as well as opulence ceases to be hereditary, the distance, both in reality and in opinion, which heretofore separated the workman from the master, is lessened every day. The workman conceives a more lofty opinion of his rights, of his future, of himself; he is filled with new ambition and new desires, he is harassed by new wants. Every instant he views with longing eyes the profits of his employer; and in order to share them, he strives to dispose of his labor at a higher rate, and he generally succeeds at length in the attempt.

In democratic countries, as well as elsewhere, most of the branches of productive industry are carried on at a small cost, by men little removed by their wealth or education above the level of those whom they employ. These manufacturing speculators are extremely numerous; their interests differ; they cannot therefore easily concert or combine their exertions. On the other hand, the workmen have always some sure resources, which enable them to refuse to work when they cannot get what they conceive to be the fair price of their labor. In the constant struggle for wages which is going on between these two classes, this strength is divided, and success alternates from one to the other.

It is even probable that, in the end, the interest of the working class will prevail; for the high wages which they have already obtained make them every day less dependent on their masters; and as they grow more independent, they have greater facilities for obtaining a further increase of wages.

I shall take for example that branch of productive industry which is still, at the present day, the most generally followed in France, and in almost all the countries of the world;—I mean the cultivation of the soil. In France most of those who labor for hire in agriculture are themselves owners of certain plots of ground, which just enable them to subsist without working for any one else. When these laborers come to offer their services to a neighboring land-owner or farmer, if he refuses them a certain rate of wages, they retire to their own small property and await another opportunity.

I think that, upon the whole, it may be asserted that a slow and gradual rise of wages is one of the general laws of democratic communities. In proportion as social conditions become more equal, wages rise; and as wages are higher, social conditions become more equal.

But a great and gloomy exception occurs in our own time. I have shown, in a preceding chapter, that aristocracy, expelled from political society, has taken refuge in certain departments of productive industry, and has established its sway there under another form; this powerfully affects the rate of wages.

As a large capital is required to embark in the great manufacturing speculations to which I allude, the number of persons who enter upon them is exceedingly limited: as their number is small, they can easily concert together, and fix the rate of wages as they please.

Their workmen, on the contrary, are exceedingly numerous, and the number of them is always increasing; for, from time to time, an extraordinary run of business takes place, during which wages are inordinately high, and they attract the surrounding population to the factories. But, when men have once embraced that line of life, we have already seen that they cannot quit it again, because they soon contract habits of body and mind which unfit them for any other sort of toil. These men have generally but little education and industry, with but few resources; they stand, therefore, almost at the mercy of the master.

When competition, or other fortuitous circumstances, lessen his profits, he can reduce the wages of his workmen almost at

pleasure, and make from them what he loses by the chances
of business. Should the workmen strike, the master, who is a
rich man, can very well wait, without being ruined, until
necessity brings them back to him; but they must work day
by day or they die, for their only property is in their hands.
They have long been impoverished by oppression, and the
poorer they become, the more easily may they be oppressed:
they can never escape from this fatal circle of cause and
consequence.

It is not surprising then that wages, after having sometimes suddenly risen, are permanently lowered in this branch
of industry; whereas, in other callings, the price of labor,
which generally increases but little, is nevertheless constantly
augmented.

This state of dependence and wretchedness, in which a
part of the manufacturing population of our time live, forms
an exception to the general rule, contrary to the state of all
the rest of the community; but, for this very reason, no
circumstance is more important or more deserving of the
especial consideration of the legislator; for when the whole
of society is in motion, it is difficult to keep any one class
stationary; and when the greater number of men are opening new paths to fortune, it is no less difficult to make the
few support in peace their wants and their desires.

38. Influence of Democracy on the Family.

I HAVE just examined the changes which the equality of conditions produce in the mutual relations of the several members of the community amongst democratic nations, and
amongst the Americans in particular. I would now go deeper,
and inquire into the closer ties of family: my object here is
not to seek for new truths, but to show in what manner facts
already known are connected with my subject.

It has been universally remarked, that, in our time, the
several members of a family stand upon an entirely new footing towards each other; that the distance which formerly
separated a father from his sons has been lessened; and that
paternal authority, if not destroyed, is at least impaired.

Something analogous to this, but even more striking, may
be observed in the United States. In America, the family, in
the Roman and aristocratic signification of the word, does not
exist. All that remains of it are a few vestiges in the first

years of childhood, when the father exercises, without opposition, that absolute domestic authority which the feebleness of his children renders necessary, and which their interest, as well as his own incontestable superiority, warrants. But as soon as the young American approaches manhood, the ties of filial obedience are relaxed day by day: master of his thoughts, he is soon master of his conduct. In America, there is, strictly speaking, no adolescence: at the close of boyhood, the man appears, and begins to trace out his own path.

It would be an error to suppose that this is preceded by a domestic struggle, in which the son has obtained by a sort of moral violence the liberty that his father refused him. The same habits, the same principles, which impel the one to assert his independence, predispose the other to consider the use of that independence as an incontestable right. The former does not exhibit any of those rancorous or irregular passions which disturb men long after they have shaken off an established authority; the latter feels none of that bitter and angry regret which is apt to survive a bygone power. The father foresees the limits of his authority long beforehand, and when the time arrives, he surrenders it without a struggle: the son looks forward to the exact period at which he will be his own master; and he enters upon his freedom without precipitation and without effort, as a possession which is his own, and which no one seeks to wrest from him.

It may, perhaps, be useful to show how these changes which take place in family relations are closely connected with the social and political revolution which is approaching its consummation under our own eyes.

There are certain great social principles which a people either introduces everywhere or tolerates nowhere. In countries which are aristocratically constituted with all the gradations of rank, the government never makes a direct appeal to the mass of the governed; as men are united together, it is enough to lead the foremost; the rest will follow. This is applicable to the family, as well as to all aristocracies which have a head. Amongst aristocratic nations, social institutions recognize, in truth, no one in the family but the father; children are received by society at his hands; society governs him, he governs them. Thus, the parent has not only a natural right, but he acquires a political right, to command them: he is the author and the support of his family; but he is also its constituted ruler.

In democracies, where the government picks out every individual singly from the mass to make him subservient to the general laws of the community, no such intermediate person is required: a father is there, in the eye of the law, only a member of the community, older and richer than his sons.

When most of the conditions of life are extremely unequal, and the inequality of these conditions is permanent, the notion of a superior grows upon the imaginations of men; if the law invested him with no privileges, custom and public opinion would concede them. When, on the contrary, men differ but little from each other, and do not always remain in dissimilar conditions of life, the general notion of a superior becomes weaker and less distinct: it is vain for legislation to strive to place him who obeys very much beneath him who commands; the manners of the time bring the two men nearer to one another, and draw them daily towards the same level.

Although the legislation of an aristocratic people should grant no peculiar privileges to the heads of families, I shall not be the less convinced that their power is more respected and more extensive than in a democracy; for I know that, whatsoever the laws may be, superiors always appear higher, and inferiors lower, in aristocracies than amongst democratic nations.

When men live more for the remembrance of what has been than for the care of what is, and when they are more given to attend to what their ancestors thought than to think themselves, the father is the natural and necessary tie between the past and the present,—the link by which the ends of these two chains are connected. In aristocracies, then, the father is not only the civil head of the family, but the organ of its traditions, the expounder of its customs, the arbiter of its manners. He is listened to with deference, he is addressed with respect, and the love which is felt for him is always tempered with fear.

When the condition of society becomes democratic, and men adopt as their general principle that it is good and lawful to judge of all things for one's self, using former points of belief not as a rule of faith, but simply as a means of information, the power which the opinions of a father exercise over those of his sons diminishes, as well as his legal power.

Perhaps the subdivision of estates which democracy brings about contributes more than anything else to change the relations existing between a father and his children. When the property of the father of a family is scanty, his son and himself constantly live in the same place, and share the same occupations: habit and necessity bring them together, and force them to hold constant communication; the inevitable consequence is a sort of familiar intimacy, which renders authority less absolute, and which can ill be reconciled with the external forms of respect.

Now, in democratic countries, the class of those who are possessed of small fortunes is precisely that which gives strength to the notions and a particular direction to the manners of the community. That class makes its opinions preponderate as universally as its will; and even those who are most inclined to resist its commands are carried away in the end by its example. I have known eager opponents of democracy, who allowed their children to address them with perfect colloquial equality.

Thus, at the same time that the power of aristocracy is declining, the austere, the conventional, and the legal part of parental authority vanishes, and a species of equality prevails around the domestic hearth. I know not, upon the whole, whether society loses by the change, but I am inclined to believe that man individually is a gainer by it. I think that, in proportion as manners and laws become more democratic, the relation of father and son becomes more intimate and more affectionate; rules and authority are less talked of, confidence and tenderness are oftentimes increased, and it would seem that the natural bond is drawn closer in proportion as the social bond is loosened.

In a democratic family, the father exercises no other power than that which is granted to the affection and the experience of age; his orders would perhaps be disobeyed, but his advice is for the most part authoritative. Though he be not hedged in with ceremonial respect, his sons at least accost him with confidence; they have no settled form of addressing him, but they speak to him constantly, and are ready to consult him every day: the master and the constituted ruler have vanished; the father remains.

Nothing more is needed in order to judge of the difference between the two states of society in this respect, than to peruse the family correspondence of aristocratic ages. The style is always correct, ceremonious, stiff, and so cold that the natural warmth of the heart can hardly be felt in the language. In democratic countries, on the contrary, the language addressed by a son to his father is always marked by mingled freedom, familiarity, and affection, which at once show that new relations have sprung up in the bosom of the family.

A similar revolution takes place in the mutual relations of children. In aristocratic families, as well as in aristocratic society, every place is marked out beforehand. Not only does the father occupy a separate rank, in which he enjoys extensive privileges, but even the children are not equal amongst themselves. The age and sex of each irrevocably determine his rank, and secure to him certain privileges: most of these distinctions are abolished or diminished by democracy.

In aristocratic families, the eldest son, inheriting the greater part of the property, and almost all the rights of the family, becomes the chief, and, to a certain extent, the master, of his brothers. Greatness and power are for him; for them, mediocrity and dependence. But it would be wrong to suppose that, amongst aristocratic nations, the privileges of the eldest son are advantageous to himself alone, or that they excite nothing but envy and hatred around him. The eldest son commonly endeavors to procure wealth and power for his brothers, because the general splendor of the house is reflected back on him who represents it; the younger sons seek to back the elder brother in all his undertakings, because the greatness and power of the head of the family better enable him to provide for all its branches. The different members of an aristocratic family are therefore very closely bound together; their interests are connected, their minds agree, but their hearts are seldom in harmony.

Democracy also binds brothers to each other, but by very different means. Under democratic laws, all the children are perfectly equal, and consequently independent: nothing brings them forcibly together, but nothing keeps them apart; and as they have the same origin, as they are trained under the same roof, as they are treated with the same care, and as no peculiar privilege distinguishes or divides them, the affectionate and frank intimacy of early years easily springs up between them. Scarcely anything can occur to break the tie thus formed at the outset of life, for brotherhood brings them daily together, without embarrassing them. It is not then by interest, but by common associations and by the free sympathy of opinion and of taste, that democracy unites brothers to each other. It divides their inheritance, but allows their hearts and minds to unite.

Such is the charm of these democratic manners, that even the partisans of aristocracy are attracted by it; and after having experienced it for some time, they are by no means tempted to revert to the respectful and frigid observances of aristocratic families. They would be glad to retain the domestic habits of democracy, if they might throw off its social conditions and its laws; but these elements are indissolubly united, and it is impossible to enjoy the former without enduring the latter.

The remarks I have made on filial love and fraternal affection are applicable to all the passions which emanate spontaneously from human nature itself.

If a certain mode of thought or feeling is the result of some peculiar condition of life, when that condition is altered nothing whatever remains of the thought or feeling. Thus, a law may bind two members of the community very closely to one another; but that law being abolished, they stand asunder. Nothing was more strict than the tie which united the vassal to the lord under the feudal system: at the present day, the two men know not each other; the fear, the gratitude, and the affection which formerly connected them have vanished, and not a vestige of the tie remains.

Such, however, is not the case with those feelings which are natural to mankind. Whenever a law attempts to tutor these feelings in any particular manner, it seldom fails to weaken them; by attempting to add to their intensity, it robs them of some of their elements, for they are never stronger than when left to themselves.

Democracy, which destroys or obscures almost all the old conventional rules of society, and which prevents men from readily assenting to new ones, entirely effaces most of the feelings to which these conventional rules have given rise; but it only modifies some others, and frequently imparts to them a degree of energy and sweetness unknown before.

Perhaps it is not impossible to condense into a single proposition the whole purport of this chapter, and of several others that preceded it. Democracy loosens social ties, but tightens natural ones; it brings kindred more closely together, whilst it throws citizens more apart.

39. Young Women in a Democracy.

No free communities ever existed without morals; and, as I observed in the former part of this work, morals are the work of women. Consequently, whatever affects the condition of women, their habits and their opinions, has great political importance in my eyes.

Amongst almost all Protestant nations, young women are far more the mistresses of their own actions than they are in Catholic countries. This independence is still greater in Protestant countries like England, which have retained or acquired the right of self-government; freedom is then infused into the domestic circle by political habits and by religious opinions. In the United States, the doctrines of Protestantism are combined with great political liberty and a most democratic state

of society; and nowhere are young women surrendered so early
or so completely to their own guidance.

Long before an American girl arrives at the marriageable
age, her emancipation from maternal control begins: she has
scarcely ceased to be a child, when she already thinks for
herself, speaks with freedom, and acts on her own impulse.
The great scene of the world is constantly open to her view:
far from seeking to conceal it from her, it is every day disclosed more completely, and she is taught to survey it with a
firm and calm gaze. Thus the vices and dangers of society are
early revealed to her; as she sees them clearly, she views them
without illusion, and braves them without fear; for she is full
of reliance on her own strength, and her confidence seems to
be shared by all around her.

An American girl scarcely ever displays that virginal softness in the midst of young desires, or that innocent and
ingenuous grace, which usually attend the European woman
in the transition from girlhood to youth. It is rare that an
American woman, at any age, displays childish timidity or
ignorance. Like the young women of Europe, she seeks to
please, but she knows precisely the cost of pleasing. If she
does not abandon herself to evil, at least she knows that it
exists; and she is remarkable rather for purity of manners than
for chastity of mind.

I have been frequently surprised, and almost frightened,
at the singular address and happy boldness with which young
women in America contrive to manage their thoughts and
their language, amidst all the difficulties of free conversation;
a philosopher would have stumbled at every step along the
narrow path which they trod without accident and without
effort. It is easy, indeed, to perceive that, even amidst the
independence of early youth, an American woman is always
mistress of herself: she indulges in all permitted pleasures,
without yielding herself up to any of them; and her reason
never allows the reins of self-guidance to drop, though it often
seems to hold them loosely.

In France, where traditions of every age are still so strangely
mingled in the opinions and tastes of the people, women commonly receive a reserved, retired, and almost conventual education, as they did in aristocratic times; and then they are
suddenly abandoned, without a guide and without assistance,
in the midst of all the irregularities inseparable from democratic society.

The Americans are more consistent. They have found out
that, in a democracy, the independence of individuals cannot
fail to be very great, youth premature, tastes ill-restrained, cus-

toms fleeting, public opinion often unsettled and powerless, paternal authority weak, and marital authority contested. Under these circumstances, believing that they had little chance of repressing in woman the most vehement passions of the human heart, they held that the surer way was to teach her the art of combating those passions for herself. As they could not prevent her virtue from being exposed to frequent danger, they determined that she should know how best to defend it; and more reliance was placed on the free vigor of her will than on safeguards which have been shaken or over-thrown. Instead then of inculcating mistrust of herself, they constantly seek to enhance her confidence in her own strength of character. As it is neither possible nor desirable to keep a young woman in perpetual and complete ignorance, they hasten to give her a precocious knowledge on all subjects. Far from hiding the corruptions of the world from her, they prefer that she should see them at once, and train herself to shun them; and they hold it of more importance to protect her conduct, than to be over-scrupulous of the innocence of her thoughts.

Although the Americans are a very religious people, they do not rely on religion alone to defend the virtue of woman; they seek to arm her reason also. In this respect they have followed the same method as in several others: they first make vigorous efforts to cause individual independence to control itself, and they do not call in the aid of religion until they have reached the utmost limits of human strength.

I am aware that an education of this kind is not without danger; I am sensible that it tends to invigorate the judg-ment at the expense of the imagination, and to make cold and virtuous women instead of affectionate wives and agree-able companions to man. Society may be more tranquil and better regulated, but domestic life has often fewer charms. These, however, are secondary evils, which may be braved for the sake of higher interests. At the stage at which we are now arrived, the choice is no longer left to us; a democratic education is indispensable to protect women from the dangers with which democratic institutions and manners surround them.

In America, the independence of woman is irrecoverably lost in the bonds of matrimony. If an unmarried woman is less constrained there than elsewhere, a wife is subjected to stricter obligations. The former makes her father's house an abode of freedom and of pleasure; the latter lives in the home of her husband as if it were a cloister. Yet these two different con-ditions of life are perhaps not so contrary as may be supposed, and it is natural that the American women should pass through the one to arrive at the other.

Religious communities and trading nations entertain peculiarly serious notions of marriage: the former consider the regularity of woman's life as the best pledge and most certain sign of the purity of her morals; the latter regard it as the highest security for the order and prosperity of the household. The Americans are, at the same time, a puritanical people and a commercial nation; their religious opinions, as well as their trading habits, consequently lead them to require much abnegation on the part of women, and a constant sacrifice of her pleasures to her duties, which is seldom demanded of her in Europe. Thus, in the United States, the inexorable opinion of the public carefully circumscribes woman within the narrow circle of domestic interests and duties, and forbids her to step beyond it.

Upon her entrance into the world, a young American woman finds these notions firmly established; she sees the rules which are derived from them; she is not slow to perceive that she cannot depart for an instant from the established usages of her contemporaries, without putting in jeopardy her peace of mind, her honor, nay, even her social existence; and she finds the energy required for such an act of submission in the firmness of her understanding, and in the virile habits which her education has given her. It may be said that she has learned, by the use of her independence, to surrender it without a struggle and without a murmur when the time comes for making the sacrifice.

But no American woman falls into the toils of matrimony as into a snare held out to her simplicity and ignorance. She had been taught beforehand what is expected of her, and voluntarily and freely enters upon this engagement. She supports her new condition with courage, because she chose it. As, in America, paternal discipline is very relaxed and the conjugal tie very strict, a young woman does not contract the latter without considerable circumspection and apprehension. Precocious marriages are rare. American women do not marry until their understandings are exercised and ripened; whereas, in other countries, most women generally only begin to exercise and ripen their understandings after marriage.

I by no means suppose, however, that the great change which takes place in all the habits of women in the United States, as soon as they are married, ought solely to be attributed to the constraint of public opinion; it is frequently imposed upon themselves by the sole effort of their own will. When the time for choosing a husband is arrived, that cold and stern reasoning power which has been educated and invigorated by the free observation of the world teaches an American woman that a spirit of levity and independence in the bonds of marriage is a constant subject of annoyance, not of pleasure; it tells her that the amusements of the girl cannot become the recreations of the wife, and that the sources of a married woman's happiness are in the home of her husband. As she clearly discerns beforehand the only road which can lead to domestic happiness, she enters upon it at once, and follows it to the end without seeking to turn back.

The same strength of purpose which the young wives of America display, in bending themselves at once and without repining to the austere duties of their new condition, is no less manifest in all the great trials of their lives. In no country in the world are private fortunes more precarious than in the United States. It is not uncommon for the same man, in the course of his life, to rise and sink again through all the grades which lead from opulence to poverty. American women support these vicissitudes with calm and unquenchable energy: it would seem that their desires contract as easily as they expand with their fortunes.

The greater part of the adventurers who migrate every year to people the Western wilds belong, as I observed in the former part of this work, to the old Anglo-American race of the Northern States. Many of these men, who rush so boldly onwards in pursuit of wealth, were already in the enjoyment of a competency in their own part of the country. They take their wives along with them, and make them share the countless perils and privations which always attend the commencement of these expeditions. I have often met, even on the verge of the wilderness, with young women who, after having been brought up amidst all the comforts of the large towns of New England, had passed, almost without any intermediate stage, from the wealthy abode of their parents to a comfortless hovel in a forest. Fever, solitude, and a tedious life had not broken the springs of their courage. Their features were impaired and faded, but their looks were firm; they appeared to be at once sad and resolute. I do not doubt that these young American women had amassed, in the education of their early years, that inward strength which they displayed under these circumstances. The early culture of the girl may still, therefore, be traced, in the United States, under the aspect of marriage; her part is changed, her habits are different, but her character is the same.

40. How Equality of Condition Contributes to Maintain Good Morals in America.

SOME philosophers and historians have said or hinted that the strictness of female morality was increased or diminished simply by the distance of a country from the equator. This solution of the difficulty was an easy one; and nothing was required but a globe and a pair of compasses to settle in an instant one of the most difficult problems in the condition of mankind. But I am not sure that this principle of the materialists is supported by facts. The same nations have been chaste or dissolute, at different periods of their history; the strictness or the laxity of their morals depended, therefore, on some variable cause, and not alone on the natural qualities of their country, which were invariable. I do not deny that, in certain climates, the passions which are occasioned by the mutual attraction of the sexes are peculiarly intense; but I believe that this natural intensity may always be excited or restrained by the condition of society, and by political institutions.

Although the travellers who have visited North America differ on many points, they all agree in remarking that morals are far more strict there than elsewhere. It is evident that, on this point, the Americans are very superior to their progenitors, the English. A superficial glance at the two nations will establish the fact.

In England, as in all other countries of Europe, public malice is constantly attacking the frailties of women. Philosophers and statesmen are heard to deplore that morals are not sufficiently strict, and the literary productions of the country constantly lead one to suppose so. In America, all books, novels not excepted, suppose women to be chaste, and no one thinks of relating affairs of gallantry.

No doubt, this great regularity of American morals is due in part to qualities of country, race, and religion; but all these causes, which operate elsewhere, do no suffice to account for it: recourse must be had to some special reason. This reason appears to me to be the principle of equality, and the institutions derived from it. Equality of condition does not of itself produce regularity of morals, but it unquestionably facilitates and increases it.

Amongst aristocratic nations, birth and fortune frequently make two such different beings of man and woman, that they can never be united to each other. Their passions draw them together, but the condition of society, and the notions suggested by it, prevent them from contracting a permanent and ostensible tie. The necessary consequence is a great number of transient and clandestine connections. Nature secretly avenges herself for the constraint imposed upon her by the laws of man.

This is not so much the case when the equality of conditions has swept away all the imaginary or the real barriers which separated man from woman. No girl then believes that she cannot become the wife of the man who loves her; and this renders all breaches of morality before marriage very uncommon: for, whatever be the credulity of the passions, a woman will hardly be able to persuade herself that she is beloved, when her lover is perfectly free to marry her and does not.

The same cause operates, though more indirectly, on married life. Nothing better serves to justify an illicit passion, either to the minds of those who have conceived it or to the world which looks on, than marriages made by compulsion or chance.

In a country in which a woman is always free to exercise her choice, and where education has prepared her to choose rightly, public opinion is inexorable to her faults. The rigor of the Americans arises in part from this cause. They consider marriages as a covenant which is often onerous, but every condition of which the parties are strictly bound to fulfil, because they knew all those conditions beforehand, and were perfectly free not to have contracted them.

The very circumstances which render matrimonial fidelity more obligatory, also render it more easy.

In aristocratic countries, the object of marriage is rather to unite property than persons; hence the husband is sometimes at school and the wife at nurse when they are betrothed. It cannot be wondered at if the conjugal tie which holds the fortunes of the pair united allows their hearts to rove; this is the result of the nature of the contract. When, on the contrary, a man always chooses a wife for himself, without any external coercion, or even guidance, it is generally a conformity of tastes and opinions which brings a man and a woman together, and this same conformity keeps and fixes them in close habits of intimacy.

Our forefathers had conceived a strange opinion on the subject of marriage; as they had remarked that the small number of love-matches which occurred in their time almost always turned out ill, they resolutely inferred that it was dangerous to listen to the dictates of the heart on the subject. Accident appeared to them a better guide than choice.

Yet it was not difficult to perceive that the examples which they witnessed in fact proved nothing at all. For, in the first place, if democratic nations leave a woman at liberty to choose her husband, they take care to give her mind sufficient knowledge, and her will sufficient strength, to make so important a choice; whereas the young women who, amongst aristocratic nations, furtively elope from the authority of their parents to throw themselves of their own accord into the arms of men whom they have had neither time to know, nor ability to judge of, are totally without those securities. It is not surprising that they make a bad use of their freedom of action the first time they avail themselves of it; nor that they fall into such cruel mistakes when, not having received a democratic education, they choose to marry in conformity to democratic customs. But this is not all. When a man and woman are bent upon marriage in spite of the differences of an aristocratic state of society, the difficulties to be overcome are enormous. Having broken or relaxed the bonds of filial obedience, they have then to emancipate themselves by a final effort from the sway of custom and the tyranny of opinion; and when at length they have succeeded in this arduous task, they stand estranged from their natural friends and kinsmen: the prejudice they have crossed separates them from all, and places them in a situation which soon breaks their courage and sours their hearts.

If, then, a couple married in this manner are first unhappy and afterwards criminal, it ought not to be attributed to the freedom of their choice, but rather to their living in a community in which this freedom of choice is not admitted.

Moreover, it should not be forgotten that the same effort which makes a man violently shake off a prevailing error, commonly impels him beyond the bounds of reason; that, to dare to declare war, in however just a cause, against the opinion of one's age and country, a violent and adventurous spirit is required, and that men of this character seldom arrive at happiness or virtue, whatever be the path they follow. (And this, it may be observed by the way, is the reason why, in the most necessary and righteous revolutions, it is so rare to meet with virtuous or moderate revolutionary characters.) There is, then, no just ground for surprise if a man who, in an age of aristocracy, chooses to consult nothing but his own opinion and his own taste in the choice of a wife, soon finds that infractions of morality and domestic wretchedness invade his household; but when this same line of action is in the natural and ordinary, course of things,—when it is sanctioned by parental authority, and backed by public opinion,—it cannot be doubted that the internal peace of families will be increased by it, and conjugal fidelity more rigidly observed.

Almost all men in democracies are engaged in public or professional life; and on the other hand, the limited income obliges a wife to confine herself to the house, in order to watch in person, and very closely, over the details of domestic economy. All these distinct and compulsory occupations are so many natural barriers, which, by keeping the two sexes asunder, render the solicitations of the one less frequent and less ardent, the resistance of the other more easy.

The equality of conditions cannot, it is true, ever succeed in making men chaste, but it may impart a less dangerous character to their breaches of morality. As no one has then either sufficient time or opportunity to assail a virtue armed in self-defence, there will be at the same time a great number of courtesans and a great number of virtuous women. This state of things causes lamentable cases of individual hardship, but it does not prevent the body of society from being strong and alert: it does not destroy family ties, or enervate the morals of the nation. Society is endangered, not by the great profligacy of a few, but by laxity of morals amongst all. In the eyes of a legislator, prostitution is less to be dreaded than intrigue.

The tumultuous and constantly harassed life which equality makes men lead, not only distracts them from the passion of love, by denying them time to indulge it, but it diverts them from it by another more secret but more certain road. All men who live in democratic times more or less contract the ways of thinking of the manufacturing and trading classes; their minds take a serious, deliberate, and positive turn; they are apt to relinquish the ideal, in order to pursue some visible and proximate object, which appears to be the natural and necessary aim of their desires. Thus, the principle of equality does not destroy the imagination, but lowers its flight to the level of the earth.

No men are less addicted to reverie than the citizens of a democracy; and few of them are ever known to give way to those idle and solitary meditations which commonly precede and produce the great emotions of the heart. It is true they attach great importance to procuring for themselves that sort of deep, regular, and quiet affection, which consti-

tutes the charm and safeguard of life; but they are not apt
to run after those violent and capricious sources of excitement which disturb and abridge it.

I am aware that all this is applicable in its full extent only
to America, and cannot at present be extended to Europe. In
the course of the last half-century, whilst laws and customs
have impelled several European nations with unexampled force
towards democracy, we have not had occasion to observe
that the relations of man and woman have become more
orderly or more chaste. In some places, the very reverse may
be detected: some classes are more strict, the general morality
of the people appears to be more lax. I do not hesitate to
make the remark, for I am as little disposed to flatter my
contemporaries as to malign them.

This fact must distress, but it ought not to surprise us. The
propitious influence which a democratic state of society may
exercise upon orderly habits is one of those tendencies which
can only be discovered after a time. If equality of condition is
favorable to purity of morals, the social commotion by which
conditions are rendered equal is adverse to it. In the last fifty
years, during which France has been undergoing this transformation, it has rarely had freedom, always disturbance.
Amidst this universal confusion of notions and this general
stir of opinions,—amidst this incoherent mixture of the just
and the unjust, of truth and falsehood, of right and might,—
public virtue has become doubtful, and private morality waver-
ing. But all revolutions, whatever may have been their object
or their agents, have at first produced similar consequences;
even those which have in the end drawn tighter the bonds of
morality, began by loosening them. The violations of morality
which the French frequently witness do not appear to me to
have a permanent character; and this is already betokened by
some curious signs of the times.

Nothing is more wretchedly corrupt than an aristocracy
which retains its wealth when it has lost its power, and which
still enjoys a vast deal of leisure after it is reduced to mere
vulgar pastimes. The energetic passions and great conceptions
which animated it heretofore leave it then; and nothing remains to it but a host of petty consuming vices, which cling
about it like worms upon a carcass.

No one denies that the French aristocracy of the last century was extremely dissolute; yet established habits and ancient belief still preserved some respect for morality amongst
the other classes of society. Nor will it be denied that, at the
present day, the remnants of that same aristocracy exhibit a
certain severity of morals; whilst laxity of morals appears to

have spread amongst the middle and lower ranks. Thus the same families which were most profligate fifty years ago are now-a-days the most exemplary, and democracy seems only to have strengthened the morality of the aristocratic classes. The French Revolution, by dividing the fortunes of the nobility, by forcing them to attend assiduously to their affairs and to their families, by making them live under the same roof with their children, and, in short, by giving a more rational and serious turn to their minds, has imparted to them, almost without their being aware of it, a reverence for religious belief, a love of order, of tranquil pleasures, of domestic endearments, and of comfort; whereas the rest of the nation, which had naturally these same tastes, was carried away into excesses by the effort which was required to overthrow the laws and political habits of the country.

The old French aristocracy has undergone the consequences of the revolution, but it neither felt the revolutionary passions, nor shared the anarchical excitement which produced it; it may easily be conceived that this aristocracy feels the salutary influence of the revolution on its manners, before those who achieved it. It may therefore be said, though at first it seems paradoxical, that, at the present day, the most anti-democratic classes of the nation principally exhibit the kind of morality which may reasonably be anticipated from democracy. I cannot but think that, when we shall have obtained all the effects of this democratic revolution, after having got rid of the tumult it has caused, the observations which are now only applicable to the few will gradually become true of the whole community.

41. How the Americans Understand the Equality of the Sexes.

I HAVE shown how democracy destroys or modifies the different inequalities which originate in society; but is that all? or does it not ultimately affect that great inequality of man and woman which has seemed, up to the present day, to be eternally based in human nature? I believe that the social changes which bring nearer to the same level the father and son, the master and servant, and, in general, superiors and inferiors, will raise woman, and make her more and more the equal of man. But here, more than ever, I feel the necessity of making myself clearly understood; for there is no subject on which the coarse and lawless fancies of our age have taken a freer range.

There are people in Europe who, confounding together the different characteristics of the sexes, would make man and woman into beings not only equal, but alike. They would give to both the same functions, impose on both the same duties, and grant to both the same rights; they would mix them in all things,—their occupations, their pleasures, their business. It may readily be conceived, that, by thus attempting to make one sex equal to the other, both are degraded; and from so preposterous a medley of the works of nature, nothing could ever result but weak men and disorderly women.

It is not thus that the Americans understand that species of democratic equality which may be established between the sexes. They admit that, as nature has appointed such wide differences between the physical and moral constitution of man and woman, her manifest design was to give a distinct employment to their various faculties; and they hold that improvement does not consist in making beings so dissimilar do pretty nearly the same things, but in causing each of them to fulfil their respective tasks in the best possible manner. The Americans have applied to the sexes the great principle of political economy which governs the manufactures of our age, by carefully dividing the duties of man from those of woman, in order that the great work of society may be the better carried on.

In no country has such constant care been taken as in America to trace two clearly distinct lines of action for the two sexes, and to make them keep pace one with the other, but in two pathways which are always different. American women never manage the outward concerns of the family, or conduct a business, or take a part in political life; nor are they, on the other hand, ever compelled to perform the rough labor of the fields, or to make any of those laborious exertions which demand the exertion of physical strength. No families are so poor as to form an exception to this rule. If, on the one hand, an American woman cannot escape from the quiet circle of domestic employments, she is never forced, on the other, to go beyond it. Hence it is, that the women of America, who often exhibit a masculine strength of understanding and a manly energy, generally preserve great delicacy of personal appearance, and always retain the manners of women, although they sometimes show that they have the hearts and minds of men.

Nor have the Americans ever supposed that one consequence of democratic principles is the subversion of marital power, or the confusion of the natural authorities in families. They hold that every association must have a head in order to accomplish its object, and that the natural head of the conjugal association is man. They do not therefore deny him the right of directing his partner; and they maintain that, in the smaller association of husband and wife, as well as in the great social community, the object of democracy is to regulate and legalize the powers which are necessary, and not to subvert all power.

This opinion is not peculiar to one sex, and contested by the other: I never observed that the women of America consider conjugal authority as a fortunate usurpation of their rights, nor that they thought themselves degraded by submitting to it. It appeared to me, on the contrary, that they attach a sort of pride to the voluntary surrender of their own will, and make it their boast to bend themselves to the yoke,—not to shake it off. Such, at least, is the feeling expressed by the most virtuous of their sex; the others are silent; and, in the United States, it is not the practice for a guilty wife to clamor for the rights of women, whilst she is trampling on her own holiest duties.

It has often been remarked, that in Europe a certain degree of contempt lurks even in the flattery which men lavish upon women: although a European frequently affects to be the slave of woman, it may be seen that he never sincerely thinks her his equal. In the United States, men seldom compliment women, but they daily show how much they esteem them. They constantly display an entire confidence in the understanding of a wife, and a profound respect for her freedom; they have decided that her mind is just as fitted as that of a man to discover the plain truth, and her heart as firm to embrace it; and they have never sought to place her virtue, any more than his, under the shelter of prejudice, ignorance, and fear.

It would seem that, in Europe, where man so easily submits to the despotic sway of women, they are nevertheless deprived of some of the greatest attributes of the human species, and considered as seductive but imperfect beings; and (what may well provoke astonishment) women ultimately look upon themselves in the same light, and almost consider it as a privilege that they are entitled to show themselves futile, feeble, and timid. The women of America claim no such privileges.

Again, it may be said that in our morals we have reserved strange immunities to man; so that there is, as it were, one virtue for his use, and another for the guidance of his partner;

and that, according to the opinion of the public, the very same
act may be punished alternately as a crime, or only as a fault.
The Americans know not this iniquitous division of duties
and rights; amongst them, the seducer is as much dishonored
as his victim.

It is true that the Americans rarely lavish upon women
those eager attentions which are commonly paid them in
Europe; but their conduct to women always implies that they
suppose them to be virtuous and refined; and such is the
respect entertained for the moral freedom of the sex, that in
the presence of a woman the most guarded language is used,
lest her ear should be offended by an expression. In America,
a young unmarried woman may, alone and without fear, undertake a long journey.

The legislators of the United States, who have mitigated
almost all the penalties of criminal law, still make rape a
capital offence, and no crime is visited with more inexorable
severity by public opinion. This may be accounted for; as the
Americans can conceive nothing more precious than a woman's honor, and nothing which ought so much to be respected
as her independence, they hold that no punishment is too
severe for the man who deprives her of them against her will.
In France, where the same offence is visited with far milder
penalties, it is frequently difficult to get a verdict from a jury
against the prisoner. Is this a consequence of contempt of
decency, or contempt of women? I cannot but believe that it
is a contempt of both.

Thus, the Americans do not think that man and woman
have either the duty or the right to perform the same offices,
but they show an equal regard for both their respective parts;
and though their lot is different, they consider both of them as
beings of equal value. They do not give to the courage of
woman the same form or the same direction as to that of man;
but they never doubt her courage: and if they hold that man
and his partner ought not always to exercise their intellect
and understanding in the same manner, they at least believe
the understanding of the one to be as sound as that of the
other, and her intellect to be as clear. Thus, then, whilst they
have allowed the social inferiority of woman to subsist, they
have done all they could to raise her morally and intellectually
to the level of man; and in this respect they appear to me to
have excellently understood the true principle of democratic
improvement.

As for myself, I do not hesitate to avow, that, although
the women of the United States are confined within the
narrow circle of domestic life, and their situation is, in some

respects, one of extreme dependence, I have nowhere seen woman occupying a loftier position; and if I were asked, now that I am drawing to the close of this work, in which I have spoken of so many important things done by the Americans, to what the singular prosperity and growing strength of that people ought mainly to be attributed, I should reply, To the superiority of their women.

42. How the Principle of Equality Naturally Divides the Americans into a Multitude of Small Private Circles.

IT might be supposed that the final and necessary effect of democratic institutions would be to confound together all the members of the community in private as well as in public life, and to compel them all to live alike; but this would be to ascribe a very coarse and oppressive form to the equality which originates in democracy. No state of society or laws can render men so much alike, but that education, fortune, and tastes will interpose some differences between them; and, though different men may sometimes find it their interest to combine for the same purposes, they will never make it their pleasure. They will therefore always tend to evade the provisions of law, whatever they may be; and, escaping in some respect from the circle in which the legislator sought to confine them, they will set up, close by the great political community, small private societies, united together by similitude of conditions, habits, and manners.

In the United States, the citizens have no sort of pre-eminence over each other; they owe each other no mutual obedience or respect; they all meet for the administration of justice, for the government of the state, and, in general, to treat of the affairs which concern their common welfare; but I never heard that attempts have been made to bring them all to follow the same diversions, or to amuse themselves promiscuously in the same places of recreation.

The Americans, who mingle so readily in their political assemblies and courts of justice, are wont carefully to separate into small distinct circles, in order to indulge by themselves in the enjoyments of private life. Each of them willingly acknowledges all his fellow-citizens as his equals, but will only receive a very limited number of them as his friends or his guests. This appears to me to be very natural. In proportion as the circle of public society is extended, it may be anticipated that the sphere of private intercourse will be contracted; far from supposing that the members of modern society will ultimately live in common, I am afraid they will end by forming only small coteries.

Amongst aristocratic nations, the different classes are like vast enclosures, out of which it is impossible to get, into which it is impossible to enter. These classes have no communication with each other, but within them men necessarily live in daily contact; even though they would not naturally suit, the general conformity of a similar condition brings them near together.

But when neither law nor custom professes to establish frequent and habitual relations between certain men, their intercourse originates in the accidental similarity of opinions and tastes; hence private society is infinitely varied. In democracies, where the members of the community never differ much from each other, and naturally stand so near that they may all at any time be confounded in one general mass, numerous artificial and arbitrary distinctions spring up, by means of which every man hopes to keep himself aloof, lest he should be carried away against his will in the crowd.

This can never fail to be the case; for human institutions can be changed, but man cannot: whatever may be the general endeavor of a community to render its members equal and alike, the personal pride of individuals will always seek to rise above the line, and to form somewhere an inequality to their own advantage.

In aristocracies, men are separated from each other by lofty stationary barriers: in democracies, they are divided by many small and almost invisible threads, which are constantly broken or moved from place to place. Thus, whatever may be the progress of equality, in democratic nations a great number of small private associations will always be formed within the general pale of political society; but none of them will bear any resemblance in its manners to the higher class in aristocracies.

43. Some Reflections on American Manners.

NOTHING seems at first sight less important than the outward form of human actions, yet there is nothing upon which men set more store: they grow used to everything except to living in a society which has not their own manners. The influence of the social and political state of a country upon manners is therefore deserving of serious examination.

Manners are generally the product of the very basis of character but they are also sometimes the result of an arbitrary convention between certain men; thus they are at once natural and acquired.

When some men perceive that they are the foremost persons in society, without contest and without effort,—when they are constantly engaged on large objects, leaving the more minute details to others,—and when they live in the enjoyment of wealth which they did not amass and do not fear to lose,— it may be supposed that they feel a kind of haughty disdain of the petty interests and practical cares of life, and that their thoughts assume a natural greatness, which their language and their manners denote. In democratic countries, manners are generally devoid of dignity, because private life is there extremely petty in its character; and they are frequently low, because the mind has few opportunities of rising above the engrossing cares of domestic interests.

True dignity in manners consists in always taking one's proper station, neither too high nor too low; and this is as much within the reach of a peasant as of a prince. In democracies, all stations appear doubtful; hence it is that the manners of democracies, though often full of arrogance, are commonly wanting in dignity, and, moreover, they are never either well-trained or accomplished.

The men who live in democracies are too fluctuating for a certain number of them ever to succeed in laying down a code of good breeding, and in forcing people to follow it. Every man therefore behaves after his own fashion, and there is always a certain incoherence in the manners of such times, because they are moulded upon the feelings and notions of each individual, rather than upon an ideal model proposed for general imitation. This, however, is much more perceptible when an aristocracy has just been overthrown, than after it has long been destroyed. New political institutions and new social elements then bring to the same places of resort, and frequently compel to live in common, men whose education and habits are still amazingly dissimilar, and this renders the motley composition of society peculiarly visible. The existence of a former strict code of good breeding is still remembered, but what it contained, or where it is to be found, is already forgotten. Men have lost the common law of manners, and they have not yet made up their minds to do without it; but every one endeavors to make to himself some sort of arbitrary and variable rule, from the remnant of former usages; so that manners have neither the regularity and the dignity which they often display amongst aristocratic nations, nor the simplicity and freedom which they sometimes assume in democracies; they are at once constrained and without constraint.

This, however, is not the normal state of things. When the equality of conditions is long established and complete, as all men entertain nearly the same notions and do nearly the same things, they do not require to agree, or to copy from one another, in order to speak or act in the same manner; their manners are constantly characterized by a number of lesser diversities, but not by any great differences. They are never perfectly alike, because they do not copy from the same pattern; they are never very unlike, because their social condition is the same. At first sight, a traveller would say that the manners of all Americans are exactly similar; it is only upon close examination that the peculiarities in which they differ may be detected.

The English make game of the manners of the Americans; but it is singular that most of the writers who have drawn these ludicrous delineations belonged themselves to the middle classes in England, to whom the same delineations are exceedingly applicable; so that these pitiless censors furnish, for the most part, an example of the very thing they blame in the United States: they do not perceive that they are deriding themselves, to the great amusement of the aristocracy of their own country.

Nothing is more prejudicial to democracy than its outward forms of behavior; many men would willingly endure its vices, who cannot support its manners. I cannot, however, admit that there is nothing commendable in the manners of a democratic people.

Amongst aristocratic nations, all who live within reach of the first class in society commonly strain to be like it, which gives rise to ridiculous and insipid limitations. As a democratic people do not possess any models of high breeding, at least they escape the daily necessity of seeing wretched copies of them. In democracies, manners are never so refined as amongst aristocratic nations, but, on the other hand, they are never so coarse. Neither the coarse oaths of the populace, nor the elegant and choice expressions of the nobility, are to be heard there: the manners of such a people are often vulgar, but they are neither brutal nor mean.

I have already observed that, in democracies, no such thing as a regular code of good breeding can be laid down; this has some inconveniences and some advantages. In aristocracies, the rules of propriety impose the same demeanor on every one;

they make all the members of the same class appear alike, in spite of their private inclinations; they adorn and they conceal the natural man. Amongst a democratic people, manners are neither so tutored nor so uniform, but they are frequently more sincere. They form, as it were, a light and loosely-woven veil, through which the real feelings and private opinions of each individual are easily discernible. The form and the substance of human actions, therefore, often stand there in closer relation; and if the great picture of human life be less embellished, it is more true. Thus it may be said, in one sense, that the effect of democracy is not exactly to give men any particular manners, but to prevent them from having manners at all.

The feelings, the passions, the virtues, and the vices of an aristocracy may sometimes reappear in a democracy, but not its manners; they are lost, and vanish forever, as soon as the democratic revolution is completed. It would seem that nothing is more lasting than the manners of an aristocratic class, for they are preserved by that class for some time after it has lost its wealth and its power,—nor so fleeting, for no sooner have they disappeared, than not a trace of them is to be found; and it is scarcely possible to say what they have been, as soon as they have ceased to be. A change in the state of society works this miracle, and a few generations suffice to consummate it. The principal characteristics of aristocracy are handed down by history after an aristocracy is destroyed; but the light and exquisite touches of manners are effaced from men's memories almost immediately after its fall. Men can no longer conceive what these manners were, when they have ceased to witness them; they are gone, and their departure was unseen, unfelt; for in order to feel that refined enjoyment which is derived from choice and distinguished manners, habit and education must have prepared the heart, and the taste for them is lost almost as easily as the practice of them. Thus, not only a democratic people cannot have aristocratic manners, but they neither comprehend nor desire them; and as they never have thought of them, it is to their minds as if such things had never been. Too much importance should not be attached to this loss, but it may well be regretted.

I am aware that it has not unfrequently happened that the same men have had very high-bred manners and very low-born feelings: the exterior of courts has sufficiently shown what imposing externals may conceal the meanest hearts. But though the manners of aristocracy do not constitute virtue, they sometimes embellish virtue itself. It was no ordinary sight to see a numerous and powerful class of men, whose every outward action seemed constantly to be dictated by a natural elevation of thought and feeling, by delicacy and regularity of taste, and by urbanity of manners. Those manners threw a pleasing illusory charm over human nature; and though the picture was often a false one, it could not be viewed without a noble satisfaction.

44. Why the National Vanity of the Americans Is More Restless and Captious Than That of the English.

ALL free nations are vainglorious, but national pride is not displayed by all in the same manner. The Americans, in their intercourse with strangers, appear impatient of the smallest censure, and insatiable of praise. The most slender eulogium is acceptable to them, the most exalted seldom contents them; they unceasingly harass you to extort praise, and if you resist their entreaties, they fall to praising themselves. It would seem as if, doubting their own merit, they wished to have it constantly exhibited before their eyes. Their vanity is not only greedy, but restless and jealous; it will grant nothing, whilst it demands everything, but is ready to beg and to quarrel at the same time.

If I say to an American that the country he lives in is a fine one, "Ay," he replies, "there is not its equal in the world." If I applaud the freedom which its inhabitants enjoy, he answers, "Freedom is a fine thing, but few nations are worthy to enjoy it." If I remark the purity of morals which distinguishes the United States, "I can imagine," says he, "that a stranger, who has witnessed the corruption that prevails in other nations, should be astonished at the difference." At length, I leave him to the contemplation of himself; but he returns to the charge, and does not desist till he has got me to repeat all I had just been saying. It is impossible to conceive a more troublesome or more garrulous patriotism; it wearies even those who are disposed to respect it.

Such is not the case with the English. An Englishman calmly enjoys the real or imaginary advantages which, in his opinion, his country possesses. If he grants nothing to other nations, neither does he solicit anything for his own. The censure of foreigners does not affect him, and their praise hardly flatters him; his position with regard to the rest of the world is one of disdainful and ignorant reserve: his pride requires no sustenance,—it nourishes itself. It is remarkable that two nations,

so recently sprung from the same stock, should be so opposite
to one another in their manner of feeling and conversing.

In aristocratic countries the great possess immense privileges, upon which their pride rests, without seeking to rely
upon the lesser advantages which accrue to them. As these
privileges came to them by inheritance, they regard them in
some sort as a portion of themselves, or at least as a natural
right inherent in their own persons. They therefore entertain
a calm sense of their own superiority; they do not dream of
vaunting privileges which every one perceives and no one
contests, and these things are not sufficiently new to be made
topics of conversation. They stand unmoved in their solitary
greatness, well assured that they are seen of all the world
without any effort to show themselves off, and that no one will
attempt to drive them from that position. When an aristocracy
carries on the public affairs, its national pride naturally assumes this reserved, indifferent, and haughty form, which is
imitated by all the other classes of the nation.

When, on the contrary, social conditions differ but little,
the slightest privileges are of some importance; as every man
sees around himself a million of people enjoying precisely
similar or analogous advantages, his pride becomes craving
and jealous, he clings to mere trifles, and doggedly defends
them. In democracies, as the conditions of life are very fluctuating, men have almost always recently acquired the advantages which they possess; the consequence is, that they feel
extreme pleasure in exhibiting them, to show others and convince themselves that they really enjoy them. As at any instant
these same advantages may be lost, their possessors are constantly on the alert, and make a point of showing that they
still retain them. Men living in democracies love their country
just as they love themselves, and they transfer the habits of
their private vanity to their vanity as a nation.

The restless and insatiable vanity of a democratic people
originates so entirely in the equality and precariousness of
their social condition, that the members of the haughtiest nobility display the very same passion in those lesser portions of
their existence in which there is anything fluctuating or contested. An aristocratic class always differs greatly from the
other classes of the nation, by the extent and perpetuity of its
privileges; but it often happens that the only differences between the members who belong to it consist in small, transient
advantages, which may any day be lost or acquired. The
members of a powerful aristocracy, collected in a capital or
a court, have been known to contest with virulence those frivolous privileges which depend on the caprice of fashion or the

will of their master. These persons then displayed towards each
other precisely the same puerile jealousies which animate the
men of democracies, the same eagerness to snatch the smallest
advantages which their equals contested, and the same desire
to parade ostentatiously those of which they were in possession.

If national pride ever entered into the minds of courtiers,
I do not question that they would display it in the same
manner as the members of a democratic community.

45. How the Aspect of Society in the United States Is at Once Excited and Monotonous.

IT would seem that nothing could be more adapted to stimulate
and to feed curiosity than the aspect of the United States.
Fortunes, opinions, and laws are there in ceaseless variation:
it is as if immutable Nature herself were mutable, such are the
changes worked upon her by the hand of man. Yet, in the end,
the spectacle of this excited community becomes monotonous,
and, after having watched the moving pageant for a time, the
spectator is tired of it.

Amongst aristocratic nations, every man is pretty nearly
stationary in his own sphere; but men are astonishingly unlike
each other,—their passions, their notions, their habits, and
their tastes are essentially different: nothing changes, but everything differs. In democracies, on the contrary, all men are alike,
and do things pretty nearly alike. It is true that they are subject
to great and frequent vicissitudes; but as the same events of
good or adverse fortune are continually recurring, the name
of the actors only is changed, the piece is always the same. The
aspect of American society is animated, because men and
things are always changing; but it is monotonous, because all
these changes are alike.

Men living in democratic times have many passions, but
most of their passions either end in the love of riches, or
proceed from it. The cause of this is, not that their souls are
narrower, but that the importance of money is really greater
at such times. When all the members of a community are
independent of or indifferent to each other, the co-operation
of each of them can be obtained only by paying for it: this
infinitely multiplies the purposes to which wealth may be
applied, and increases its value. When the reverence which
belonged to what is old has vanished, birth, condition, and
profession no longer distinguish men, or scarcely distinguish

them: hardly anything but money remains to create strongly marked differences between them, and to raise some of them above the common level. The distinction originating in wealth is increased by the disappearance or diminution of all other distinctions. Amongst aristocratic nations, money reaches only to a few points on the vast circle of man's desires: in democracies, it seems to lead to all.

The love of wealth is therefore to be traced, either as a principal or an accessory motive, at the bottom of all that the Americans do: this gives to all their passions a sort of family likeness, and soon renders the survey of them exceedingly wearisome. This perpetual recurrence of the same passion is monotonous; the peculiar methods by which this passion seeks its own gratification are no less so.

In an orderly and peaceable democracy like the United States, where men cannot enrich themselves by war, by public office, or by political confiscation, the love of wealth mainly drives them into business and manufactures. Although these pursuits often bring about great commotions and disasters, they cannot prosper without strictly regular habits and a long routine of petty uniform acts. The stronger the passion is, the more regular are these habits, and the more uniform are these acts. It may be said that it is the vehemence of their desires which makes the Americans so methodical; it perturbs their minds, but it disciplines their lives.

The remark I here apply to America may indeed be addressed to almost all our contemporaries. Variety is disappearing from the human race; the same ways of acting, thinking, and feeling are to be met with all over the world. This is not only because nations work more upon each other, and copy each other more faithfully; but as the men of each country relinquish more and more the peculiar opinions and feelings of a caste, a profession, or a family, they simultaneously arrive at something nearer to the constitution of man, which is everywhere the same. Thus they become more alike, even without having imitated each other. Like travellers scattered about some large wood, intersected by paths converging to one point, if all of them keep their eyes fixed upon that point, and advance towards it, they insensibly draw nearer together,— though they seek not, though they see not and know not each other; and they will be surprised at length to find themselves all collected on the same spot. All the nations which take, not any particular man, but Man himself, as the object of their researches and their imitations, are tending in the end to a similar state of society, like these travellers converging to the central plot of the forest.

46. Why So Many Ambitious Men and So Little Lofty Ambition Are to Be Found in the United States.

THE first thing which strikes a traveller in the United States is the innumerable multitude of those who seek to emerge from their original condition; and the second is the rarity of lofty ambition to be observed in the midst of the universally ambitious stir of society. No Americans are devoid of a yearning desire to rise; but hardly any appear to entertain hopes of great magnitude, or to pursue very lofty aims. All are constantly seeking to acquire property, power, and reputation; few contemplate these things upon a great scale; and this is the more surprising, as nothing is to be discerned in the manners or laws of America to limit desire, or to prevent it from spreading its impulses in every direction. It seems difficult to attribute this singular state of things to the equality of social condition; for as soon as that same equality was established in France, the flight of ambition became unbounded. Nevertheless, I think that we may find the principal cause of this fact in the social condition and democratic manners of the Americans.

All revolutions enlarge the ambition of men: this is more peculiarly true of those revolutions which overthrow an aristocracy. When the former barriers which kept back the multitude from fame and power are suddenly thrown down, a violent and universal movement takes place towards that eminence so long coveted and at length to be enjoyed. In this first burst of triumph, nothing seems impossible to any one: not only are desires boundless, but the power of satisfying them seems almost boundless too. Amidst the general and sudden change of laws and customs, in this vast confusion of all men and all ordinances, the various members of the community rise and sink again with excessive rapidity, and power passes so quickly from hand to hand that none need despair of catching it in turn.

It must be recollected, moreover, that the people who destroy an aristocracy have lived under its laws; they have witnessed its splendor, and they have unconsciously imbibed the feelings and notions which it entertained. Thus, at the moment when an aristocracy is dissolved, its spirit still pervades the mass of the community, and its tendencies are

256

retained long after it has been defeated. Ambition is therefore always extremely great as long as a democratic revolution lasts, and it will remain so for some time after the revolution is consummated.

The reminiscence of the extraordinary events which men have witnessed is not obliterated from their memory in a day. The passions which a revolution has roused do not disappear at its close. A sense of instability remains in the midst of re-established order; a notion of easy success survives the strange vicissitudes which gave it birth; desires still remain extremely enlarged, while the means of satisfying them are diminished day by day. The taste for large fortunes subsists, though large fortunes are rare; and on every side we trace the ravages of inordinate and unsuccessful ambition kindled in hearts which it consumes in secret and in vain.

At length, however, the last vestiges of the struggle are effaced; the remains of aristocracy completely disappear; the great events by which its fall was attended are forgotten; peace succeeds to war, and the sway of order is restored in the new realm; desires are again adapted to the means by which they may be fulfilled; the wants, the opinions, and the feelings of men cohere once more; the level of the community is perma-nently determined, and democratic society established.

A democratic nation, arrived at this permanent and regular state of things, will present a very different spectacle from that which we have just described; and we may readily conclude that, if ambition becomes great whilst the conditions of soci-ety are growing equal, it loses that quality when they have grown so.

As wealth is subdivided and knowledge diffused, no one is entirely destitute of education or of property; the privileges and disqualifications of caste being abolished, and men having shattered the bonds which once held them fixed, the notion of advancement suggests itself to every mind, the desire to rise swells in every heart, and all men want to mount above their station; ambition is the universal feeling.

But if the equality of conditions gives some resources to all the members of the community, it also prevents any of them from having resources of great extent, which necessarily cir-cumscribes their desires within somewhat narrow limits. Thus, amongst democratic nations, ambition is ardent and continual, but its aim is not habitually lofty; and life is generally spent in eagerly coveting small objects which are within reach.

What chiefly diverts the men of democracies from lofty ambition is not the scantiness of their fortunes, but the vehe-mence of the exertions they daily make to improve them. They strain their faculties to the utmost to achieve paltry results, and this cannot fail speedily to limit their range of view, and to circumscribe their powers. They might be much poorer, and still be greater.

The small number of opulent citizens who are to be found amidst a democracy do not constitute an exception to this rule. A man who raises himself by degrees to wealth and power, contracts, in the course of this protracted labor, habits of prudence and restraint which he cannot afterwards shake off. A man cannot gradually enlarge his mind as he does his house.

The same observation is applicable to the sons of such a man: they are born, it is true, in a lofty position, but their parents were humble; they have grown up amidst feelings and notions which they cannot afterwards easily get rid of; and it may be presumed that they will inherit the propensities of their father, as well as his wealth.

It may happen, on the contrary, that the poorest scion of a powerful aristocracy may display vast ambition, because the traditional opinions of his race and the general spirit of his order still buoy him up for some time above his fortune.

Another thing which prevents the men of democratic periods from easily indulging in the pursuit of lofty objects, is the lapse of time which they foresee must take place before they can be ready to struggle for them. "It is a great advantage," says Pascal, "to be a man of quality, since it brings one man as forward at eighteen or twenty, as another man would be at fifty, which is a clear gain of thirty years." Those thirty years are commonly wanting to the ambitious characters of democracies. The principle of equality, which allows every man to arrive at everything, prevents all men from rapid advancement.

In a democratic society, as well as elsewhere, there are only a certain number of great fortunes to be made; and as the paths which lead to them are indiscriminately open to all, the progress of all must necessarily be slackened. As the candidates appear to be nearly alike, and as it is difficult to make a selection without infringing the principle of equality, which is the supreme law of democratic societies, the first idea which suggests itself is to make them all advance at the same rate, and submit to the same trials. Thus, in proportion as men become more alike, and the principle of equality is more peaceably and deeply infused into the institutions and manners of the country, the rules for advancement become more inflexible, advancement itself slower, the difficulty of arriving quickly at a certain height far greater. From hatred of privilege and from the embarrassment of choosing, all men are at last constrained, whatever may be their standard, to pass the same ordeal; all are indiscriminately subjected to a multitude of petty preliminary exercises, in which their youth is wasted and their imagination quenched, so that they despair of ever fully attaining what is held out to them; and when at length they are in a condition to perform any extraordinary acts, the taste for such things has forsaken them.

In China, where the equality of conditions is very great and very ancient, no man passes from one public office to another without undergoing a competitive trial. This probation occurs afresh at every stage of his career; and the notion is now so rooted in the manners of the people, that I remember to have read a Chinese novel in which the hero, after numberless crosses, succeeds at length in touching the heart of his mistress by taking honors. A lofty ambition breathes with difficulty in such an atmosphere.

The remark I apply to politics extends to everything: equality everywhere produces the same effects; where the laws of a country do not regulate and retard the advancement of men by positive enactment, competition attains the same end.

In a well-established democratic community, great and rapid elevation is therefore rare; it forms an exception to the common rule; and it is the singularity of such occurrences that makes men forget how rarely they happen.

Men living in democracies ultimately discover these things; they find out at last that the laws of their country open a boundless field of action before them, but that no one can hope to hasten across it. Between them and the final object of their desires they perceive a multitude of small intermediate impediments, which must be slowly surmounted: this prospect wearies and discourages their ambition at once. They therefore give up hopes so doubtful and remote, to search nearer to themselves for less lofty and more easy enjoyments. Their horizon is not bounded by the laws, but narrowed by themselves.

I have remarked that lofty ambitions are more rare in the ages of democracy than in times of aristocracy: I may add, that when, in spite of these natural obstacles, they do spring into existence, their character is different. In aristocracies, the career of ambition is often wide, but its boundaries are determined. In democracies, ambition commonly ranges in a narrower field, but, if once it gets beyond that, hardly any limits can be assigned to it. As men are individually weak,—as they live asunder, and in constant motion,—as precedents are of little authority, and laws but of short duration,—resistance to novelty is languid, and the fabric of society never appears perfectly erect or firmly consolidated. So that, when

once an ambitious man has the power in his grasp, there is
nothing he may not dare; and when it is gone from him, he
meditates the overthrow of the state to regain it. This gives to
great political ambition a character of revolutionary violence,
which it seldom exhibits to an equal degree in aristocratic
communities. The common aspect of democratic nations will
present a great number of small and very rational objects of
ambition, from amongst which a few ill-controlled desires
of a larger growth will at intervals break out; but no such a
thing as ambition, conceived and regulated on a vast scale, is
to be met with there.

I have shown elsewhere by what secret influence the principle of equality makes the passion for physical gratification
and the exclusive love of the present predominate in the human
heart: these different propensities mingle with the sentiment
of ambition, and tinge it, as it were, with their hues.

I believe that ambitious men in democracies are less engrossed than any others with the interests and the judgment
of posterity; the present moment alone engages and absorbs
them. They are more apt to complete a number of undertakings
with rapidity, than to raise lasting monuments of their achievements; and they care much more for success than for fame.
What they most ask of men is obedience, what they most covet
is empire. Their manners have, in almost all cases, remained
below their station; the consequence is, that they frequently
carry very low tastes into their extraordinary fortunes, and
that they seem to have acquired the supreme power only to
minister to their coarse or paltry pleasures.

I think that, in our time, it is very necessary to purify, to
regulate, and to proportion the feeling of ambition, but that
it would be extremely dangerous to seek to impoverish and to
repress it over much. We should attempt to lay down certain
extreme limits, which it should never be allowed to outstep;
but its range within those established limits should not be too
much checked.

I confess that I apprehend much less for democratic society
from the boldness than from the mediocrity of desires. What
appears to me most to be dreaded is, that, in the midst of the
small, incessant occupations of private life, ambition should
lose its vigor and its greatness; that the passions of man should
abate, but at the same time be lowered; so that the march
of society should every day become more tranquil and less
aspiring.

I think, then, that the leaders of modern society would be
wrong to seek to lull the community by a state of too uniform
and too peaceful happiness: and that it is well to expose it from

time to time to matters of difficulty and danger, in order to raise ambition, and to give it a field of action.

Moralists are constantly complaining that the ruling vice of the present time is pride. This is true in one sense, for indeed every one thinks that he is better than his neighbor, or refuses to obey his superior; but it is extremely false in another, for the same man who cannot endure subordination or equality, has so contemptible an opinion of himself that he thinks he is born only to indulge in vulgar pleasures. He willingly takes up with low desires, without daring to embark in lofty enterprises, of which he scarcely dreams.

Thus, far from thinking that humility ought to be preached to our contemporaries, I would have endeavors made to give them a more enlarged idea of themselves and of their kind. Humility is unwholesome to them; what they most want is, in my opinion, pride. I would willingly exchange several of our small virtues for this one vice.

47. The Trade of Place-Hunting in Certain Democratic Countries.

IN the United States, as soon as a man has acquired some education and pecuniary resources, he either endeavors to get rich by commerce or industry, or he buys land in the bush and turns pioneer. All that he asks of the state is, not to be disturbed in his toil, and to be secure of his earnings. Amongst most European nations, when a man begins to feel his strength and to extend his desires, the first thing that occurs to him is to get some public employment. These opposite effects, originating in the same cause, deserve our passing notice.

When public employments are few in number, ill-paid, and precarious, whilst the different kinds of business are numerous and lucrative, it is to business, and not to official duties, that the new and eager desires created by the principle of equality turn from every side. But if, whilst the ranks of society are becoming more equal, the education of the people remains incomplete, or their spirit the reverse of bold,—if commerce and industry, checked in their growth, afford only slow and arduous means of making a fortune,—the various members of the community, despairing of ameliorating their own condition, rush to the head of the state and demand its assistance. To relieve their own necessities at the cost of the public treasury appears to them the easiest and most open, if not the only, way of rising above a condition which no longer contents them; place-hunting becomes the most generally followed of all trades.

This must especially be the case in those great centralized monarchies, in which the number of paid offices is immense, and the tenure of them tolerably secure, so that no one despairs of obtaining a place, and of enjoying it as undisturbedly as an hereditary fortune.

I shall not remark that the universal and inordinate desire for place is a great social evil; that it destroys the spirit of independence in the citizen, and diffuses a venal and servile humor throughout the frame of society; that it stifles the manlier virtues: nor shall I be at the pains to demonstrate that this kind of traffic only creates an unproductive activity, which agitates the country without adding to its resources: all these things are obvious. But I would observe, that a government which encourages this tendency risks its own tranquillity, and places its very existence in great jeopardy.

I am aware that, at a time like our own, when the love and respect which formerly clung to authority are seen gradually to decline, it may appear necessary to those in power to lay a closer hold on every man by his own interest, and it may seem convenient to use his own passions to keep him in order and in silence; but this cannot be so long, and what may appear to be a source of strength for a certain time will assuredly become, in the end, a great cause of embarrassment and weakness.

Amongst democratic nations, as well as elsewhere, the number of official appointments has, in the end, some limits; but amongst those nations, the number of aspirants is unlimited; it perpetually increases, with a gradual and irresistible rise, in proportion as social conditions become more equal, and is only checked by the limits of the population.

Thus, when public employments afford the only outlet for ambition, the government necessarily meets with a permanent opposition at last; for it is tasked to satisfy with limited means unlimited desires. It is very certain that, of all people in the world, the most difficult to restrain and to manage are a people of office-hunters. Whatever endeavors are made by rulers, such a people can never be contented; and it is always to be apprehended that they will ultimately overturn the constitution of the country, and change the aspect of the state, for the sole purpose of making a clearance of places.

The sovereigns of the present age, who strive to fix upon themselves alone all those novel desires which are aroused by equality, and to satisfy them, will repent in the end, if I am not mistaken, that ever they embarked in this policy: they will one day discover that they have hazarded their own power by making it so necessary, and that the more safe and honest course would have been to teach their subjects the art of providing for themselves.

48. Why Great Revolutions Will Become More Rare.

A PEOPLE who have existed for centuries under a system of castes and classes, can only arrive at a democratic state of society by passing through a long series of more or less critical transformations, accomplished by violent efforts, and after numerous vicissitudes; in the course of which, property, opinions, and power are rapidly transferred from one to another. Even after this great revolution is consummated, the revolutionary habits produced by it may long be traced, and it will be followed by deep commotion. As all this takes place at the very time when social conditions are becoming more equal, it is inferred that some concealed relation and secret tie exists between the principle of equality itself and revolution, insomuch that the one cannot exist without giving rise to the other.

On this point, reasoning may seem to lead to the same result as experience. Amongst a people whose ranks are nearly equal, no ostensible bond connects men together, or keeps them settled in their station. None of them have either a permanent right or power to command, none are forced by their condition to obey; but every man, finding himself possessed of some education and some resources, may choose his own path, and proceed apart from all his fellow-men. The same causes which make the members of the community independent of each other, continually impel them to new and restless desires, and constantly spur them onwards. It therefore seems natural that, in a democratic community, men, things, and opinions should be forever changing their form and place, and that democratic ages should be times of rapid and incessant transformation.

But is this really the case? Does the equality of social conditions habitually and permanently lead men to revolution? Does that state of society contain some perturbing principle, which prevents the community from ever subsiding into calm, and disposes the citizens to alter incessantly their laws, their principles, and their manners? I do not believe it; and as the subject is important, I beg for the reader's close attention.

Almost all the revolutions which have changed the aspect of nations have been made to consolidate or to destroy social inequality. Remove the secondary causes which have produced the great convulsions of the world, and you will almost always find the principle of inequality at the bottom. Either the poor have attempted to plunder the rich, or the rich to enslave the poor. If, then, a state of society can ever be founded in which every man shall have something to keep, and little to take from others, much will have been done for the peace of the world.

I am aware that, amongst a great democratic people, there will always be some members of the community in great poverty, and others in great opulence; but the poor, instead of forming the immense majority of the nation, as is always the case in aristocratic communities, are comparatively few in number, and the laws do not bind them together by the ties of irremediable and hereditary penury.

The wealthy, on their side, are few and powerless; they have no privileges which attract public observation; even their wealth, as it is no longer incorporated and bound up with the soil, is impalpable, and, as it were, invisible. As there is no longer a race of poor men, so there is no longer a race of rich men; the latter spring up daily from the multitude, and relapse into it again. Hence they do not form a distinct class, which may be easily marked out and plundered; and, moreover, as they are connected with the mass of their fellow-citizens by a thousand secret ties, the people cannot assail them without inflicting an injury upon themselves.

Between these two extremes of democratic communities stand an innumerable multitude of men almost alike, who, without being exactly either rich or poor, are possessed of sufficient property to desire the maintenance of order, yet not enough to excite envy. Such men are the natural enemies of violent commotions; their stillness keeps all beneath them and above them still, and secures the balance of the fabric of society.

Not, indeed, that even these men are contented with what they have gotten, or that they feel a natural abhorrence for a revolution in which they might share the spoil without sharing the calamity; on the contrary, they desire, with unexampled ardor, to get rich, but the difficulty is to know from whom riches can be taken. The same state of society which constantly prompts desires, restrains these desires within necessary limits; it gives men more liberty of changing, and less interest in change.

Not only are the men of democracies not naturally desirous of revolutions, but they are afraid of them. All revolutions more or less threaten the tenure of property: but most of those who live in democratic countries are possessed of property; not only are they possessed of property, but they live in the condition where men set the greatest store upon their property.

If we attentively consider each of the classes of which society is composed, it is easy to see that the passions created by property are keenest and most tenacious amongst the middle classes. The poor often care but little for what they possess, because they suffer much more from the want of what they have not, than they enjoy the little they have. The rich have many other passions besides that of riches to satisfy; and, besides, the long and arduous enjoyment of a great fortune sometimes makes them in the end insensible to its charms. But the men who have a competency, alike removed from opulence and from penury, attach an enormous value to their possessions. As they are still almost within the reach of poverty, they see its privations near at hand, and dread them; between poverty and themselves there is nothing but a scanty fortune, upon which they immediately fix their apprehensions and their hopes. Every day increases the interest they take in it, by the constant cares which it occasions; and they are the more attached to it by their continual exertions to increase the amount. The notion of surrendering the smallest part of it is insupportable to them, and they consider its total loss as the worst of misfortunes.

Now, these eager and apprehensive men of small property constitute the class which is constantly increased by the equality of conditions. Hence, in democratic communities, the majority of the people do not clearly see what they have to gain by a revolution, but they continually and in a thousand ways feel that they might lose by one.

I have shown, in another part of this work, that the equality of conditions naturally urges men to embark in commercial and industrial pursuits, and that it tends to increase and to distribute real property: I have also pointed out the means by which it inspires every man with an eager and constant desire to increase his welfare. Nothing is more opposed to revolutionary passions than these things. It may happen that the final result of a revolution is favorable to commerce and manufactures; but its first consequence will almost always be the ruin of manufactures and mercantile men, because it must always change at once the general principles of consumption, and temporarily upset the existing proportion between supply and demand.

I know of nothing more opposite to revolutionary manners than commercial manners. Commerce is naturally adverse to all the violent passions; it loves to temporize, takes delight in compromise, and studiously avoids irritation. It is patient, insinuating, flexible, and never has recourse to extreme measures until obliged by the most absolute necessity. Commerce renders men independent of each other, gives them a lofty notion of their personal importance, leads them to seek to conduct their own affairs, and teaches how to conduct them well; it therefore prepares men for freedom, but preserves them from revolutions.

In a revolution, the owners of personal property have more to fear than all others; for, on the one hand, their property is often easy to seize; and, on the other, it may totally disappear at any moment,—a subject of alarm to which the owners of real property are less exposed, since, although they may lose the income of their estates, they may hope to preserve the land itself through the greatest vicissitudes. Hence the former are much more alarmed at the symptoms of revolutionary commotion than the latter. Thus, nations are less disposed to make revolutions in proportion as personal property is augmented and distributed amongst them, and as the number of those possessing it is increased.

Moreover, whatever profession men may embrace, and whatever species of property they may possess, one characteristic is common to them all. No one is fully contented with his present fortune; all are perpetually striving, in a thousand ways, to improve it. Consider any one of them at any period of his life, and he will be found engaged with some new project for the purpose of increasing what he has; talk not to him of the interests and the rights of mankind, this small domestic concern absorbs for the time all his thoughts, and inclines him to defer political agitations to some other season. This not only prevents men from making revolutions, but deters men from desiring them. Violent political passions have but little hold on those who have devoted all their faculties to the pursuit of their well-being. The ardor which they display in small matters calms their zeal for momentous undertakings.

From time to time, indeed, enterprising and ambitious men will arise in democratic communities, whose unbounded aspirations cannot be contented by following the beaten track. Such men like revolutions, and hail their approach; but they have great difficulty in bringing them about, unless extraordinary events come to their assistance. No man can struggle with advantage against the spirit of his age and country; and, however powerful he may be supposed to be, he will find it difficult to make his contemporaries share in feelings and opinions which are repugnant to all their feelings and desires.

It is a mistake to believe that, when once the equality of condition has become the old and uncontested state of society, and has imparted its characteristics to the manners of a nation, men will easily allow themselves to be thrust into perilous risks by an imprudent leader or a bold innovator. Not indeed that they will resist him openly, by well-contrived schemes, or even by a premeditated plan of resistance. They will not struggle energetically against him,—sometimes they will even applaud him; but they do not follow him. To his vehemence they secretly oppose their inertia, to his revolutionary tendencies their conservative interests, their homely tastes to his adventurous passions, their good sense to the flights of his genius, to his poetry their prose. With immense exertion he raises them for an instant, but they speedily escape from him, and fall back, as it were, by their own weight. He strains himself to rouse the indifferent and distracted multitude, and finds at last that he is reduced to impotence, not because he is conquered, but because he is alone.

I do not assert that men living in democratic communities are naturally stationary; I think, on the contrary, that a perpetual stir prevails in the bosom of those societies, and that rest is unknown there; but I think that men bestir themselves within certain limits, beyond which they hardly ever go. They are forever varying, altering, and restoring secondary matters; but they carefully abstain from touching what is fundamental. They love change, but they dread revolutions.

Although the Americans are constantly modifying or abrogating some of their laws, they by no means display revolutionary passions. It may be easily seen, from the promptitude with which they check and calm themselves when public excitement begins to grow alarming, and at the very moment when passions seem most roused, that they dread a revolution as the worst of misfortunes, and that every one of them is inwardly resolved to make great sacrifices to avoid such a catastrophe. In no country in the world is the love of property more active and more anxious than in the United States; nowhere does the majority display less inclination for those principles which threaten to alter, in whatever manner, the laws of property.

I have often remarked, that theories which are of a revolutionary nature, since they cannot be put in practice without a complete and sometimes a sudden change in the state of property and persons, are much less favorably viewed in the United States than in the great monarchical countries of Europe: if some men profess them, the bulk of the people reject them with instinctive abhorrence. I do not hesitate to say, that most of the maxims commonly called democratic in

France would be proscribed by the democracy of the United States. This may easily be understood; in America, men have the opinions and passions of democracy; in Europe, we have still the passions and opinions of revolution.

If ever America undergoes great revolutions, they will be brought about by the presence of the black race on the soil of the United States; that is to say, they will owe their origin, not to the equality, but to the inequality of condition.

When social conditions are equal, every man is apt to live apart, centred in himself and forgetful of the public. If the rulers of democratic nations were either to neglect to correct this fatal tendency, or to encourage it from a notion that it weans men from political passions and thus wards off revolutions, they might eventually produce the evil they seek to avoid, and a time might come when the inordinate passions of a few men, aided by the unintelligent selfishness or the pusillanimity of the greater number, would ultimately compel society to pass through strange vicissitudes. In democratic communities, revolutions are seldom desired except by a minority; but a minority may sometimes effect them.

I do not assert that democratic nations are secure from revolutions; I merely say that the state of society in those nations does not lead to revolutions, but rather wards them off. A democratic people left to itself will not easily embark in great hazards; it is only led to revolutions unawares; it may sometimes undergo them, but it does not make them: and I will add, that, when such a people has been allowed to acquire sufficient knowledge and experience, it will not suffer them to be made.

I am well aware that, in this respect, public institutions may themselves do much; they may encourage or repress the tendencies which originate in the state of society. I therefore do not maintain, I repeat, that a people is secure from revolutions simply because conditions are equal in the community; but I think that, whatever the institutions of such a people may be, great revolutions will always be far less violent and less frequent than is supposed; and I can easily discern a state of polity which, when combined with the principle of equality, would render society more stationary than it has ever been in our western part of the world.

The observations I have here made on events may also be applied in part to opinions. Two things are surprising in the United States,—the mutability of the greater part of human actions, and the singular stability of certain principles. Men are in constant motion; the mind of man appears almost unmoved. When once an opinion has spread over the country and struck root there, it would seem that no power on earth is strong enough to eradicate it. In the United States, general principles in religion, philosophy, morality, and even politics, do not vary, or at least are only modified by a hidden and often an imperceptible process: even the grossest prejudices are obliterated with incredible slowness, amidst the continual friction of men and things.

I hear it said that it is in the nature and the habits of democracies to be constantly changing their opinions and feelings. This may be true of small democratic nations, like those of the ancient world, in which the whole community could be assembled in a public place, and then excited at will by an orator. But I saw nothing of the kind amongst the great democratic people which dwells upon the opposite shores of the Atlantic Ocean. What struck me in the United States was, the difficulty of shaking the majority in an opinion once conceived, or of drawing it off from a leader once adopted. Neither speaking nor writing can accomplish it; nothing but experience will avail, and even experience must be repeated.

This is surprising at first sight, but a more attentive investigation explains the fact. I do not think that it is as easy as is supposed to uproot the prejudices of a democratic people, to change its belief, to supersede principles once established by new principles in religion, politics, and morals,—in a word, to make great and frequent changes in men's minds. Not that the human mind is there at rest,—it is in constant agitation; but it is engaged in infinitely varying the consequences of known principles, and in seeking for new consequences, rather than in seeking for new principles. Its motion is one of rapid circumvolution, rather than of straightforward impulse by rapid and direct effort; it extends its orbit by small continual and hasty movements, but it does not suddenly alter its position.

Men who are equal in rights, in education, in fortune, or, to comprise all in one word, in their social condition, have necessarily wants, habits, and tastes which are hardly dissimilar. As they look at objects under the same aspect, their minds naturally tend to similar conclusions; and, though each of them may deviate from his contemporaries and form opinions of his own, they will involuntarily and unconsciously concur in a certain number of received opinions. The more attentively I consider the effects of equality upon the mind, the more am I persuaded that the intellectual anarchy which we witness about us is not, as many men suppose, the natural state of democratic nations. I think it is rather to be regarded as an accident peculiar to their youth, and that it only breaks out at that period of transition when men have already snapped the former ties which bound them together, but are still amazingly different in origin, education, and manners; so that, having retained opinions, propensities, and tastes of great diversity, nothing any longer prevents men from avowing them openly. The leading opinions of men become similar in proportion as their conditions assimilate: such appears to me to be the general and permanent law; the rest is casual and transient.

I believe that it will rarely happen to any man, in a democratic community, suddenly to frame a system of notions very remote from that which his contemporaries have adopted; and if some such innovator appeared, I apprehend that he would have great difficulty in finding listeners, still more in finding believers. When the conditions of men are almost equal, they do not easily allow themselves to be persuaded by each other. As they all live in close intercourse, as they have learned the same things together, and as they lead the same life, they are not naturally disposed to take one of themselves for a guide, and to follow him implicitly. Men seldom take the opinion of their equal, or of a man like themselves, upon trust.

Not only is confidence in the superior attainments of certain individuals weakened amongst democratic nations, as I have elsewhere remarked, but the general notion of the intellectual superiority which any man whatsoever may acquire in relation to the rest of the community is soon overshadowed. As men grow more like each other, the doctrine of the equality of the intellect gradually infuses itself into their opinions; and it becomes more difficult for any innovator to acquire or to exert much influence over the minds of a people. In such communities, sudden intellectual revolutions will therefore be rare; for, if we read aright the history of the world, we shall find that great and rapid changes in human opinions have been produced far less by the force of reasoning than by the authority of a name.

Observe, too, that, as the men who live in democratic societies are not connected with each other by any tie, each of them must be convinced individually; whilst, in aristocratic society, it is enough to convince a few, the rest follow. If Luther had lived in an age of equality, and had not had princes and potentates for his audience, he would perhaps have found it more difficult to change the aspect of Europe.

Not, indeed, that the men of democracies are naturally strongly persuaded of the certainty of their opinions, or are unwavering in belief; they frequently entertain doubts which no one, in their eyes, can remove. It sometimes happens, at such times, that the human mind would willingly change its position; but as nothing urges or guides it forward, it oscillates to and fro without progressive motion.

Even when the confidence of a democratic people has been won, it is still no easy matter to gain their attention. It is extremely difficult to obtain a hearing from men living in democracies, unless it be to speak to them of themselves. They do not attend to the things said to them, because they are always fully engrossed with the things they are doing. For, indeed, few men are idle in democratic nations; life is passed in the midst of noise and excitement, and men are so engaged in acting that little time remains to them for thinking. I would especially remark, that they are not only employed, but that they are passionately devoted to their employments. They are always in action, and each of their actions absorbs their faculties: the zeal which they display in business puts out the enthusiasm they might otherwise entertain for ideas.

I think that it is extremely difficult to excite the enthusiasm of a democratic people for any theory which has not a palpable, direct, and immediate connection with the daily occupations of life: therefore they will not easily forsake their old opinions; for it is enthusiasm which flings the minds of men out of the beaten track, and effects the great revolutions of the intellect, as well as the great revolutions of the political world.

Thus, democratic nations have neither time nor taste to go in search of novel opinions. Even when those they possess become doubtful, they still retain them, because it would take too much time and inquiry to change them; they retain them, not as certain, but as established.

There are yet other and more cogent reasons which prevent any great change from being easily effected in the principles of a democratic people. I have already adverted to them in the nineteenth chapter.

If the influence of individuals is weak and hardly perceptible amongst such a people, the power exercised by the mass upon the mind of each individual is extremely great,—I have already shown for what reasons. I would now observe, that it is wrong to suppose that this depends solely upon the form of government, and that the majority would lose its intellectual supremacy if it were to lose its political power.

In aristocracies, men have often much greatness and strength of their own: when they find themselves at variance with the greater number of their fellow-countrymen, they withdraw to their own circle, where they support and console themselves. Such is not the case in a democratic country; there, public favor seems as necessary as the air we breathe, and to live at

ALEXIS DE TOCQUEVILLE

variance with the multitude is, as it were, not to live. The multitude require no laws to coerce those who think not like themselves: public disapprobation is enough; a sense of their loneliness and impotence overtakes them and drives them to despair.

Whenever social conditions are equal, public opinion presses with enormous weight upon the minds of each individual; it surrounds, directs, and oppresses him; and this arises from the very constitution of society, much more than from its political laws. As men grow more alike, each man feels himself weaker in regard to all the rest; as he discerns nothing by which he is considerably raised above them, or distinguished from them, he mistrusts himself as soon as they assail him. Not only does he mistrust his strength, but he even doubts of his right; and he is very near acknowledging that he is in the wrong, when the greater number of his countrymen assert that he is so. The majority do not need to constrain him; they convince him. In whatever way, then, the powers of a democratic community may be organized and balanced, it will always be extremely difficult to believe what the bulk of the people reject, or to profess what they condemn.

This circumstance is extraordinarily favorable to the stability of opinions. When an opinion has taken root amongst a democratic people, and established itself in the minds of the bulk of the community, it afterwards subsists by itself and is maintained without effort, because no one attacks it. Those who at first rejected it as false, ultimately receive it as the general impression; and those who still dispute it in their hearts, conceal their dissent; they are careful not to engage in a dangerous and useless conflict.

It is true, that, when the majority of a democratic people change their opinions, they may suddenly and arbitrarily effect strange revolutions in men's minds; but their opinions do not change without much difficulty, and it is almost as difficult to show that they are changed.

Time, events, or the unaided individual action of the mind, will sometimes undermine or destroy an opinion, without any outward sign of the change. It has not been openly assailed, no conspiracy has been formed to make war on it, but its followers one by one noiselessly secede; day by day a few of them abandon it, until at last it is only professed by a minority. In this state it will still continue to prevail. As its enemies remain mute, or only interchange their thoughts by stealth, they are themselves unaware for a long period that a great revolution has actually been effected; and in this state of uncertainty they take no steps; they observe each other and are silent. The majority have ceased to believe what they believed before; but they still affect to believe, and this empty phantom of public opinion is strong enough to chill innovators, and to keep them silent and at a respectful distance.

We live at a time which has witnessed the most rapid changes of opinion in the minds of men; nevertheless it may be that the leading opinions of society will ere long be more settled than they have been for several centuries in our history: that time is not yet come, but it may perhaps be approaching. As I examine more closely the natural wants and tendencies of democratic nations, I grow persuaded that, if ever social equality is generally and permanently established in the world, great intellectual and political revolutions will become more difficult and less frequent than is supposed. Because the men of democracies appear always excited, uncertain, eager, changeable in their wills and in their positions, it is imagined that they are suddenly to abrogate their laws, to adopt new opinions, and to assume new manners. But if the principle of equality predisposes men to change, it also suggests to them certain interests and tastes which cannot be satisfied without a settled order of things; equality urges them on, but at the same time it holds them back; it spurs them, but fastens them to earth; it kindles their desires, but limits their powers.

This, however, is not perceived at first; the passions which tend to sever the citizens of a democracy are obvious enough; but the hidden force which restrains and unites them is not discernible at a glance.

Amidst the ruins which surround me, shall I dare to say that revolutions are not what I most fear for coming generations? If men continue to shut themselves more closely within the narrow circle of domestic interests, and to live upon that kind of excitement, it is to be apprehended that they may ultimately become inaccessible to those great and powerful public emotions which perturb nations, but which develop them and recruit them. When property becomes so fluctuating, and the love of property so restless and so ardent, I cannot but fear that men may arrive at such a state as to regard every new theory as a peril, every innovation as an irksome toil, every social improvement as a stepping-stone to revolution, and so refuse to move altogether for fear of being moved too far. I dread, and I confess it, lest they should at last so entirely give way to a cowardly love of present enjoyment, as to lose sight of the interests of their future selves and those of their descendants; and prefer to glide along the easy current of life, rather than to make, when it is necessary, a strong and sudden effort to a higher purpose.

It is believed by some that modern society will be ever changing its aspect; for myself, I fear that it will ultimately be too invariably fixed in the same institutions, the same prejudices, the same manners, so that mankind will be stopped and circumscribed; that the mind will swing backwards and forwards forever, without begetting fresh ideas; that man will waste his strength in bootless and solitary trifling; and, though in continual motion, that humanity will cease to advance.

49. Why Democratic Nations Are Naturally Desirous of Peace, and Democratic Armies of War.

THE same interests, the same fears, the same passions, which deter democratic nations from revolutions, deter them also from war; the spirit of military glory and the spirit of revolution are weakened at the same time and by the same causes. The ever-increasing numbers of men of property who are lovers of peace, the growth of personal wealth which war so rapidly consumes, the mildness of manners, the gentleness of heart, those tendencies to pity which are produced by the equality of conditions, that coolness of understanding which renders men comparatively insensible to the violent and poetical excitement of arms,—all these causes concur to quench the military spirit. I think it may be admitted as a general and constant rule, that, amongst civilized nations, the warlike passions will become more rare and less intense in proportion as social conditions shall be more equal.

War is nevertheless an occurrence to which all nations are subject, democratic nations as well as others. Whatever taste they may have for peace, they must hold themselves in readiness to repel aggression, or, in other words, they must have an army. Fortune, which has conferred so many peculiar benefits upon the inhabitants of the United States, has placed them in the midst of a wilderness, where they have, so to speak, no neighbors: a few thousand soldiers are sufficient for their wants; but this is peculiar to America, not democracy.

The equality of conditions, and the manners as well as the institutions resulting from it, do not exempt a democratic people from the necessity of standing armies, and their armies always exercise a powerful influence over their fate. It is therefore of singular importance to inquire what are the natural propensities of the men of whom these armies are composed.

Amongst aristocratic nations, especially amongst those in which birth is the only source of rank, the same inequality exists in the army as in the nation; the officer is noble, the soldier is a serf; the one is naturally called upon to command, the other to obey. In aristocratic armies, the private soldier's ambition is therefore circumscribed within very narrow limits. Nor has the ambition of the officer an unlimited range. An aristocratic body not only forms a part of the scale of ranks in the nation, but it contains a part of the scale of ranks within itself: the members of whom it is composed are placed one above another, in a particular and unvarying manner. Thus, one man is born to the command of a regiment, another to that of a company; when once they have reached the utmost object of their hopes, they stop of their own accord, and remain contented with their lot.

There is, besides, a strong cause, which, in aristocracies, weakens the officer's desire of promotion. Amongst aristocratic nations, an officer, independently of his rank in the army, also occupies an elevated rank in society; the former is almost always, in his eyes, only an appendage to the latter. A nobleman who embraces the profession of arms follows it less from motives of ambition than from a sense of the duties imposed on him by his birth. He enters the army in order to find an honorable employment for the idle years of his youth, and to be able to bring back to his home and his peers some honorable recollections of military life; but his principal object is not to obtain by that profession either property, distinction, or power, for he possesses these advantages in his own right, and enjoys them without leaving his home.

In democratic armies, all the soldiers may become officers, which makes the desire of promotion general, and immeasurably extends the bounds of military ambition. The officer, on his part, sees nothing which naturally and necessarily stops him at one grade more than at another; and each grade has immense importance in his eyes, because his rank in society almost always depends on his rank in the army. Amongst democratic nations, it often happens that an officer has no property but his pay, and no distinction but that of military honors: consequently, as often as his duties change his fortune changes, and he becomes, as it were, a new man. What was only an appendage to his position in aristocratic armies, has thus become the main point, the basis of his whole condition.

Under the old French monarchy, officers were always called by their titles of nobility; they are now always called by the title of their military rank. This little change in the forms of language suffices to show that a great revolution has taken place in the constitution of society and in that of the army.

In democratic armies, the desire of advancement is almost universal: it is ardent, tenacious, perpetual; it is strengthened by all other desires, and only extinguished with life itself. But it is easy to see, that, of all armies in the world, those in which advancement must be slowest in time of peace are the armies of democratic countries. As the number of commissions is naturally limited, whilst the number of competitors is almost unlimited, and as the strict law of equality is over all alike, none can make rapid progress,—many can make no progress at all. Thus, the desire of advancement is greater, and the opportunities of advancement fewer there than elsewhere. All the ambitious spirits of a democratic army are consequently ardently desirous of war, because war makes vacancies, and warrants the violation of that law of seniority which is the sole privilege natural to democracy.

We thus arrive at this singular consequence, that, of all armies, those most ardently desirous of war are democratic armies, and of all nations, those most fond of peace are democratic nations; and what makes these facts still more extraordinary is, that these contrary effects are produced at the same time by the principle of equality.

All the members of the community, being alike, constantly harbor the wish and discover the possibility of changing their condition and improving their welfare: this makes them fond of peace, which is favorable to industry, and allows every man to pursue his own little undertakings to their completion. On the other hand, this same equality makes soldiers dream of fields of battle, by increasing the value of military honors in the eyes of those who follow the profession of arms, and by rendering those honors accessible to all. In either case, the inquietude of the heart is the same, the taste for enjoyment as insatiable, the ambition of success as great,—the means of gratifying it alone are different.

These opposite tendencies of the nation and the army expose democratic communities to great dangers. When a military spirit forsakes a people, the profession of arms immediately ceases to be held in honor, and military men fall to the lowest rank of the public servants: they are little esteemed, and no longer understood. The reverse of what takes place in aristocratic ages then occurs; the men who enter the army are no longer those of the highest, but of the lowest rank. Military ambition is only indulged when no other is possible. Hence arises a circle of cause and consequence from which it is difficult to escape: the best part of the nation shuns the military profession because that profession is not honored, and the profession is not honored because the best part of the nation has ceased to follow it.

It is then no matter of surprise that democratic armies are often restless, ill-tempered, and dissatisfied with their lot, although their physical condition is commonly far better, and their discipline less strict, than in other countries. The soldier feels that he occupies an inferior position, and his wounded pride either stimulates his taste for hostilities which would render his services necessary, or gives him a desire for revolution, during which he may hope to win by force of arms the political influence and personal importance now denied him.

The composition of democratic armies makes this last-mentioned danger much to be feared. In democratic communities, almost every man has some property to preserve; but democratic armies are generally led by men without property, most of whom have little to lose in civil broils. The bulk of the nation is naturally much more afraid of revolutions than in the ages of aristocracy, but the leaders of the army much less so.

Moreover, as amongst democratic nations (to repeat what I have just remarked) the wealthiest, best educated, and ablest men seldom adopt the military profession, the army, taken collectively, eventually forms a small nation by itself, where the mind is less enlarged, and habits are more rude, than in the nation at large. Now, this small uncivilized nation has arms in its possession, and alone knows how to use them; for, indeed, the pacific temper of the community increases the danger to which a democratic people is exposed from the military and turbulent spirit of the army. Nothing is so dangerous as an army amidst an unwarlike nation; the excessive love of the whole community for quiet continually puts the constitution at the mercy of the soldiery.

It may therefore be asserted, generally speaking, that, if democratic nations are naturally prone to peace from their interests and their propensities, they are constantly drawn to war and revolutions by their armies. Military revolutions, which are scarcely ever to be apprehended in aristocracies, are always to be dreaded amongst democratic nations. These perils must be reckoned amongst the most formidable which beset their future fate, and the attention of statesmen should be sedulously applied to find a remedy for the evil.

When a nation perceives that it is inwardly affected by the restless ambition of its army, the first thought which occurs is to give this inconvenient ambition an object by going to war.

I do not wish to speak ill of war: war almost always enlarges the mind of a people, and raises their character. In some cases, it is the only check to the excessive growth of certain propensities which naturally spring out of the equality of conditions, and it must be considered as a necessary corrective to certain inveterate diseases to which democratic communities are liable.

War has great advantages, but we must not flatter ourselves that it can diminish the danger I have just pointed out. That peril is only suspended by it, to return more fiercely when the war is over; for armies are much more impatient of peace after having tasted military exploits. War could only be a remedy for a people who should always be athirst for military glory.

I foresee that all the military rulers who may rise up in great democratic nations will find it easier to conquer with their armies, than to make their armies live at peace after conquest. There are two things which a democratic people will always find very difficult,—to begin a war and to end it.

Again, if war has some peculiar advantages for democratic nations, on the other hand, it exposes them to certain dangers, which aristocracies have no cause to dread to an equal extent. I shall point out only two of these.

Although war gratifies the army, it embarrasses and often exasperates that countless multitude of men whose minor passions every day require peace in order to be satisfied. Thus there is some risk of its causing, under another form, the very disturbance it is intended to prevent.

No protracted war can fail to endanger the freedom of a democratic country. Not indeed that, after every victory, it is to be apprehended that the victorious generals will possess themselves by force of the supreme power, after the manner of Sylla and Cæsar: the danger is of another kind. War does not always give over democratic communities to military government, but it must invariably and immeasurably increase the powers of civil government; it must almost compulsorily concentrate the direction of all men and the management of all things in the hands of the administration. If it lead not to despotism by sudden violence, it prepares men for it more gently by their habits. All those who seek to destroy the liberties of a democratic nation ought to know that war is the surest and the shortest means to accomplish it. This is the first axiom of the science.

One remedy, which appears to be obvious when the ambition of soldiers and officers becomes the subject of alarm, is to augment the number of commissions to be distributed by increasing the army. This affords temporary relief, but it plunges the country into deeper difficulties at some future period. To increase the army may produce a lasting effect in an aristocratic community, because military ambition is there confined to one class of men, and the ambition of each individual stops, as it were, at a certain limit; so that it may be possible to satisfy all who feel its influence. But nothing is gained by increasing the army amongst a democratic people, because the number of aspirants always rises in exactly the same ratio as the army itself. Those whose claims have been satisfied by the creation of new commissions are instantly succeeded by a fresh multitude beyond all power of satisfaction; and even those who were but now satisfied soon begin to crave more advancement; for the same excitement prevails in the ranks of the army as in the civil classes of democratic society, and what men want is, not to reach a certain grade, but to have constant promotion. Though these wants may not be very vast, they are perpetually recurring. Thus a democratic nation, by augmenting its army, only allays for a time the ambition of the military profession, which soon becomes even more formidable, because the number of those who feel it is increased.

I am of opinion that a restless and turbulent spirit is an evil inherent in the very constitution of democratic armies, and beyond hope of cure. The legislators of democracies must not expect to devise any military organization capable by its influence of calming and restraining the military profession: their efforts would exhaust their powers, before the object could be attained.

The remedy for the vices of the army is not to be found in the army itself, but in the country. Democratic nations are naturally afraid of disturbance and of despotism; the object is to turn these natural instincts into intelligent, deliberate, and lasting tastes. When men have at last learned to make a peaceful and profitable use of freedom, and have felt its blessings,—when they have conceived a manly love of order, and have freely submitted themselves to discipline,— these same men, if they follow the profession of arms, bring into it, unconsciously and almost against their will, these same habits and manners. The general spirit of the nation being infused into the spirit peculiar to the army, tempers the opinions and desires engendered by military life, or represses them by the mighty force of public opinion. Teach but the citizens to be educated, orderly, firm, and free, and the soldiers will be disciplined and obedient.

Any law which, in repressing the turbulent spirit of the army, should tend to diminish the spirit of freedom in the nation, and to overshadow the notion of law and right, would defeat its object: it would do much more to favor, than to defeat the establishment of military tyranny.

After all, and in spite of all precautions, a large army amidst a democratic people will always be a source of great danger; the most effectual means of diminishing that danger would be to reduce the army, but this is a remedy which all nations are not able to apply.

50. Causes Which Render Democratic Armies Weaker Than Other Armies at the Outset of a Campaign, and More Formidable in Protracted Warfare.

ANY army is in danger of being conquered at the outset of a campaign, after a long peace; any army which has long been engaged in warfare has strong chances of victory: this truth is peculiarly applicable to democratic armies. In aristocracies, the military profession, being a privileged career, is held in honor even in time of peace. Men of great talents, great attainments, and great ambition embrace it; the army is in all respects on a level with the nation, and frequently above it.

We have seen, on the contrary, that, amongst a democratic people, the choicer minds of the nation are gradually drawn away from the military profession, to seek by other paths distinction, power, and especially wealth. After a long peace, —and in democratic times the periods of peace are long,— the army is always inferior to the country itself. In this state, it is called into active service; and, until war has altered it, there is danger for the country as well as for the army.

I have shown that, in democratic armies, and in time of peace, the rule of seniority is the supreme and inflexible law of promotion. This is a consequence, as I have before observed, not only of the constitution of these armies, but of the constitution of the people; and it will always occur.

Again, as amongst these nations, the officer derives his position in the country solely from his position in the army, and as he draws all the distinction and the competency he enjoys from the same source, he does not retire from his profession, or is not superannuated, till very near the close of life. The consequence of these two causes is, that, when a democratic people goes to war after a long interval of peace, all the leading officers of the army are old men. I speak not only of the generals, but of the non-commissioned officers, who have most of them been stationary, or have advanced only step by step. It may be remarked with surprise, that, in a democratic army, after a long peace, all the soldiers are mere boys, and all the superior officers in declining years; so that the former are wanting in experience, the latter in vigor. This is a leading cause of defeat, for the first condition of successful generalship is youth: I should not have ventured to say so, if the greatest captain of modern times had not made the observation.

These two causes do not act in the same manner upon aristocratic armies: as men are promoted in them by right of birth much more than by right of seniority, there are in all ranks a certain number of young men who bring to their profession all the early vigor of body and mind. Again, as the men who seek for military honors amongst an aristocratic people enjoy a settled position in civil society, they seldom continue in the army until old age overtakes them. After having devoted the most vigorous years of youth to the career of arms, they voluntarily retire, and spend at home the remainder of their maturer years.

A long peace not only fills democratic armies with elderly officers, but it also gives to all the officers habits both of body and mind which render them unfit for actual service. The man who has long lived amidst the calm and lukewarm atmosphere of democratic manners, can at first ill adapt himself to the harder toils and sterner duties of warfare; and if he has not absolutely lost the taste for arms, at least he has assumed a mode of life which unfits him for conquest.

Amongst aristocratic nations, the enjoyments of civil life exercise less influence on the manners of the army, because, amongst those nations, the aristocracy commands the army; and an aristocracy, however plunged in luxurious pleasures, has always many other passions besides that of its own well-being, and to satisfy those passions more thoroughly its well-being will be readily sacrificed.

I have shown that, in democratic armies, in time of peace, promotion is extremely slow. The officers at first support this state of things with impatience; they grow excited, restless, exasperated; but in the end most of them make up their minds to it. Those who have the largest share of ambition and of resources quit the army; others, adapting their tastes and their desires to their scanty fortunes, ultimately look upon the military profession in a civil point of view. The quality they value most in it is the competency and security which attend it: their whole notion of the future rests upon the cer-

ALEXIS DE TOCQUEVILLE

tainty of this little provision, and all they require is peaceably
to enjoy it. Thus, not only does a long peace fill an army with
old men, but it frequently imparts the views of old men to
those who are still in the prime of life.

I have also shown that, amongst democratic nations, in
time of peace, the military profession is held in little honor
and practised with little spirit. This want of public favor
is a heavy discouragement to the army; it weighs down
the minds of the troops, and when war breaks out at last,
they cannot immediately resume their spring and vigor. No
similar cause of moral weakness exists in aristocratic armies:
there, the officers are never lowered, either in their own eyes
or in those of their countrymen; because, independently of
their military greatness, they are personally great. But, even if
the influence of peace operated on the two kinds of armies in
the same manner, the results would still be different.

When the officers of an aristocratic army have lost their
warlike spirit and the desire of raising themselves by service,
they still retain a certain respect for the honor of their class,
and an old habit of being foremost to set an example. But
when the officers of a democratic army have no longer the
love of war and the ambition of arms, nothing whatever
remains to them.

I am therefore of opinion, that, when a democratic people engages in a war after a long peace, it incurs much more
risk of defeat than any other nation; but it ought not easily to
be cast down by its reverses, for the chances of success for
such an army are increased by the duration of the war. When
a war has at length, by its long continuance, roused the whole
community from their peaceful occupations, and ruined their
minor undertakings, the same passions which made them attach so much importance to the maintenance of peace will be
turned to arms. War, after it has destroyed all modes of speculation, becomes itself the great and sole speculation, to which
all the ardent and ambitious desires that equality engenders are
exclusively directed. Hence it is, that the selfsame democratic
nations which are so reluctant to engage in hostilities, sometimes perform prodigious achievements when once they have
taken the field.

As the war attracts more and more of public attention, and
is seen to create high reputations and great fortunes in a short
space of time, the choicest spirits of the nation enter the military profession: all the enterprising, proud, and martial minds,
no longer of the aristocracy solely, but of the whole country,
are drawn in this direction. As the number of competitors for
military honors is immense, and war drives every man to his

proper level, great generals are always sure to spring up. A long war produces upon a democratic army the same effects that a revolution produces upon a people; it breaks through regulations, and allows extraordinary men to rise above the common level. Those officers whose bodies and minds have grown old in peace, are removed, or superannuated, or they die. In their stead, a host of young men are pressing on, whose frames are already hardened, whose desires are extended and inflamed by active service. They are bent on advancement at all hazards, and perpetual advancement; they are followed by others with the same passions and desires, and after these are others, yet unlimited by aught but the size of the army. The principle of equality opens the door of ambition to all, and death provides chances for ambition. Death is constantly thinning the ranks, making vacancies, closing and opening the career of arms.

There is, moreover, a secret connection between the military character and the character of democracies, which war brings to light. The men of democracies are naturally passionately eager to acquire what they covet, and to enjoy it on easy conditions. They for the most part worship chance, and are much less afraid of death than of difficulty. This is the spirit which they bring to commerce and manufactures; and this same spirit, carried with them to the field of battle, induces them willingly to expose their lives in order to secure in a moment the rewards of victory. No kind of greatness is more pleasing to the imagination of a democratic people than military greatness,—a greatness of vivid and sudden lustre, obtained without toil, by nothing but the risk of life.

Thus, whilst the interest and the tastes of the members of a democratic community divert them from war, their habits of mind fit them for carrying on war well: they soon make good soldiers, when they are aroused from their business and their enjoyments.

If peace is peculiarly hurtful to democratic armies, war secures to them advantages which no other armies ever possess; and these advantages, however little felt at first, cannot fail in the end to give them the victory. An aristocratic nation, which, in a contest with a democratic people, does not succeed in ruining the latter at the outset of the war, always runs a great risk of being conquered by it.

51. Some Considerations on War in Democratic Communities.

WHEN the principle of equality is spreading, not only amongst a single nation, but amongst several neighboring nations at the same time, as is now the case in Europe, the inhabitants of these different countries, notwithstanding the dissimilarity of language, of customs, and of laws, still resemble each other in their equal dread of war and their common love of peace. It is in vain that ambition or anger puts arms in the hands of princes; they are appeased in spite of themselves by a species of general apathy and good-will, which makes the sword drop from their grasp, and wars become more rare.

As the spread of equality, taking place in several countries at once, simultaneously impels their various inhabitants to follow manufactures and commerce, not only do their tastes become similar, but their interests are so mixed and entangled with one another, that no nation can inflict evils on other nations without those evils falling back upon itself; and all nations ultimately regard war as a calamity almost as severe to the conqueror as the conquered.

Thus, on the one hand, it is extremely difficult in democratic times to draw nations into hostilities; but, on the other, it is almost impossible that any two of them should go to war without embroiling the rest. The interests of all are so interlaced, their opinions and their wants so much alike, that none can remain quiet when the others stir. Wars therefore become more rare, but when they break out, they spread over a larger field.

Neighboring democratic nations not only become alike in some respects, but they eventually grow to resemble each other in almost all. This similitude of nations has consequences of great importance in relation to war.

If I inquire why it is that the Helvetic Confederacy made the greatest and most powerful nations of Europe tremble in the fifteenth century, whilst, at the present day, the power of that country is exactly proportioned to its population, I perceive that the Swiss are become like all the surrounding communities, and those surrounding communities like the Swiss: so that, as numerical strength now forms the only difference between them, victory necessarily attends the largest army. Thus, one of the consequences of the democratic revolution which is going on in Europe is to make numerical strength preponderate on all fields of battle, and to constrain all small nations to incorporate themselves with large states, or at least to adopt the policy of the latter.

As numbers are the determining cause of victory, each people ought of course to strive by all the means in its power to bring the greatest possible number of men into the field. When it was possible to enlist a kind of troops superior to all others, such as the Swiss infantry or the French horse of the sixteenth century, it was not thought necessary to raise very large armies; but the case is altered when one soldier is as efficient as another.

The same cause which begets this new want also supplies means of satisfying it; for, as I have already observed, when men are all alike they are all weak, and the supreme power of the state is naturally much stronger amongst democratic nations than elsewhere. Hence, whilst these nations are desirous of enrolling the whole male population in the ranks of the army, they have the power of effecting this object: the consequence is, that, in democratic ages, armies seem to grow larger in proportion as the love of war declines.

In the same ages, too, the manner of carrying on war is likewise altered by the same causes. Machiavelli observes, in "The Prince," "that it is much more difficult to subdue a people who have a prince and his barons for their leaders, than a nation which is commanded by a prince and his slaves." To avoid offence, let us read, "public functionaries" for "slaves," and this important truth will be strictly applicable to our own time.

A great aristocratic people cannot either conquer its neighbors or be conquered by them, without great difficulty. It cannot conquer them, because all its forces can never be collected and held together for a considerable period: it cannot be conquered, because an enemy meets at every step small centres of resistance, by which invasion is arrested. War against an aristocracy may be compared to war in a mountainous country,—the defeated party has constant opportunities of rallying its forces to make a stand in a new position.

Exactly the reverse occurs amongst democratic nations: they easily bring their whole disposable force into the field, and when the nation is wealthy and populous it soon becomes victorious; but if ever it is conquered, and its territory invaded, it has few resources at command; and if the enemy takes the capital, the nation is lost. This may very well be explained: as each member of the community is individually isolated and extremely powerless, no one of the whole body can either defend himself or present a rallying-point to others. Nothing is strong in a democratic country except the state; as the military strength of the state is destroyed by the destruction of the army, and its civil power paralyzed by the capture of the chief city, all that remains is only a multitude without strength or government, unable to resist the organized power by which it is assailed. I am aware that this danger may be lessened by the creation of local liberties, and consequently of local powers; but this remedy will always be insufficient. For after such a catastrophe, not only is the population unable to carry on hostilities, but it may be apprehended that they will not be inclined to attempt it.

According to the law of nations adopted in civilized countries, the object of war is, not to seize the property of private individuals, but simply to get possession of political power. The destruction of private property is only occasionally resorted to, for the purpose of attaining the latter object.

When an aristocratic country is invaded after the defeat of its army, the nobles, although they are at the same time the wealthiest members of the community, will continue to defend themselves individually rather than submit; for if the conqueror remained master of the country he would deprive them of their political power, to which they cling even more closely than to their property. They therefore prefer fighting to submission, which is to them the greatest of all misfortunes; and they readily carry the people along with them, because the people have long been used to follow and obey them, and besides have but little to risk in the war.

Amongst a nation in which equality of condition prevails, on the contrary, each citizen has but a slender share of political power, and often has no share at all: on the other hand, all are independent, and all have something to lose; so that they are much less afraid of being conquered, and much more afraid of war, than an aristocratic people. It will always be extremely difficult to decide a democratic population to take up arms when hostilities have reached its own territory. Hence the necessity of giving to such a people the rights and the political character which may impart to every citizen some of those interests that cause the nobles to act for the public welfare in aristocratic countries.

It should never be forgotten by the princes and other leaders of democratic nations, that nothing but the love and the habit of freedom can maintain an advantageous contest with the love and the habit of physical well-being. I can conceive nothing better prepared for subjection, in case of defeat, than a democratic people without free institutions.

Formerly, it was customary to take the field with a small body of troops, to fight in small engagements, and to make long regular sieges: modern tactics consist in fighting decisive battles, and, as soon as a line of march is open before the army, in rushing upon the capital city, in order to terminate the war at a single blow. Napoleon, it is said, was the inventor of this new system; but the invention of such a system did not depend on any individual man, whoever he might be. The mode in which Napoleon carried on war was suggested to him by the state of society in his time; that mode was successful, because it was eminently adapted to that state of society, and because he was the first to employ it. Napoleon was the first commander who marched at the head of an army from capital to capital; but the road was opened for him by the ruin of feudal society. It may fairly be believed that, if that extraordinary man had been born three hundred years ago, he would not have derived the same results from his method of warfare, or, rather, that he would have had a different method.

I shall add but a few words on civil wars, for fear of exhausting the patience of the reader. Most of the remarks which I have made respecting foreign wars are applicable *a fortiori* to civil wars. Men living in democracies have not naturally the military spirit; they sometimes acquire it, when they have been dragged by compulsion to the field; but to rise in a body, and voluntarily to expose themselves to the horrors of war, and especially of civil war, is a course which the men of democracies are not apt to adopt. None but the most adventurous members of the community consent to run into such risks; the bulk of the population remain motionless.

But even if the population were inclined to act, considerable obstacles would stand in their way; for they can resort to no old and well-established influence which they are willing to obey,—no well-known leaders to rally the discontented, as well as to discipline and to lead them,—no political powers subordinate to the supreme power of the nation, which afford an effectual support to the resistance directed against the government.

In democratic countries, the moral power of the majority is immense, and the physical resources which it has at its command are out of all proportion to the physical resources which may be combined against it. Therefore, the party which occupies the seat of the majority, which speaks in its name and wields its power, triumphs instantaneously and irresistibly over all private resistance; it does not even give such opposition time to exist, but nips it in the bud.

Those who, in such nations, seek to effect a revolution by force of arms, have no other resource than suddenly to seize upon the whole engine of government as it stands, which can better be done by a single blow than by a war; for as soon as there is a regular war, the party which represents the state is always certain to conquer.

The only case in which a civil war could arise is, if the army should divide itself into two factions, the one raising the standard of rebellion, the other remaining true to its allegiance. An army constitutes a small community, very closely united together, endowed with great powers of vitality, and able to supply its own wants for some time. Such a war might be bloody, but it could not be long; for either the rebellious army would gain over the government by the sole display of its resources, or by its first victory, and then the war would be over; or the struggle would take place, and then that portion of the army which should not be supported by the organized powers of the state would speedily either disband itself, or be destroyed. It may therefore be admitted as a general truth, that, in ages of equality, civil wars will become much less frequent and less protracted.

BOOK IV

☆

INFLUENCE OF DEMOCRATIC IDEAS AND FEELINGS ON POLITICAL SOCIETY

52. Equality Naturally Gives Men a Taste for Free Institutions.

THE principle of equality, which makes men independent of each other, gives them a habit and a taste for following, in their private actions, no other guide than their own will. This complete independence, which they constantly enjoy in regard to their equals and in the intercourse of private life, tends to make them look upon all authority with a jealous eye, and speedily suggests to them the notion and the love of political freedom. Men living at such times have a natural bias to free institutions. Take any one of them at a venture, and search if you can his most deep-seated instincts; and you will find that, of all governments, he will soonest conceive and most highly value that government whose head he has himself elected, and whose administration he may control.

Of all the political effects produced by the equality of conditions, this love of independence is the first to strike the observing, and to alarm the timid; nor can it be said that their alarm is wholly misplaced, for anarchy has a more formidable aspect in democratic countries than elsewhere. As the citizens have no direct influence on each other, as soon as the supreme power of the nation fails, which kept them all in their several stations, it would seem that disorder must instantly reach its utmost pitch, and that, every man drawing aside in a different direction, the fabric of society must at once crumble away.

I am persuaded, however, that anarchy is not the principal evil which democratic ages have to fear, but the least. For the principle of equality begets two tendencies: the one leads men straight to independence, and may suddenly drive them into anarchy; the other conducts them by a longer, more secret, but more certain road, to servitude. Nations readily discern the former tendency, and are prepared to resist it; they are led away by the latter, without perceiving its drift; hence it is peculiarly important to point it out.

For myself, I am so far from urging it as a reproach to the principle of equality that it renders men intractable, that this very circumstance principally calls forth my approbation. I admire to see how it deposits in the mind and heart of man the dim conception and instinctive love of political independence, thus preparing the remedy for the evil which it produces: it is on this very account that I am attached to it.

53. That the Opinions of Democratic Nations About Government Are Naturally Favorable to the Concentration of Power.

THE notion of secondary powers, placed between the sovereign and his subjects, occurred naturally to the imagination of aristocratic nations, because those communities contained individuals or families raised above the common level, and apparently destined to command by their birth, their education, and their wealth. This same notion is naturally wanting in the minds of men in democratic ages, for converse reasons; it can only be introduced artificially, it can only be kept there with difficulty; whereas they conceive, as it were without thinking upon the subject, the notion of a single and central power, which governs the whole community by its direct influence. Moreover, in politics as well as in philosophy and in religion, the intellect of democratic nations is peculiarly open to simple and general notions. Complicated systems are repugnant to it, and its favorite conception is that of a great nation composed of citizens all formed upon one pattern, and all governed by a single power.

The very next notion to that of a single and central power, which presents itself to the minds of men in the ages of equality, is the notion of uniformity of legislation. As every man sees that he differs but little from those about him, he cannot understand why a rule which is applicable to one man should not be equally applicable to all others. Hence the slightest privileges are repugnant to his reason; the faintest dissimilarities in the political institutions of the same people offend him, and uniformity of legislation appears to him to be the first condition of good government.

I find, on the contrary, that this notion of a uniform rule, equally binding on all the members of the community, was almost unknown to the human mind in aristocratic ages; it was either never broached, or it was rejected.

These contrary tendencies of opinion ultimately turn on both sides to such blind instincts and ungovernable habits, that they still direct the actions of men, in spite of particular exceptions. Notwithstanding the immense variety of conditions in the Middle Ages, a certain number of persons existed at that period in precisely similar circumstances; but this did not prevent the laws then in force from assigning to each of them distinct duties and different rights. On the contrary, at the present time, all the powers of government are exerted to impose the same customs and the same laws on populations which have as yet but few points of resemblance.

As the conditions of men become equal amongst a people, individuals seem of less, and society of greater importance; or rather, every citizen, being assimilated to all the rest, is lost in the crowd, and nothing stands conspicuous but the great and imposing image of the people at large. This naturally gives the men of democratic periods a lofty opinion of the privileges of society, and a very humble notion of the rights of individuals; they are ready to admit that the interests of the former are everything, and those of the latter nothing. They are willing to acknowledge that the power which represents the community has far more information and wisdom than any of the members of that community; and that it is the duty, as well as the right, of that power, to guide as well as govern each private citizen.

If we closely scrutinize our contemporaries, and penetrate to the root of their political opinions, we shall detect some of the notions which I have just pointed out, and we shall perhaps be surprised to find so much accordance between men who are so often at variance.

The Americans hold, that, in every state, the supreme power ought to emanate from the people; but when once that power is constituted, they can conceive, as it were, no limits to it, and they are ready to admit that it has the right to do whatever it pleases. They have not the slightest notion of peculiar privileges granted to cities, families, or persons: their minds appear never to have foreseen that it might be possible not to apply with strict uniformity the same laws to every part of the state, and to all its inhabitants.

These same opinions are more and more diffused in Europe; they even insinuate themselves amongst those nations which most vehemently reject the principle of the sovereignty of the people. Such nations assign a different origin to the supreme power, but they ascribe to that power the same characteristics. Amongst them all, the idea of intermediate powers is weakened and obliterated; the idea of rights inherent in certain individuals is rapidly disappearing from the minds of men; the idea of the omnipotence and sole authority of society at large rises to fill its place. These ideas take root and spread in proportion as social conditions become more equal, and men more alike, they are produced by equality, and in turn they hasten the progress of equality.

In France, where the revolution of which I am speaking has gone further than in any other European country, these opinions have got complete hold of the public mind. If we listen attentively to the language of the various parties in France, we shall find that there is not one which has not adopted them. Most of these parties censure the conduct of the government, but they all hold that the government ought perpetually to act and interfere in everything that is done. Even those which are most at variance are nevertheless agreed upon this head. The unity, the ubiquity, the omnipotence of the supreme power, and the uniformity of its rules, constitute the principal characteristics of all the political systems which have been put forward in our age. They recur even in the wildest visions of political regeneration: the human mind pursues them in its dreams.

If these notions spontaneously arise in the minds of private individuals, they suggest themselves still more forcibly to the minds of princes. Whilst the ancient fabric of European society is altered and dissolved, sovereigns acquire new conceptions of their opportunities and their duties; they learn for the first time that the central power which they represent may and ought to administer, by its own agency and on a uniform plan, all the concerns of the whole community. This opinion, which, I will venture to say, was never conceived before our time by the monarchs of Europe, now sinks deeply into the minds of kings, and abides there amidst all the agitation of more unsettled thoughts.

Our contemporaries are therefore much less divided than is commonly supposed; they are constantly disputing as to the hands in which supremacy is to be vested, but they readily agree upon the duties and the rights of that supremacy. The notion they all form of government is that of a sole, simple, providential, and creative power.

All secondary opinions in politics are unsettled; this one remains fixed, invariable, and consistent. It is adopted by statesmen and political philosophers; it is eagerly laid hold of by the multitude; those who govern and those who are governed agree to pursue it with equal ardor; it is the earliest notion of their minds, it seems innate. It originates, therefore, in no caprice of the human intellect, but it is a necessary condition of the present state of mankind.

54. *That the Sentiments of Democratic Nations Accord with Their Opinions in Leading Them to Concentrate Political Power.*

IF it be true that, in ages of equality, men readily adopt the notion of a great central power, it cannot be doubted, on the other hand, that their habits and sentiments predispose them to recognize such a power, and to give it their support. This may be demonstrated in a few words, as the greater part of the reasons to which the fact may be attributed have been previously stated.

As the men who inhabit democratic countries have no superiors, no inferiors, and no habitual or necessary partners in their undertakings, they readily fall back upon themselves, and consider themselves as beings apart. I had occasion to point this out at considerable length in treating of individualism. Hence such men can never, without an effort, tear themselves from their private affairs to engage in public business; their natural bias leads them to abandon the latter to the sole visible and permanent representative of the interests of the community, that is to say, to the state. Not only are they naturally wanting in a taste for public business, but they have frequently no time to attend to it. Private life in democratic times is so busy, so excited, so full of wishes and of work, that hardly any energy or leisure remains to each individual for public life. I am the last man to contend that these propensities are unconquerable, since my chief object in writing this book has been to combat them. I only maintain that, at the present day, a secret power is fostering them in the human heart, and that, if they are not checked, they will wholly overgrow it.

I have also had occasion to show how the increasing love of well-being and the fluctuating character of property cause democratic nations to dread all violent disturbances. The love of public tranquillity is frequently the only passion which these nations retain, and it becomes more active and powerful amongst them in proportion as all other passions droop and die. This naturally disposes the members of the community constantly to give or to surrender additional rights to the central power, which alone seems to be interested in defending them by the same means that it uses to defend itself.

As in periods of equality, no man is compelled to lend his assistance to his fellow-men, and none has any right to expect much support from them, every one is at once independent and powerless. These two conditions, which must never be either separately considered or confounded together, inspire the citizen of a democratic country with very contrary propensities. His independence fills him with self-reliance and pride amongst his equals; his debility makes him feel from time to time the want of some outward assistance, which he cannot expect from any of them, because they are all impotent and unsympathizing. In this predicament, he naturally turns his eyes to that imposing power which alone rises above the level of universal depression. Of that power his wants and especially his desires continually remind him, until he ultimately views it as the sole and necessary support of his own weakness.

This may more completely explain what frequently takes place in democratic countries, where the very men who are so impatient of superiors patiently submit to a master, exhibiting at once their pride and their servility.

The hatred which men bear to privilege increases in proportion as privileges become fewer and less considerable, so that democratic passions would seem to burn most fiercely just when they have least fuel. I have already given the reason of this phenomenon. When all conditions are unequal, no inequality is so great as to offend the eye; whereas the slightest dissimilarity is odious in the midst of general uniformity: the more complete this uniformity is, the more insupportable does the sight of such a difference become. Hence it is natural that the love of equality should constantly increase together with equality itself, and that it should grow by what it feeds on.

This never-dying, ever-kindling hatred, which sets a democratic people against the smallest privileges, is peculiarly favorable to the gradual concentration of all political rights in the hands of the representative of the state alone. The sovereign, being necessarily and incontestably above all the citizens, excites not their envy, and each of them thinks that he strips his equals of the prerogative which he concedes to the crown. The man of democratic age is extremely reluctant to obey his neighbor who is his equal; he refuses to acknowledge superior ability in such a person; he mistrusts his justice, and is jealous of his power; he fears and he contemns him; and he loves continually to remind him of the common dependence in which both of them stand to the same master.

Every central power, which follows its natural tendencies, courts and encourages the principle of equality; for equality singularly facilitates, extends, and secures the influence of a central power.

In like manner, it may be said that every central government worships uniformity: uniformity relieves it from inquiry into an infinity of details, which must be attended to if rules have to be adapted to different men, instead of indiscriminately subjecting all men to the same rule: thus the government likes what the citizens like, and naturally hates what they hate. These common sentiments, which, in democratic nations, constantly unite the sovereign and every member of the community in one and the same conviction, establish a secret and lasting sympathy between them. The faults of the government are pardoned for the sake of its tastes; public confidence is only reluctantly withdrawn in the midst even of its excesses and its errors; and it is restored at the first call. Democratic nations often hate those in whose hands the central power is vested; but they always love that power itself.

Thus, by two separate paths, I have reached the same conclusion. I have shown that the principle of equality suggests to men the notion of a sole, uniform, and strong government: I have now shown that the principle of equality imparts to them a taste for it. To governments of this kind the nations of our age are therefore tending. They are drawn thither by the natural inclination of mind and heart; and in order to reach that result, it is enough that they do not check themselves in their course.

I am of opinion, that, in the democratic ages which are opening upon us, individual independence and local liberties will ever be the products of art; that centralization will be the natural government.

55. *Of Certain Peculiar and Accidental Causes, Which Either Lead a People to Complete the Centralization of Government, or Which Divert Them from It.*

IF ALL democratic nations are instinctively led to the centralization of government, they tend to this result in an unequal manner. This depends on the particular circumstances which may promote or prevent the natural consequences of that state of society,—circumstances which are exceedingly numerous, but of which I shall mention only a few.

Amongst men who have lived free long before they became equal, the tendencies derived from free institutions combat, to a certain extent, the propensities superinduced by the principle of equality; and although the central power may increase its privileges amongst such a people, the private members of such a community will never entirely forfeit their independence. But when the equality of conditions grows up amongst a people who have never known, or have long ceased to know, what freedom is, (and such is the case upon the continent of Europe,) as the former habits of the nation are suddenly combined, by some sort of natural attraction, with the new habits and principles engendered by the state of society, all powers seem spontaneously to rush to the centre. These powers accumulate there with astonishing rapidity, and the state instantly attains the utmost limits of its strength, whilst private persons allow themselves to sink as suddenly to the lowest degree of weakness.

The English who emigrated three hundred years ago to found a democratic commonwealth on the shores of the New World had all learned to take a part in public affairs in their mother country; they were conversant with trial by jury; they were accustomed to liberty of speech and of the press,—to personal freedom, to the notion of rights and the practice of asserting them. They carried with them to America these free institutions and manly customs, and these institutions preserved them against the encroachments of the state. Thus, amongst the Americans, it is freedom which is old,—equality is of comparatively modern date. The reverse is occurring in Europe, where equality, introduced by absolute power and under the rule of kings, was already infused into the habits of nations long before freedom had entered into their thoughts.

I have said that, amongst democratic nations, the notion of government naturally presents itself to the mind under the form of a sole and central power, and that the notion of intermediate powers is not familiar to them. This is peculiarly applicable to the democratic nations which have witnessed the triumph of the principle of equality by means of a violent revolution. As the classes which managed local affairs have been suddenly swept away by the storm, and as the confused mass which remains has as yet neither the organization nor the habits which fit it to assume the administration of these affairs, the state alone seems capable of taking upon itself all the details of government, and centralization becomes, as it were, the unavoidable state of the country.

Napoleon deserves neither praise nor censure for having centered in his own hands almost all the administrative power of France; for, after the abrupt disappearance of the nobility and the higher rank of the middle classes, these powers devolved on him of course: it would have been almost as difficult for him to reject as to assume them. But a similar necessity has never been felt by the Americans, who, having passed through no revolution, and having governed themselves from the first, never had to call upon the state to act for a time as their guardian. Thus, the progress of centralization amongst a democratic people depends not only on the progress of equality, but on the manner in which this equality has been established.

At the commencement of a great democratic revolution, when hostilities have but just broken out between the different classes of society, the people endeavor to centralize the public administration in the hands of the government, in order to wrest the management of local affairs from the aristocracy. Towards the close of such a revolution, on the contrary, it is usually the conquered aristocracy who endeavor to make over the management of all affairs to the state, because such an aristocracy dread the tyranny of a people who have become their equal, and not unfrequently their master. Thus, it is not always the same class of the community which strives to increase the prerogative of the government; but as long as the democratic revolution lasts, there is always one class in the nation, powerful in numbers or in wealth, who are induced, by peculiar passions or interests, to centralize the public administration, independently of that hatred of being governed by one's neighbor which is a general and permanent feeling amongst democratic nations.

It may be remarked, that, at the present day, the lower orders in England are striving with all their might to destroy local independence, and to transfer the administration from all the points of the circumference to the centre; whereas the higher classes are endeavoring to retain this administration within its ancient boundaries. I venture to predict that a time will come when the very reverse will happen.

These observations explain why the supreme power is always stronger, and private individuals weaker, amongst a democratic people, who have passed through a long and arduous struggle to reach a state of equality, than amongst a democratic community in which the citizens have been equal from the first. The example of the Americans completely demonstrates the fact. The inhabitants of the United States were never divided by any privileges; they have never known the mutual relation of master and inferior; and as they neither dread nor hate each other, they have never known the necessity of calling in the supreme power to manage their affairs. The lot of the Americans is singular: they have derived from the aristocracy of England the notion of private rights and the taste for local freedom; and they have been able to retain both, because they have had no aristocracy to combat.

If education enables men at all times to defend their independence, this is most especially true in democratic times. When all men are alike, it is easy to found a sole and all-powerful government by the aid of mere instinct. But men require much intelligence, knowledge, and art to organize and to maintain secondary powers under similar circumstances, and to create, amidst the independence and individual weakness of the citizens, such free associations as may be able to struggle against tyranny without destroying public order.

Hence the concentration of power and the subjection of individuals will increase amongst democratic nations, not only in the same proportion as their equality, but in the same proportion as their ignorance. It is true that, in ages of imperfect civilization, the government is frequently as wanting in the knowledge required to impose a despotism upon the people, as the people are wanting in the knowledge required to shake it off; but the effect is not the same on both sides. However rude a democratic people may be, the central power which rules them is never completely devoid of cultivation, because it readily draws to its own uses what little cultivation is to be found in the country, and, if necessary, may seek assistance elsewhere. Hence, amongst a nation which is ignorant as well as democratic, an amazing difference cannot fail speedily to arise between the intellectual capacity of the ruler and that of each of his subjects. This completes the easy concentration of all power in his hands: the administrative function of the state is perpetually extended, because the state alone is competent to administer the affairs of the country.

Aristocratic nations, however unenlightened they may be, never afford the same spectacle, because, in them, instruction is nearly equally diffused between the monarch and the leading members of the community.

The Pacha who now rules in Egypt found the population of that country composed of men exceedingly ignorant and equal, and he has borrowed the science and ability of Europe to govern that people. As the personal attainments of the sovereign are thus combined with the ignorance and democratic weakness of his subjects, the utmost centralization has been established without impediment, and the Pacha has made the country his manufactory, and the inhabitants his workmen.

I think that extreme centralization of government ultimately enervates society, and thus, after a length of time, weakens the government itself; but I do not deny that a centralized social power may be able to execute great undertakings with facility in a given time and on a particular point. This is more especially true of war, in which success depends much more on the means of transferring all the resources of a nation to one single point, than on the extent of those resources. Hence it is chiefly in war that nations desire, and frequently need, to increase the powers of the central government. All men of military genius are fond of centralization, which increases their strength; and all men of centralizing genius are fond of war, which compels nations to combine all their powers in the hands of the government. Thus, the democratic tendency which leads men unceasingly to multiply the privileges of the state, and to circumscribe the rights of private persons, is much more rapid and constant amongst those democratic nations which are exposed by their position to great and frequent wars, than amongst all others.

I have shown how the dread of disturbance and the love of well-being insensibly lead democratic nations to increase the functions of central government, as the only power which appears to be intrinsically sufficiently strong, enlightened, and secure to protect them from anarchy. I would now add, that all the particular circumstances which tend to make the state of a democratic community agitated and precarious, enhance this general propensity, and lead private persons more and more to sacrifice their rights to their tranquillity.

A people are therefore never so disposed to increase the functions of central government as at the close of a long and bloody revolution, which, after having wrested property from the hands of its former possessors, has shaken all belief, and filled the nation with fierce hatreds, conflicting interests, and contending factions. The love of public tranquillity becomes at such times an indiscriminate passion, and the members of the community are apt to conceive a most inordinate devotion to order.

I have already examined several of the incidents which may concur to promote the centralization of power, but the principal cause still remains to be noticed. The foremost of the incidental causes which may draw the management of all affairs into the hands of the ruler in democratic countries, is the origin of that ruler himself, and his own propensities. Men who live in the ages of equality are naturally fond of

central power, and are willing to extend its privileges; but
if it happens that this same power faithfully represents their
own interests, and exactly copies their own inclinations, the
confidence they place in it knows no bounds, and they think
that whatever they bestow upon it is bestowed upon themselves.

The attraction of administrative powers to the centre will
always be less easy and less rapid under the reign of kings who
are still in some way connected with the old aristocratic order,
than under new princes, the children of their own achievements, whose birth, prejudices, propensities, and habits appear
to bind them indissolubly to the cause of equality. I do not
mean that princes of aristocratic origin who live in democratic
ages do not attempt to centralize; I believe they apply themselves as diligently as any others to that object. For them,
the sole advantages of equality lie in that direction; but their
opportunities are less great, because the community, instead
of volunteering compliance with their desires, frequently obey
them with reluctance. In democratic communities, the rule is,
that centralization must increase in proportion as the sovereign
is less aristocratic.

When an ancient race of kings stands at the head of an
aristocracy, as the natural prejudices of the sovereign perfectly accord with the natural prejudices of the nobility, the
vices inherent in aristocratic communities have a free course,
and meet with no corrective. The reverse is the case when the
scion of a feudal stock is placed at the head of a democratic
people. The sovereign is constantly led, by his education, his
habits, and his associations, to adopt sentiments suggested
by the inequality of conditions, and the people tend as constantly, by their social condition, to those manners which
are engendered by equality. At such times, it often happens
that the citizens seek to control the central power far less
as a tyrannical than as an aristocratical power, and that they
persist in the firm defence of their independence, not only
because they would remain free, but especially because they
are determined to remain equal.

A revolution which overthrows an ancient regal family
in order to place new men at the head of a democratic people
may temporarily weaken the central power; but, however
anarchical such a revolution may appear at first, we need
not hesitate to predict that its final and certain consequence
will be to extend and to secure the prerogatives of that power.

The foremost, or indeed the sole condition, which is required in order to succeed in centralizing the supreme power

in a democratic community, is to love equality, or to get men to believe you love it. Thus, the science of despotism, which was once so complex, is simplified, and reduced, as it were, to a single principle.

56. What Sort of Despotism Democratic Nations Have to Fear.

I HAD remarked during my stay in the United States, that a democratic state of society, similar to that of the Americans, might offer singular facilities for the establishment of despotism; and I perceived, upon my return to Europe, how much use had already been made, by most of our rulers, of the notions, the sentiments, and the wants created by this same social condition, for the purpose of extending the circle of their power. This led me to think that the nations of Christendom would perhaps eventually undergo some oppression like that which hung over several of the nations of the ancient world.

A more accurate examination of the subject, and five years of further meditation, have not diminished my fears, but have changed the object of them.

No sovereign ever lived in former ages so absolute or so powerful as to undertake to administer by his own agency, and without the assistance of intermediate powers, all the parts of a great empire: none ever attempted to subject all his subjects indiscriminately to strict uniformity of regulation, and personally to tutor and direct every member of the community. The notion of such an undertaking never occurred to the human mind; and if any man had conceived it, the want of information, the imperfection of the administrative system, and, above all, the natural obstacles caused by the inequality of conditions, would speedily have checked the execution of so vast a design.

When the Roman Emperors were at the height of their power, the different nations of the empire still preserved manners and customs of great diversity; although they were subject to the same monarch, most of the provinces were separately administered; they abounded in powerful and active municipalities; and although the whole government of the empire was centred in the hands of the Emperor alone, and he always remained, in case of need, the supreme arbiter in all matters, yet the details of social life and private occupations lay for the most part beyond his control. The Emperors possessed, it is true, an immense and unchecked power, which allowed them to gratify all their whimsical tastes, and to employ for that purpose the whole strength of the state. They frequently abused that power arbitrarily to deprive their subjects of property or of life: their tyranny was extremely onerous to the few, but it did not reach the many; it was fixed to some few main objects, and neglected the rest; it was violent, but its range was limited.

It would seem that, if despotism were to be established amongst the democratic nations of our days, it might assume a different character; it would be more extensive and more mild; it would degrade men without tormenting them. I do not question, that, in an age of instruction and equality like our own, sovereigns might more easily succeed in collecting all political power into their own hands, and might interfere more habitually and decidedly with the circle of private interests, than any sovereign of antiquity could ever do. But this same principle of equality which facilitates despotism, tempers its rigor. We have seen how the manners of society become more humane and gentle, in proportion as men become more equal and alike. When no member of the community has much power or much wealth, tyranny is, as it were, without opportunities and a field of action. As all fortunes are scanty, the passions of men are naturally circumscribed, their imagination moderates the sovereign himself, and checks within certain limits the inordinate stretch of his desires.

Independently of these reasons, drawn from the nature of the state of society itself, I might add many others arising from causes beyond my subject; but I shall keep within the limits I have laid down.

Democratic governments may become violent, and even cruel, at certain periods of extreme effervescence or of great danger; but these crises will be rare and brief. When I consider the petty passions of our contemporaries, the mildness of their manners, the extent of their education, the purity of their religion, the gentleness of their morality, their regular and industrious habits, and the restraint which they almost all observe in their vices no less than in their virtues, I have no fear that they will meet with tyrants in their rulers, but rather with guardians.

I think, then, that the species of oppression by which democratic nations are menaced is unlike anything which ever before existed in the world: our contemporaries will find no prototype of it in their memories. I seek in vain for an expression which will accurately convey the whole of the idea I have formed of it; the old words despotism and tyranny are inappropriate: the thing itself is new, and since I cannot name, I must attempt to define it.

I seek to trace the novel features under which despotism may appear in the world. The first thing that strikes the observation is an innumerable multitude of men, all equal and alike, incessantly endeavoring to procure the petty and paltry pleasures with which they glut their lives. Each of them, living apart, is as a stranger to the fate of all the rest,—his children and his private friends constitute to him the whole of mankind; as for the rest of his fellow-citizens, he is close to them, but he sees them not; he touches them, but he feels them not; he exists but in himself and for himself alone; and if his kindred still remain to him, he may be said at any rate to have lost his country.

Above this race of men stands an immense and tutelary power, which takes upon itself alone to secure their gratifications, and to watch over their fate. That power is absolute, minute, regular, provident, and mild. It would be like the authority of a parent, if, like that authority, its object was to prepare men for manhood; but it seeks, on the contrary, to keep them in perpetual childhood: it is well content that the people should rejoice, provided they think of nothing but rejoicing. For their happiness such a government willingly labors, but it chooses to be the sole agent and the only arbiter of that happiness; it provides for their security, foresees and supplies their necessities, facilitates their pleasures, manages their principal concerns, directs their industry, regulates the descent of property, and subdivides their inheritances: what remains, but to spare them all the care of thinking and all the trouble of living?

Thus, it every day renders the exercise of the free agency of man less useful and less frequent; it circumscribes the will within a narrower range, and gradually robs a man of all the uses of himself. The principle of equality has prepared men for these things; it has predisposed men to endure them, and oftentimes to look on them as benefits.

After having thus successively taken each member of the community in its powerful grasp, and fashioned him at will, the supreme power then extends its arm over the whole community. It covers the surface of society with a network of small complicated rules, minute and uniform, through which the most original minds and the most energetic characters cannot penetrate, to rise above the crowd. The will of man is not shattered, but softened, bent, and guided; men are seldom forced by it to act, but they are constantly restrained from acting: such a power does not destroy, but it prevents existence; it does not tyrannize, but it compresses, enervates, extinguishes, and stupefies a people, till each nation is reduced to be nothing better than a flock of timid and industrious animals, of which the government is the shepherd.

I have always thought that servitude of the regular, quiet, and gentle kind which I have just described might be combined more easily than is commonly believed with some of the outward forms of freedom, and that it might even establish itself under the wing of the sovereignty of the people.

Our contemporaries are constantly excited by two conflicting passions; they want to be led, and they wish to remain free: as they cannot destroy either the one or the other of these contrary propensities, they strive to satisfy them both at once. They devise a sole, tutelary, and all-powerful form of government, but elected by the people. They combine the principle of centralization and that of popular sovereignty; this gives them a respite: they console themselves for being in tutelage by the reflection that they have chosen their own guardians. Every man allows himself to be put in leading-strings, because he sees that it is not a person or a class of persons but the people at large, who hold the end of his chain.

By this system, the people shake off their state of dependence just long enough to select their master, and then relapse into it again. A great many persons at the present day are quite contented with this sort of compromise between administrative despotism and the sovereignty of the people; and they think they have done enough for the protection of individual freedom when they have surrendered it to the power of the nation at large. This does not satisfy me: the nature of him I am to obey signifies less to me than the fact of extorted obedience.

I do not, however, deny that a constitution of this kind appears to me to be infinitely preferable to one which, after having concentrated all the powers of government, should vest them in the hands of an irresponsible person or body of persons. Of all the forms which democratic despotism could assume, the latter would assuredly be the worst.

When the sovereign is elective, or narrowly watched by a legislature which is really elective and independent, the oppression which he exercises over individuals is sometimes greater, but it is always less degrading; because every man, when he is oppressed and disarmed, may still imagine that, whilst he yields obedience, it is to himself he yields it, and that it is to one of his own inclinations that all the rest give way. In like manner, I can understand that, when the sovereign represents the nation, and is dependent upon the people, the rights and the power of which every citizen is deprived not only serve the head of the state, but the state itself; and that private persons derive some return from the sacrifice of their independence which they have made to the public. To create a representation of the people in every centralized country is, therefore, to diminish the evil which extreme centralization may produce, but not to get rid of it.

I admit that, by this means, room is left for the intervention of individuals in the more important affairs; but it is not the less suppressed in the smaller and more private ones. It must not be forgotten that it is especially dangerous to enslave men in the minor details of life. For my own part, I should be inclined to think freedom less necessary in great things than in little ones, if it were possible to be secure of the one without possessing the other.

Subjection in minor affairs breaks out every day, and is felt by the whole community indiscriminately. It does not drive men to resistance, but it crosses them at every turn, till they are led to surrender the exercise of their own will. Thus their spirit is gradually broken and their character enervated; whereas that obedience which is exacted on a few important but rare occasions, only exhibits servitude at certain intervals, and throws the burden of it upon a small number of men. It is in vain to summon a people, who have been rendered so dependent on the central power, to choose from time to time the representatives of that power; this rare and brief exercise of their free choice, however important it may be, will not prevent them from gradually losing the faculties of thinking, feeling, and acting for themselves, and thus gradually falling below the level of humanity.

I add, that they will soon become incapable of exercising the great and only privilege which remains to them. The democratic nations which have introduced freedom into their political constitution, at the very time when they were augmenting the despotism of their administrative constitution, have been led into strange paradoxes. To manage those minor affairs in which good sense is all that is wanted,—the people are held to be unequal to the task; but when the government of the country is at stake, the people are invested with immense powers; they are alternately made the playthings of their ruler, and his masters,—more than kings, and less than men. After having exhausted all the different modes of election, without finding one to suit their purpose, they are still amazed, and still bent on seeking further; as if the evil they remark did not originate in the constitution of the country, far more than in that of the electoral body.

It is, indeed, difficult to conceive how men who have entirely given up the habit of self-government should succeed in making a proper choice of those by whom they are to be governed; and no one will ever believe that a liberal, wise, and energetic government can spring from the suffrages of a subservient people.

A constitution which should be republican in its head, and ultra-monarchical in all its other parts, has ever appeared to me to be a short-lived monster. The vices of rules and the inaptitude of the people would speedily bring about its ruin; and the nation, weary of its representatives and of itself, would create freer institutions, or soon return to stretch itself at the feet of a single master.

I believe that it is easier to establish an absolute and despotic government amongst a people in which the conditions of society are equal, than amongst any other; and I think that, if such a government were once established amongst such a people, it would not only oppress men, but would eventually strip each of them of several of the highest qualities of humanity. Despotism, therefore, appears to me peculiarly to be dreaded in democratic times. I should have loved freedom, I believe, at all times, but in the time in which we live I am ready to worship it.

On the other hand, I am persuaded that all who shall attempt, in the ages upon which we are entering, to base freedom upon aristocratic privilege, will fail; that all who shall attempt to draw and to retain authority within a single class, will fail. At the present day, no ruler is skilful or strong enough to found a despotism by re-establishing permanent distinctions of rank amongst his subjects: no legislator is wise or powerful enough to preserve free institutions, if he does not take equality for his first principle and his watchword. All of our contemporaries who would establish or secure the independence and the dignity of their fellow-men, must show themselves the friends of equality; and the only worthy means of showing themselves as such is to be so: upon this depends the success of their holy enterprise. Thus, the question is not how to reconstruct aristocratic society, but how to make liberty proceed out of that democratic state of society in which God has placed us.

These two truths appear to me simple, clear, and fertile in consequences; and they naturally lead me to consider what kind of free government can be established amongst a people in which social conditions are equal.

It results, from the very constitution of democratic nations and from their necessities, that the power of government amongst them must be more uniform, more centralized, more extensive, more searching, and more efficient than in other countries. Society at large is naturally stronger and more active, the individual more subordinate and weak; the former does more, the latter less; and this is inevitably the case.

It is not, therefore, to be expected that the range of private independence will ever be as extensive in democratic as in aristocratic countries;—nor is this to be desired; for amongst aristocratic nations, the mass is often sacrificed to the individual, and the prosperity of the greater number to the greatness of the few. It is both necessary and desirable that the government of a democratic people should be active and powerful: and our object should not be to render it weak or indolent, but solely to prevent it from abusing its aptitude and its strength.

The circumstance which most contributed to secure the independence of private persons in aristocratic ages was, that the supreme power did not affect to take upon itself alone the government and administration of the community; those functions were necessarily partially left to the members of the aristocracy: so that, as the supreme power was always divided, it never weighed with its whole weight and in the same manner on each individual.

Not only did the government not perform everything by its immediate agency; but, as most of the agents who discharged its duties derived their power, not from the state, but from the circumstance of their birth, they were not perpetually under its control. The government could not make or unmake them in an instant, at pleasure, or bend them in strict uniformity to its slightest caprice;—this was an additional guaranty of private independence.

I readily admit that recourse cannot be had to the same means at the present time; but I discover certain democratic expedients which may be substituted for them. Instead of vesting in the government alone all the administrative powers of which corporations and nobles have been deprived, a portion of them may be intrusted to secondary public bodies temporarily composed of private citizens: thus the liberty of private persons will be more secure, and their equality will not be diminished.

The Americans, who care less for words than the French, still designate by the name of County the largest of their administrative districts; but the duties of the count or lord-lieutenant are in part performed by a provincial assembly.

At a period of equality like our own, it would be unjust and unreasonable to institute hereditary officers; but there is nothing to prevent us from substituting elective public officers to a certain extent. Election is a democratic expedient, which insures the independence of the public officer in relation to the government as much as hereditary rank can insure it amongst aristocratic nations, and even more so.

Aristocratic countries abound in wealthy and influential persons who are competent to provide for themselves, and who cannot be easily or secretly oppressed: such persons restrain a government within general habits of moderation and reserve. I am well aware that democratic countries contain no such persons naturally; but something analogous to them may be created by artificial means. I firmly believe that an aristocracy cannot again be founded in the world; but I think that private citizens, by combining together, may constitute bodies of great wealth, influence, and strength, corresponding to the persons of an aristocracy. By this means, many of the greatest political advantages of aristocracy would be obtained, without its injustice or its dangers. An association for political, commercial, or manufacturing purposes, or even for those of science and literature, is a powerful and enlightened member of the community, which cannot be disposed of at pleasure, or oppressed without remonstrance; and which, by defending its own rights against the encroachments of the government, saves the common liberties of the country.

In periods of aristocracy, every man is always bound so closely to many of his fellow-citizens that he cannot be assailed without their coming to his assistance. In ages of equality, every man naturally stands alone; he has no hereditary friends whose co-operation he may demand; no class upon whose sympathy he may rely: he is easily got rid of, and he is trampled on with impunity. At the present time, an oppressed member of the community has therefore only one method of self-defence,—he may appeal to the whole nation; and if the whole nation is deaf to his complaint, he may appeal to mankind: the only means he has of making this appeal is by the press. Thus, the liberty of the press is infinitely more valuable amongst democratic nations than amongst all others; it is the only cure for the evils which equality may produce. Equality sets men apart and weakens them; but the press places a powerful weapon within every man's reach, which the weakest and loneliest of them all may use. Equality deprives a man of the support of his connections; but the press enables him to summon all his fellow-countrymen and all his fellow-men to his assistance. Printing has accelerated the progress of equality, and it is also one of its best correctives.

I think that men living in aristocracies may, strictly speaking, do without the liberty of the press: but such is not the case with those who live in democratic countries. To protect their personal independence I trust not to great political assemblies, to parliamentary privilege, or to the assertion of popular sovereignty. All these things may, to a certain extent, be reconciled with personal servitude. But that servitude cannot be complete if the press is free: the press is the chief democratic instrument of freedom.

Something analogous may be said of the judicial power. It is a part of the essence of judicial power to attend to private interests, and to fix itself with predilection on minute objects submitted to its observation: another essential quality of judicial power is never to volunteer its assistance to the oppressed, but always to be at the disposal of the humblest of those who solicit it; their complaint, however feeble they may themselves be, will force itself upon the ear of justice and claim redress, for this is inherent in the very constitution of courts of justice.

A power of this kind is therefore peculiarly adapted to the wants of freedom, at a time when the eye and finger of the government are constantly intruding into the minutest details of human actions, and when private persons are at once too weak to protect themselves, and too much isolated for them to reckon upon the assistance of their fellows. The strength of the courts of law has even been the greatest security which can be offered to personal independence; but this is more especially the case in democratic ages: private rights and interests are in constant danger, if the judicial power does not grow more extensive and more strong to keep pace with the growing equality of conditions.

Equality awakens in men several propensities extremely dangerous to freedom, to which the attention of the legislator ought constantly to be directed. I shall only remind the reader of the most important amongst them.

Men living in democratic ages do not readily comprehend the utility of forms: they feel an instinctive contempt for them,—I have elsewhere shown for what reasons. Forms excite their contempt, and often their hatred; as they commonly aspire to none but easy and present gratifications, they rush onwards to the object of their desires, and the slightest

delay exasperates them. This same temper, carried with them
into political life, renders them hostile to forms, which perpetually retard or arrest them in some of their projects.

Yet this objection, which the men of democracies make
to forms, is the very thing which renders forms so useful
to freedom; for their chief merit is to serve as a barrier between the strong and the weak, the ruler and the people, to
retard the one, and give the other time to look about him.
Forms become more necessary in proportion as the government becomes more active and more powerful, whilst private
persons are becoming more indolent and more feeble. Thus
democratic nations naturally stand more in need of forms
than other nations, and they naturally respect them less. This
deserves most serious attention.

Nothing is more pitiful than the arrogant disdain of most
of our contemporaries for questions of form; for the smallest questions of form have acquired in our time an importance which they never had before: many of the greatest
interests of mankind depend upon them. I think, that, if the
statesmen of aristocratic ages could sometimes contemn forms
with impunity, and frequently rise above them, the statesmen
to whom the government of nations is now confided ought
to treat the very least among them with respect, and not
neglect them without imperious necessity. In aristocracies, the
observance of forms was superstitious; amongst us, they
ought to be kept up with a deliberate and enlightened
deference.

Another tendency, which is extremely natural to democratic nations and extremely dangerous, is that which leads
them to despise and undervalue the rights of private persons. The attachment which men feel to a right, and the respect which they display for it, is generally proportioned to
its importance, or to the length of time during which they
have enjoyed it. The rights of private persons amongst democratic nations are commonly of small importance, of recent
growth, and extremely precarious; the consequence is, that
they are often sacrificed without regret, and almost always
violated without remorse.

But it happens that, at the some period and amongst the
same nations in which men conceive a natural contempt for
the rights of private persons, the rights of society at large
are naturally extended and consolidated: in other words, men
become less attached to private rights just when it is most
necessary to retain and defend what little remains of them.
It is therefore most especially in the present democratic times,
that the true friends of the liberty and the greatness of man

ought constantly to be on the alert, to prevent the power of government from lightly sacrificing the private rights of individuals to the general execution of its designs. At such times, no citizen is so obscure that it is not very dangerous to allow him to be oppressed; no private rights are so unimportant that they can be surrendered with impunity to the caprices of a government. The reason is plain:—if the private right of an individual is violated at a time when the human mind is fully impressed with the importance and the sanctity of such rights, the injury done is confined to the individual whose right is infringed; but to violate a right at the present day is deeply to corrupt the manners of the nation, and to put the whole community in jeopardy, because the very notion of this kind of right constantly tends amongst us to be impaired and lost.

There are certain habits, certain notions, and certain vices which are peculiar to a state of revolution, and which a protracted revolution cannot fail to create and to propagate, whatever be, in other respects, its character, its purpose, and the scene on which it takes place. When any nation has, within a short space of time, repeatedly varied its rules, its opinions, and its laws, the men of whom it is composed eventually contract a taste for change, and grow accustomed to see all changes effected by sudden violence. Thus they naturally conceive a contempt for forms which daily prove ineffectual; and they do not support, without impatience, the dominion of rules which they have so often seen infringed.

As the ordinary notions of equity and morality no longer suffice to explain and justify all the innovations daily begotten by a revolution, the principle of public utility is called in, the doctrine of political necessity is conjured up, and men accustom themselves to sacrifice private interests without scruple, and to trample on the rights of individuals in order more speedily to accomplish any public purpose.

These habits and notions, which I shall call revolutionary, because all revolutions produce them, occur in aristocracies just as much as amongst democratic nations; but amongst the former they are often less powerful and always less lasting, because there they meet with habits, notions, defects, and impediments, which counteract them: they consequently disappear as soon as the revolution is terminated, and the nation reverts to its former political courses. This is not always the case in democratic countries, in which it is ever to be feared that revolutionary tendencies, becoming more gentle and more regular, without entirely disappearing from society, will be gradually transformed into habits of subjection to the adminis-

trative authority of the government. I know of no countries in
which revolutions are more dangerous than in democratic
countries; because, independently of the accidental and transient evils which must always attend them, they may always
create some evils which are permanent and unending.

I believe that there are such things as justifiable resistance
and legitimate rebellion: I do not therefore assert, as an absolute proposition, that the men of democratic ages ought never
to make revolutions; but I think that they have especial reason to hesitate before they embark in them, and that it is far
better to endure many grievances in their present condition,
than to have recourse to so perilous a remedy.

I shall conclude by one general idea, which comprises not
only all the particular ideas which have been expressed in the
present chapter, but also most of those which it is the object
of this book to treat of. In the ages of aristocracy which
preceded our own, there were private persons of great power,
and a social authority of extreme weakness. The outline of
society itself was not easily discernible, and constantly confounded with the different powers by which the community
was ruled. The principal efforts of the men of those times were
required to strengthen, aggrandize, and secure the supreme
power; and, on the other hand, to circumscribe individual
independence within narrower limits, and to subject private
interests to the interests of the public. Other perils and other
cares await the men of our age. Amongst the greater part of
modern nations, the government, whatever may be its origin,
its constitution, or its name, has become almost omnipotent,
and private persons are falling, more and more, into the lowest
stage of weakness and dependence.

In olden society, everything was different; unity and uniformity were nowhere to be met with. In modern society,
everything threatens to become so much alike, that the peculiar characteristics of each individual will soon be entirely lost
in the general aspect of the world. Our forefathers were
ever prone to make an improper use of the notion that private
rights ought to be respected; and we are naturally prone, on
the other hand, to exaggerate the idea that the interest of a
private individual ought always to bend to the interest of the
many.

The political world is metamorphosed: new remedies must
henceforth be sought for new disorders. To lay down extensive
but distinct and settled limits to the action of the government;
to confer certain rights on private persons, and to secure
to them the undisputed enjoyment of those rights; to enable
individual man to maintain whatever independence, strength,

and original power he still possesses; to raise him by the side of society at large, and uphold him in that position,—these appear to me the main objects of legislators in the ages upon which we are now entering.

It would seem as if the rulers of our time sought only to use men in order to make things great; I wish that they would try a little more to make great men; that they would set less value on the work, and more upon the workman; that they would never forget that a nation cannot long remain strong when every man belonging to it is individually weak; and that no form or combination of social polity has yet been devised to make an energetic people out of a community of pusillanimous and enfeebled citizens.

I trace amongst our contemporaries two contrary notions which are equally injurious. One set of men can perceive nothing in the principle of equality but the anarchical tendencies which it engenders: they dread their own free agency, they fear themselves. Other thinkers, less numerous but more enlightened, take a different view: beside that track which starts from the principle of equality to terminate in anarchy, they have at last discovered the road which seems to lead men to inevitable servitude. They shape their souls beforehand to this necessary condition; and, despairing of remaining free, they already do obeisance in their hearts to the master who is soon to appear. The former abandon freedom because they think it dangerous; the latter, because they hold it to be impossible.

If I had entertained the latter conviction, I should not have written this book, but I should have confined myself to deploring in secret the destiny of mankind. I have sought to point out the dangers to which the principle of equality exposes the independence of man, because I firmly believe that these dangers are the most formidable, as well as the least foreseen, of all those which futurity holds in store; but I do not think that they are insurmountable.

The men who live in the democratic ages upon which we are entering have naturally a taste for independence; they are naturally impatient of regulation, and they are wearied by the permanence even of the condition they themselves prefer. They are fond of power; but they are prone to despise and hate those who wield it, and they easily elude its grasp by their own mobility and insignificance.

These propensities will always manifest themselves, because they originate in the groundwork of society, which will undergo no change: for a long time they will prevent the establishment of any despotism, and they will furnish fresh

‚weapons to each succeeding generation which shall struggle
in favor of the liberty of mankind. Let us, then, look forward
to the future with that salutary fear which makes men keep
watch and ward for freedom, not with that faint and idle terror which depresses and enervates the heart.

57. General Survey of the Subject.

BEFORE closing forever the subject that I have now discussed,
I would fain take a parting survey of all the different characteristics of modern society, and appreciate at last the general
influence to be exercised by the principle of equality upon the
fate of mankind; but I am stopped by the difficulty of the
task, and, in presence of so great a theme, my sight is troubled,
and my reason fails.

The society of the modern world, which I have sought
to delineate, and which I seek to judge, has just come into
existence. Time has not yet shaped it into perfect form; the
great revolution by which it has been created is not yet over;
and, amidst the occurrences of our time, it is almost impossible to discern what will pass away with the revolution itself, and what will survive its close. The world which is rising
into existence is still half encumbered by the remains of the
world which is waning into decay; and, amidst the vast perplexity of human affairs, none can say how much of ancient
institutions and former manners will remain, or how much
will completely disappear.

Although the revolution which is taking place in the social
condition, the laws, the opinions, and the feelings of men
is still very far from being terminated, yet its results already
admit of no comparison with anything that the world has
ever before witnessed. I go back from age to age up to the
remotest antiquity, but I find no parallel to what is occurring
before my eyes: as the past has ceased to throw its light upon
the future, the mind of man wanders in obscurity.

Nevertheless, in the midst of a prospect so wide, so novel,
and so confused, some of the more prominent characteristics may already be discerned and pointed out. The good
things and the evils of life are more equally distributed in
the world: great wealth tends to disappear, the number
of small fortunes to increase; desires and gratifications are
multiplied, but extraordinary prosperity and irremediable
penury are alike unknown. The sentiment of ambition is

universal, but the scope of ambition is seldom vast. Each individual stands apart in solitary weakness; but society at large is active, provident, and powerful: the performances of private persons are insignificant, those of the state immense.

There is little energy of character, but manners are mild, and laws humane. If there be few instances of exalted hero- ism or of virtues of the highest, brightest, and purest temper, men's habits are regular, violence is rare, and cruelty almost unknown. Human existence becomes longer, and property more secure: life is not adorned with brilliant trophies, but it is extremely easy and tranquil. Few pleasures are either very refined or very coarse; and highly polished manners are as uncommon as great brutality of tastes. Neither men of great learning, nor extremely ignorant communities, are to be met with; genius becomes more rare, information more diffused. The human mind is impelled by the small efforts of all man- kind combined together, not by the strenuous activity of a few men. There is less perfection, but more abundance, in all the productions of the arts. The ties of race, of rank, and of country are relaxed; the great bond of humanity is strengthened.

If I endeavor to find out the most general and most promi- nent of all these different characteristics, I perceive that what is taking place in men's fortunes manifests itself under a thou- sand other forms. Almost all extremes are softened or blunted: all that was most prominent is superseded by some middle term, at once less lofty and less low, less brilliant and less obscure, than what before existed in the world.

When I survey this countless multitude of beings, shaped in each other's likeness, amidst whom nothing rises and noth- ing falls, the sight of such universal uniformity saddens and chills me, and I am tempted to regret that state of society which has ceased to be. When the world was full of men of great importance and extreme insignificance, of great wealth and extreme poverty, of great learning and extreme ignorance, I turned aside from the latter to fix my observation on the former alone, who gratified my sympathies. But I admit that this gratification arose from my own weakness: it is because I am unable to see at once all that is around me, that I am al- lowed thus to select and separate the objects of my predilection from among so many others. Such is not the case with that Almighty and Eternal Being, whose gaze necessarily includes the whole of created things, and who surveys distinctly, though at once, mankind and man.

We may naturally believe that it is not the singular pros- perity of the few, but the greater well-being of all, which is

most pleasing in the sight of the Creator and Preserver of men.
What appears to me to be man's decline is, to His eye, advancement; what afflicts me is acceptable to Him. A state of
equality is perhaps less elevated, but it is more just: and its
justice constitutes its greatness and its beauty. I would strive,
then, to raise myself to this point of the Divine contemplation, and thence to view and to judge the concerns of men.

No man, upon the earth, can as yet affirm, absolutely and
generally, that the new state of the world is better than its
former one; but it is already easy to perceive that this state
is different. Some vices and some virtues were so inherent
in the constitution of an aristocratic nation, and are so opposite to the character of a modern people, that they can
never be infused into it; some good tendencies and some bad
propensities which were unknown to the former, are natural
to the latter; some ideas suggest themselves spontaneously
to the imagination of the one, which are utterly repugnant to
the mind of the other. They are like two distinct orders of
human being, each of which has its own merits and defects,
its own advantages and its own evils. Care must therefore be
taken not to judge the state of society which is now coming
into existence, by notions derived from a state of society
which no longer exists; for, as these states of society are
exceedingly different in their structure, they cannot be submitted to a just or fair comparison. It would be scarcely more
reasonable to require of our contemporaries the peculiar virtues which originated in the social condition of their forefathers, since that social condition is itself fallen, and has
drawn into one promiscuous ruin the good and evil which
belonged to it.

But as yet these things are imperfectly understood. I find
that a great number of my contemporaries undertake to make
a selection from amongst the institutions, the opinions, and
the ideas which originated in the aristocratic constitution of
society as it was: a portion of these elements they would willingly relinquish, but they would keep the remainder and transplant them into their new world. I apprehend that such men
are wasting their time and their strength in virtuous but
unprofitable efforts. The object is, not to retain the peculiar
advantages which the inequality of conditions bestows upon
mankind, but to secure the new benefits which equality may
supply. We have not to seek to make ourselves like our progenitors, but to strive to work out that species of greatness
and happiness which is our own.

For myself, who now look back from this extreme limit
of my task, and discover from afar, but at once, the various

objects which have attracted my more attentive investigation upon my way, I am full of apprehensions and of hopes. I perceive mighty dangers which it is possible to ward off,— mighty evils which may be avoided or alleviated; and I cling with a firmer hold to the belief, that, for democratic nations to be virtuous and prosperous, they require but to will it.

I am aware that many of my contemporaries maintain that nations are never their own masters here below, and that they necessarily obey some insurmountable and unintelligent power, arising from anterior events, from their race, or from the soil and climate of their country. Such principles are false and cowardly; such principles can never produce aught but feeble men and pusillanimous nations. Providence has not created mankind entirely independent or entirely free. It is true, that around every man a fatal circle is traced, beyond which he cannot pass; but within the wide verge of that circle he is powerful and free: as it is with man, so with communities. The nations of our time cannot prevent the conditions of men from becoming equal; but it depends upon themselves whether the principle of equality is to lead them to servitude or freedom, to knowledge or barbarism, to prosperity or wretchedness.

THE AMERICAN SCENE

☐ **BEFORE FREEDOM edited and with an Introduction by Belinda Hurmence.** The oral history of American slavery in the powerful words of former slaves. "Eloquent . . . historically valuable." Including the two volumes *Before Freedom, When I Can Just Remember* and *My Folks Don't Want Me to Talk About Slavery.* "Eloquent . . . historically valuable."—*Los Angeles Times Book Review* (627814—$4.95)

☐ **BROTHER, CAN YOU SPARE A DIME? The Great Depression 1929-1933 by Milton Meltzer.** Meltzer weaves first-hand accounts into a moving history of the terrible depression. Black Thursday, 1929, the stock market crash; 1930, the auto industry's drastic shrinkage; 1932, more than one fourth of the nation's banks closed and no planned relief; and finally 1933, the beginning of Roosevelt's New Deal. (628179—$4.99)

☐ **THE MAKING OF THE PRESIDENT® 1960 by Theodore H. White.** The masterful Pulitzer Prize winning account of the 1960 campaign and election of John F. Kennedy. (627164—$5.95)

☐ **JEFFERSON by Saul K. Padover.** Abridged. In this stirring portrait, Professor Padover deftly reveals the personality of Thomas Jefferson, the devoted husband and father, the farmer and philosopher, as well as the crises and achievements of his brilliant career as a statesman. An absorbing, highly readable book of a great American's life and ideas. (627970—$4.95)

☐ **WITH MALICE TOWARD NONE: The Life of Abraham Lincoln by Stephen B. Oates.** Oates reaches through the legend to the man himself, incorporating the history of the era into a fascinating portrait of one of America's great presidents. (628152—$5.95)

Prices slightly higher in Canada

There's an epidemic with 27 million victims. And no visible symptoms.

It's an epidemic of people who can't read.

Believe it or not, 27 million Americans are functionally illiterate, about one adult in five.

The solution to this problem is you... when you join the fight against illiteracy. So call the Coalition for Literacy at toll-free **1-800-228-8813** and volunteer.

Volunteer Against Illiteracy. The only degree you need is a degree of caring.